The Blue Guides

G000129269

Please write in with your comments, suggestions and corrections for the next edition of the Blue Guide. Writers of the most helpful letters will be awarded a free Blue Guide of their choice.

City Guide
Vienna

Nicholas T. Parsons

A&C Black • London
WW Norton • New York

Second edition 2002
First edition 1997

Published by A & C Black Publishers Limited
Alderman House, 37 Soho Square, London W1D 3QZ

www.acblack.com

Maps and plans © A & C Black, drawn by Hen Blas Consultants Ltd and RJS Associates
Illustrations © Jim Urquhart

A CIP catalogue record of this book is available from the British Library.

ISBN 0–7136–6128–3

Published in the United States of America by
WW Norton and Company, Inc
500 Fifth Avenue, New York, NY 10110

Published simultaneously in Canada by
Penguin Books Canada Limited
10 Alcorn Avenue, Toronto
Ontario M4V 3B2

ISBN 0–393–32346–3 USA

The author and the publishers have done their best to ensure the accuracy of all the information in *Blue Guide Vienna*; however, they can accept no responsibility for any loss, injury
or inconvenience sustained by any traveller as a result of information or advice contained
in the guide.

Cover photograph: *Tree of Life* (Stoclet Frieze) c 1905–09 by Gustav Klimt,
Österreichische Galerie, Vienna/Bridgeman Art Library.

Nicholas T. Parsons has known Vienna intimately for fourteen years and has written
extensively on the city, as well as on other cities and countries of Central Europe. He works
as a feature journalist and translator and is also author of *Blue Guide Austria*.

A & C Black uses paper produced with elemental chlorine-free pulp, harvested from
managed sustainable forests.

Printed and bound in Great Britain by Butler & Tanner, Frome and London.

Contents

The Guide

Maps and plans

Preface

My aim in writing this city guide to Vienna in the Blue Guide series is to place the city in its historical and cultural context and to provide the visitor with a carefully organised programme of sightseeing. While I believe the text supplies the depth of information traditionally expected from Blue Guides, every effort has been made to evoke the city as a living entity with a vivid and turbulent past; by the same token, I have tried to avoid treating Vienna simply as a museum of famous sights that the tourist views largely divorced from the historical events or circumstances that have given rise to them.

Since the first edition the pace of change has quickened in Austria. In February 2000, the long-standing Social Democratic–Conservative coalition was replaced by a Centre Right government of conservatives partnered by the controversial Freedom Party (FPÖ). Countries of the European Union applied 'sanctions' against this democratically elected government, which however were lifted after a report on Austria's political climate and the Freedom Party commissioned by the European Union made only relatively minor criticisms of the FPÖ and none of the government itself. Vienna has meanwhile seen further investment in infrastructure (always one of the city's strengths) and has opened an ambitious *MuseumsQuartier*, which will no doubt rival Mitterand's self-aggrandising Parisian legacy, just as Schönbrunn was once built to emulate and rival Versailles. Many of the existing museums have been given a face-lift under a rolling plan of refurbishment initiated by the previous government, and many too have begun to offer a broad programme of ancillary events. Vienna is now more lively and culturally diverse, more prosperous and more imaginative in its self-presentation, than ever before.

Acknowledgements

Over the years that I have lived in Vienna many people have enlightened me with regard to various aspects of the city's history and culture. Their names are too numerous to mention, but an exception should be made in the case of Wolfgang Bahr, who once systematically guided me round each district of the city and gave me the benefit of his immense local knowledge; and Helmut Katzmann, who has so often saved me from error or helped me to a greater insight of Viennese peculiarities. For indispensable assistance in checking specific aspects of the text, I am greatly indebted to Trixie and Géza Hajós and Michael Krapf. Dr M.P.A Sheaffer wrote me several letters and I have incorporated some of her suggestions, where appropriate. I have also taken note of some helpful comments by James Stow. Peter Branscombe's enormous knowledge of matters Viennese has proved invaluable. Louis Parsons provided high quality photographic references for the illustrations; I am grateful for all his hard work. I am obliged to Gemma Davies and Miranda Robson at A & C Black for much forbearance and cheerful support. Last but not least, I would like to thank my wife, Ilona Sármány-Parsons, for her critical insights and many valuable suggestions, which have hopefully refined my unsophisticated judgements and corrected my false or misleading assumptions. Any errors which remain are entirely my own.

Introduction

Vienna, a city whose origin lies in pre-Roman times, was latterly the most important of the four great cultural centres of the Habsburg Empire. Unlike the other three (Budapest, Prague and Cracow) it escaped the deadening Communist yoke; as a result, its architectural heritage had, until recently, been somewhat better preserved and the city enjoyed growing prosperity over more than half a century from tourism and the service industries. The city has miraculously preserved a huge amount of its architectural heritage. The mingling of historical periods that will be everywhere apparent to visitors is paralleled by a mingling of influences that have shaped the unique character of the Viennese themselves: racially mixed, they are to a large degree culturally homogeneous. In the hope of conveying a better understanding of these often enigmatic people and their enduringly beautiful city, I have paid particular attention to chronology and history (pp 43–73). Like all the great cities of Central Europe, Vienna has been continually buffeted by outside forces, a geo-politically exposed outpost of Western Europe, or the suffering heart and focus of Central Europe, according to one's point of view.

Today Vienna is a modern city with around 1.8 million inhabitants enjoying the fruits of a new era, which began when Austria joined the European Union in January 1995. Its hard core of Viennese is supplemented by a vast international population of officials, diplomats, immigrant workers and others. By the beginning of the new millennium, officially, over 16 per cent of the city's population or about 300,000 people was non-Viennese. The figure is in fact far higher, as there are many people living unregistered, which is technically illegal. However panic about 'foreigners' (*Ausländer*) has subsided, despite the best efforts of the Freedom Party (FPÖ) to stir it up; ironically the People's Party (ÖVP) the centre-right wing of the government, even found itself debating with its more right-wing partners in 2001 about the possibility of bringing in more skilled workers to solve the shortage of qualified labour in areas like software and computer technology. Despite the image of Austria propagated abroad, there has only been one case of terrorism against minorities in twenty years, a lone bomber who targeted Romanies and liberal politicians renowned for their support for asylum-seekers. There was also one death in police custody of an illegal immigrant being deported. This may be contrasted with continual outbreaks of violence and intolerance against minorities in other countries which belong to the European Union. Austrians have every right to feel that a double standard is frequently applied to them, although it is true that the opportunistic Jörg Haider, with his adroit exploitation of chauvinism, xenophobia and the various grievances of the 'little man', together with his apparent cosmeticization of Austria's role in Nazism, has a lot to answer for.

In a way that reflects the local genius, the people and the authorities of Vienna are adept at gracefully combining respect for the great aesthetic achievements of the Habsburgs' '*Residenzstadt*' (the Royal Seat and therefore centre of administration and patronage) with a determination to open up their city to the future. The latter process was given extra impetus by the late Chancellor Bruno Kreisky and his supporters, who, in the 1970s, persuaded both fellow Austrians and the international community that Vienna should become a third seat of the UNO after New York and Geneva. Vienna's UNO-city is dominated by the dramatic glass and concrete blocks for UNIDO and the IAEO, built beyond the Danube on land provided by the City of Vienna, where they disturb no Baroque perspective. A nominal annual rent of one Austrian schilling is levied by the Austrian Republic.

However, modernity has arrived in the Old City as well. Nowadays, inside many an immaculately restored palace, flickering computer screens co-exist with elegant Baroque vaulting, lavish stucco or coffered ceilings: an image of a city with one foot in the past and one in the future.

Vienna's architecture

The Roman camp of *Vindobona* lay at the heart of what was to become the **Innere Stadt** (Inner City); today's fashionable **Graben** formed part of its southern perimeter. While there is little Romanesque architecture that has survived, the city boasts some magnificent Gothic buildings, most notably the cathedral, (**Stephansdom**), which is one of the glories of Central Europe. Much of the money that might have gone into Renaissance building works was in fact spent on the star-shaped fortification (*tracé italien*; 1531–66) that was designed to protect the city from the Turkish armies in the 16C and 17C. The finest Renaissance work, the two-storeyed arcade of the **Stallburg** is to be found in the **Hofburg**, the Habsburgs' ever-expanding imperial residence. However the most enduring images of the city for many visitors are supplied by the Baroque period of the 17C and 18C—magnificent churches like Fischer von Erlach's 18C **Karlskirche**, or great palaces like Hildebrandt's 18C **Belvedere**, built for Prince Eugene of Savoy.

The crucial change for the city from an essentially medieval layout to modern metropolis occurred when Emperor Franz Joseph ordered the destruction of the bastions in 1857 and thus inaugurated the **Ringstraßen era** with its sumptuous Historicist architecture by Theophil Hansen, Heinrich Ferstel, and Friedrich Schmidt. The great boulevard on the Parisian model that gave its name to the era encircled the old city almost entirely (hence 'Ringstraße'). Most of the city's public and official buildings date from this period and were located on this boulevard (the neo-Renaissance **Oper** and **Burgtheater**, the classical **Parlament**, the neo-Gothic **Rathaus** and **Votivkirche**). Between the Ringstraße and the former outer line of defence (Linienwall, now the **Gürtel** traffic artery) the suburbs gradually became more overbuilt and integrated in the late 19C.

Towards the end of the 19C, Jugendstil and the Secession marked a reaction against Historicism. Otto Wagner was the dominant figure of the Secession, as far as architecture was concerned, and the walks featured in the book illustrate the development of his style from late Historicism—buildings he designed or constructed on the **Graben**—to full-blown Secession style with functionalist elements like the **Kirche am Steinhof**. Functionalist theory was taken further by Adolf Loos, who was impressed by the modernity and efficiency of America (cf. the **Loos Bar** in the Kärntner Durchgang and the **Loos Haus** on Michaelerplatz). Loos also played a minor role in realising the ambitious programme of social housing of the city's Social Democratic council in the 1920s (although he was not involved with the famous **Gemeindebauten**, or blocks of council apartments built to uniform specifications).

Green space also expanded as the city developed and civic independence increased. Many of the imperial parks (**Augarten**, **Belvedere**, **Schönbrunn** and the **Prater**) were thrown open to the public in the age of Enlightenment (specifically during the reign of Joseph II, 1780–90). After the Napoleonic Wars, the **Volksgarten** (1821–23), Vienna's first public park, was laid out and in the Founders' Period bourgeois initiative resulted in the delightful **Stadtpark** (1862–63) being created alongside the Ringstraße. Today, Vienna is one of the more ecologically aware cities of Europe, carefully preserving and tending its open spaces and creating completely new recreation areas, such as the island resulting from modern regulation of the Danube. This concern with the environment carries over into pedestrian zones in the Inner City and the use of environmentally friendly forms of public transport such as the delightful trams.

The Arts in Vienna

Visitors to the city can enjoy one of the richest ongoing programmes of music, theatre and exhibitions in Europe (for venues see the monthly *Wien Programm*, available at Tourist Information offices). Apart from the new productions and repertory at the **Oper** and the **Volksoper**, or the concert programmes of the **Musikverein** and the **Konzerthaus**, there are the imaginatively varied offerings of the **Wiener Festwochen** (mid-May to mid-June), which comprise musical and dramatic productions built round a central theme. The midsummer music festival features inter alia free open-air opera, projected onto a gigantic screen in front of the **Rathaus** (City Hall). There are also regular Haydn and Schubert festivals for devotees, and special events associated with Mozart.

The quality and quantity of the visual arts in Vienna hardly needs stressing. The world-famous permanent collections of the **Kunsthistorisches Museum**, the **Österreichische Galerie** (Klimt, Schiele, Biedermeier portraiture) in the Belvedere and the **Museum Moderner Kunst,** now transferred to the new **MuseumsQuartier** (see *Vienna's Highlights*, p 11–12), are supplemented by numerous temporary exhibitions either in-house or at such venues as the **Secession or Kunsthalle**. Although the age of mega-shows, for example *Traum und Wirklichkeit: Wien 1870–1930* (*Dream and Reality: Vienna 1870–1930*), which inspired similar shows in Paris and New York, now seems to be over, the Viennese are good at staging smaller or thematic ones, often in the **Kunstforum** or the **Jüdisches Museum der Stadt Wien**. (See also *Vienna's museums* on p 37.)

Vienna's Highlights

Vienna has the advantage over some cities in that the most important sights are concentrated in the **Innere Stadt**, the historic core of the city inside the **Ringstraße**. But there are many sights which lie beyond the Ring worth visiting.

The walks described in the Guide are mostly designed to take two to three hours, depending on how much time is spent on individual sights. However, the most important museums (*see below*) require a morning or afternoon to themselves: the **Kunsthistorisches Museum** (p 138) on the Ring, the **Upper and Lower Belvedere** (Oberes und Unteres Belvedere; p 172) to the south, the **Historical Museum of the City of Vienna** (Historisches Museum der Stadt Wien, p 169) on Karlsplatz and **Schönbrunn** (p 191), to the west and the new **MuseumsQuartier** (p 181).

Any sightseeing plan should allow half a day to see the various sights and museums of the **Hofburg** (p 77) where tours of the Sacred and Secular Imperial Treasuries and the Kaiserappartements should not be missed, and about one and a half hours for St Stephen's cathedral or **Stephansdom** (p 104), assuming the catacombs and tower are included. Both of these have individual sections devoted to them in the Guide and all seven Inner City Walks start or end at Stephansplatz or the Hofburg.

Vienna has many lovely **churches**, but the following merit inclusion in any itinerary. In the **Inner City** (listed from west to east): **Maria am Gestade** (p 111), **Michaelerkirche** (p 91), **Peterskirche** (p 116), **Kapuzinerkirche und Kapuzinergruft** (p 122), **Jesuitenkirche** (p 127) and **Dominikaner-kirche** (p 124) are the finest Gothic and Baroque churches.

Outside the Ring, the outstanding church is Fischer von Erlachs' **Karlskirche** (p 167) on Karlsplatz. The **Servitenkirche** (p 187) to the north-west is also well worth the detour as is the **Piaristenkirche Maria Treu** (p 184) in the Josefstadtdistrict. If you have a Saturday morning free, consider a visit to Otto Wagner's remarkable **Kirche am Steinhof** (p 196) on Baumgartner Höhe in the western suburb of Penzing.

Other highlights of the city

Listed from west to east, other sights that should not be missed if time permits are: the **Strudlhofstiege** and nearby **Liechtenstein Summer Palace** (p 186, outside the Ring), the latter no longer housing the Museum of Modern Art (but shortly to house the Liechtenstein's personal collection), its English landscape park is due to be opened to the public after renovation; the so-called **Ferstel** and the **Harrach Palace**, together with the **Schottenstift** (church and picture gallery, pp 96–98), all of which are on Freyung; the **Loos-Haus** on Michaelerplatz (p 92), the **Anker Clock** on Hoher Markt (p 110), the **Plague Column** on Graben (p 115), the **Secession** on Friedrichstraße (p 165) and, nearby, the **Academy of Fine Arts** (Akademie der Bildenden Künste, including gallery, p 150); the Mecca for Wiener Schnitzel lovers (**Figlmüller**, p 124) and a typical wine cellar such as the **Zwölf Apostel-Keller** on Sonnenfelsgasse (p 127–128); Otto Wagner's **Postsparkassenamt** (Post Office Savings Bank, p 157) and the **Stadtpark** (p 155). Perhaps you will not feel you have really 'done' Vienna without a visit to **Hotel Sacher** (p 117) behind the Opera House and tea at **Demel** on the Kohlmarkt (p 104).

Outside Vienna

If you are motoring to Vienna from the west, it is easy to take in a number of attractive sights en route, including the Baroque monastery at **Melk**, the beautiful **Wachau** region, together with historic **Dürnstein** and **Krems**. If you motor on east to Hungary from Vienna, a sweep to the southeast could include **Eisenstadt** (Esterhazy Palace), the **Neusiedler See**, and the offshoot of the Austrian gallery at **Schloss Halbturn**. However, be warned that this will involve a considerably longer route to Budapest within Hungary than the direct motorway via Nickelsdorf and Győr; (on the other hand, this route allows for visits to interesting Hungarian sights, such as the **Esterhazy Schloss** at Fertőd, the town of **Sopron**, the Romanesque cathedral at **Ják**, and so on). If you are heading south from Vienna, detours could include **Baden**, **Heiligenkreuz** and **Mayerling**.

Using the Guide

Abbreviations

The following abbreviations occur in the guide:
FPÖ Freiheitliche Partei Österreichs
ÖVP Österreichische Volkspartei
IAEO International Atomic Energy Agency
UNIDO United Nations Industrial Development Organisation

The following symbols have been used:
☎ telephone
✉ e-mail/web-site addresses
🗐 fax
€ Euro

PRACTICAL INFORMATION

 Planning your trip

When to go

Vienna is uncomfortably hot (frequently 30°C or more) in July and August and often formidably cold in December, January and February (around zero, often below in January). The most pleasant time for a visit is the long Indian summer of September and early October.

Migraine sufferers and those with blood pressure problems can expect discomfort prompted by the sudden onsets of the *Föhn*, a warm wind blowing off the Alps.

Passports and formalities

Citizens of the European Union, USA and Canada may enter Austria with a valid passport. A stay of 90 days is allowed without further formalities.

No vaccinations are required, but intending hikers in the Wienerwald or elsewhere in Austria should inquire about inoculation against *Zecken*, a form of tick from whose infection a potentially fatal encephalitis can result.

Customs

Austria joined the European Union on 1 January 1995 and border controls (except at airports) for EU citizens have been abolished. Non-EU citizens are subject to the traditional limits, but enjoy the advantage of being able to reclaim VAT on purchases made in Austria.

Whatever your status, if you import more than 7000 Euros, it is sensible to declare it to the authorities, especially if you think you will be depositing or re-exporting large sums.

Currency

From January 2002, only the Euro has been legal tender. On 1 January 2001, the Austrian Schilling (ATS) was matched with the Euro (€) at a rate of 13,7603 ATS (13 schillings, 76 Groschen) to one Euro, but the Schilling remained in circulation for a year with prices being shown in both currencies. For those only familiar with the old currency, relative prices may be calculated by thinking of 100 ATS as about seven and one quarter Euros.

Austrian National Tourist Board offices

UK
Information about Vienna and Austria may be obtained from the Austrian National Tourist Office at 14 Cork Street, London W1. ☎ 020 7629 0461. 🗐 020 7499 6038. ✉ info@anto.co.uk.

USA
P.O.Box 1142. New York NY 10108–1142. ☎ 212 944 6885. 🗐 212 730 4568. ✉ antony@ibm.net. ✉ www.anto.com.

Canada
2 Bloor St East, Suite 3330, Toronto, Ontario M4W IA8. ☎ 416 967 3381.
🖷 416 967 4101. ✉ anto-tor@sympatico.at.
Australia
36 Carrington Street, 1st Floor, Sydney NSW 2000. ☎ 02 9299 3621.
🖷 02 9299 3808. ✉ oewsyd@world.net.

Contact the Tourist Board in Vienna for advance information, brochures etc.
They will also make hotel reservations. **Tourist-Info, Albertinaplatz 1**,Wien-
Tourismus, A-1025 Wien. ☎ 3 1 24 555. 🖷 43 1 24 555 666.
✉ info@info.wien.at, and ✉ www.info.wien.at.

Tourist information websites
✉ **www.anto.com** and ✉ **www.austria-tourism.at**
Austrian National Tourist Office.

✉ **www.austria-info.at/amusa/index.html**
Art and music news from Austria.

✉ **www.info.wien.at**
Information specifically for **Vienna**: events and current attractions, museum
opening times, gastronomy, newsletter (free subscription), Vienna for the disabled, see also **www.accessibleeverything.com** and **www.atlholidays**
childrens' attractions from the Wiener Tourismusverband.

✉ **www.wien.gv.at**
Another website dedicated to all that is going on in Vienna: culture, education, getting around, history of, high tech Vienna, media, politics, tourist
information etc.

✉ **www.austria-tourism.at**
Accommodation for the whole of **Austria**. The Osterreich
Werbung/Urlaubsinformation Osterreich office in Vienna is in Margarethenstrasse 1/Rilkeplatz 5, A-1040 Wien (a short walk from Karlsplatz), ☎ (00
431) 587 20 00. 🖷 1 588 66 48. ✉ oeinfo@oewwien.via at. Open Mon–Fri,
10.00–17.00 (to 18.00 Thur).

Tour operators
Austria Travel, 46 Queen Anne's Gate, London SW1 9AU. ☎ 020 7222 2430.
🖷 020 7233 0293. City breaks.
Austrian Holidays, 5th Floor, 10 Wardour Street, London W1 4BQ. ☎ 020
7434 7399. 🖷 020 7434 7393. *Austrian Airlines Group* package tour sub-
sidiary. Mostly city breaks.
Danube Travel, 45 Great Cumberland Place, London W1R 7LH.
Habsburg Heritage Cultural Tours, 158 Rosendale Road, London SE21 8LG.
☎ 020 8761 0444. 🖷 020 8766 6151. Specialises in music festivals and
Danube cruises.
Klassik Tours, 141 Glendower Road, Plymouth PL3 4LB. ☎ 01752 311979.
🖷 01752 311980. Tours include 'Mozart in Salzburg and Vienna',
'Schubertiades' etc.
Martin Randall Travel, 10 Barley Mow Passage, London W4 4PH. ☎ 020 8742
3355. 🖷 020 8742 1066.

Prospect Music and Art Tours Ltd, 36 Manchester Street, London W1M 5PE.
☎ 020 7486 5704. 📠 020 7486 5686.
Reality and Beyond Ltd, Quenington Old Rectory, Cirencester, Gloucestershire
GL7 5BN. ☎ 01285 750 888. 📠 01285 750 540.

Health and insurance
Although there is a reciprocal agreement with the UK covering emergency treatment, it is advisable to have full travel and health insurance for peace of mind
and to avoid tedious bureaucracy. Charges for private treatment are high.

Travellers with disabilities
Two new websites designed to assist disabled travellers are **www.atlholidays**,
offering holiday information and **www.accessibleeverything.com** offering
general information on planning holidays.

The main U-Bahn stations in Vienna have lifts, but buses and trams remain
generally inaccessible for those in wheelchairs travelling without assistance.
Many of the major museums that are just completing, or have recently completed, renovations (e.g. the Belvedere) have improved facilities for the disabled.
The Tourist Information Offices have a brochure for assisting disabled travellers
in Vienna, or call City Information, ☎ 525 500. *Bizeps* (☎ 5238 92123) is a
multilingual support group, and *Fahrtendienst Haas* (☎ 27 700. Open Mon–Fri
06.00–21.00, Sat, Sun, 08.00–21.00) is a taxi service equipped to accommodate wheelchairs.

Getting there

By air
The costs of return flights to Vienna have decreased considerably in real terms
over the last decade, although the current slump means flights have been
reduced and fares are on their way up again. The most favourable deals are for
minimum stays of a week booked at least two weeks ahead, or packages such as
'weekend breaks' with hotel included. There are several flights daily from
Heathrow with *Austrian Airlines (AUA)* and *British Airways (BA)*. All flights
land at Schwechat airport.

AUA and *Delta Airlines* operate non-stop flights from New York–Vienna. One-
stop flights are operated from Chicago, Los Angeles and Miami to Vienna by both
airlines.

UK
Austrian Airlines Group, 10 Wardour Street, London W1D 6BQ. Information on
☎ 020 7434 7350. Reservations ☎ 0845 601 0948. 📠 020 7434 7363.
✉ www.austrianairlines.co.uk.
British Airways, 156 Regent Street, London W1R 5TA. ☎ 0845 7799977.
✉ www.britishairways.co.uk.

USA/Canada
Austrian Airlines Group, 17–20 Whitestone Expressway, Whitestone, New York, NY. ☎ 1-800 843 0002. Also at: Suite 740, 4000 MacArthur Blvd, Newport Beach, CA 92660, ☎ same as the New York office.
Delta Airlines. Toll-free enquiries for North America and Canada. ☎ 1-800/241 4141.

Airline offices in Vienna

Austrian Airlines Group, Kärntner Ring 18. Booking and reservations ☎ 05 1789. 🖷 05 1766-42 30.
British Airways, Kärntner Ring 10. ☎ 795 67-567. 🖷 504 20 84. Customer Services ☎ 505 76 95.
Delta Airlines, Kärntner Ring 17. ☎ 795 67-023. 🖷 795 67-312.

Flight information at Schwechat Airport, ☎ 70 07-222 31/2/3.
Arrival information ☎ 70 07 221 97.

By rail

Travelling to Vienna by rail is a relatively expensive option, but there are comfortable overnight sleepers from the major European cities. The Austria Night Express leaves London's Victoria Station at noon and takes about 22 hours. For enquiries and reservations contact the *International Rail Centre*, Victoria Station, London SW1V 1JY ☎ 0990 848 848 or *Eurotrain*, 52 Grosvenor Gardens, London SW1 ☎ 020 7730 3402.

By coach

The cheapest way to travel is by coach. Contact *Eurolines*, 52 Grosvenor Gardens, London SW1W OAU. ☎ 0990 14319. Departure is from London Victoria.

By car

Vienna is about 1287km (800 miles) from Calais, via Belgium, the entire journey being on motorway. The French stretch of express route is technically not motorway, and charges no toll, and the Belgian and German motorways are as yet toll-free. Autobahn tolls are now levied in Austria. Stickers (called *Vignetten*) valid for shorter or longer periods up to a calendar year may be purchased at the border.

Arriving in Vienna

By air

All flights land at Schwechat (airport) airport, which is about 19km east of the city centre. From Schwechat there are half-hourly transfer buses into town (one to the Hilton/City Terminal and one to the Westbahnhof via the Südbahnhof); also an hourly *Schnellbahn* (Rapid Transit Train) to Wien Mitte and a minibus service bookable at the airport or in advance through your airline. Journey time into town is approximately 25 minutes, depending on traffic.

By rail

Trains coming from the west will arrive at the Westbahnhof, from the east at either the Süd- or the Westbahnhof, from the south at the Südbahnhof and from the Czech Republic and points east in Austria at the Franz-Josefs-Bahnhof or the Südbahnhof. None of the stations is far from the city centre and all have good traffic connections (Tram and/or *U-Bahn, Schnellbahn*). Check your tickets carefully before leaving your hotel to determine which station your train *leaves from*—they are not close to each other. For train information, ☎ 05-1717 (ÖBB). ✉ www.oeb.at.

By coach

Coaches arrive at Wien Mitte, Landstraßer Hauptstraße, which is well provided with traffic connections for all areas of the city. Travel agents will also have details of package coach tours.

Getting around

Local tourist information offices

The most convenient tourist office in Vienna is located on the corner of the Albertinaplatz (**Tourist-Info, Albertinaplatz 1**, open daily 09.00–19.00 including holidays, Wien-Tourismus, A-1025 Wien. ☎ 3 1 24 555. ▤ 43 1 24 555 666. ✉ info@info.wien.at. ✉ www.info.wien.at), behind the Opera house and close to the U-Bahn connections at Karlsplatz/Oper (U1, U2, U4). It is designed to offer the individual traveller a comprehensive service that includes hotel booking, sightseeing and ticket agencies, round trips with Intropa, the *Wien Karte* (Vienna Card) and currency exchange. The office also has an abundant supply of brochures.

A smaller office is located at **Schwechat Airport** (Jun–Sept 08.30–23.00 daily, Oct–May 08.30–22.00 daily).

Maps and plans

A large selection of **city plans** (including plans of **individual districts**) is available at *Freytag-Berndt und Artaria* at Kohlmarkt 9 (nearest U-Bahn, Stephansplatz U1, U3). The most detailed and sophisticated general plan is the sectionalised fold-out system of *Falk*, which is constantly updated. The shop also contains a large number of general and specialist guides and travel books on Vienna/Austria in several languages. Basic street plans are available gratis at tourist information centres.

Public transport

Buses and trams

Viennese public transport is generally reliable and clean, as well as being safe at night. Trams and buses can be disrupted by sudden snowfall or blizzards in the winter months, but otherwise the network (which operates between about 05.00 and midnight) is a model of efficiency. Maps and timetables of the system can be obtained at U-Bahn stations.

Hopper buses (1A, 2A and 3A) traverse the Innere Stadt (inner city) with end-stations at Schwedenplatz, Schottentor and Schwarzenbergplatz. **Trams** fan out from the Ringstraße to the suburbs, while two lines travel on the Ring itself (No. 1 clockwise, No. 2 anti-clockwise). The interstices between tram lines are covered by **bus** routes.

The **night service** is continually being extended and improved: there are now 22 bus routes operating at half-hourly intervals from some time after midnight until the commencement of the daytime service after 05.00. One of these strategic routes will almost certainly pass within walking distance of your destination. A special ticket supplement must be purchased, either in advance (see below) or on the bus. Stops serviced by a night bus will have the number(s) and route advertised on them (e.g. *N.4*). Many routes start from Schwedenplatz or Schottentor. A leaflet detailing routes is available at U-bahn information offices.

The U-Bahn

The modern U-Bahn now has five lines (two of them partly adaptations of the 19C Stadtbahn and mostly above ground). The newish **U3** runs between Ottakring in the west and Semmering in the east. The **U2,** currently linking Karlsplatz and Schottenring, is to be extended across the Danube to Aspern by the end of 2008. It serves the new MuseumsQuartier. The **Schnellbahn** runs from railheads to outlying suburbs.

Tickets and discount travel

It is strongly advisable for visitors to buy either a 24-hour, 72-hour (the **Wien-Karte/Vienna Card**), or weekly pass (all transferable). These can be bought at one of the **Tabak/Trafik** outlets in the city or at the railway stations, U-Bahn ticket offices, (Karlsplatz, Stephansplatz, Schwedenplatz, Schottentor, Westbahnhof and elsewhere), and some hotel reception desks, tourist information and Vienna transport information offices. These tickets enable you to travel all over the network on all forms of city transport for the period specified.

The **Wien-Karte/Vienna Card** (currently around 16 Euros) is a useful combination card that entitles the holder to 72 hours of network travel on the underground, buses and trams and it offers discounts on tickets for a large number of performances, events, permanent and temporary exhibitions (these last may be charged extra to the regular admission fee). It is also valid in some shops.

Tickets for individual journeys can also be bought in blocks. If you are going out of town and returning, the convenient (but expensive) **Umwelt-Streifennetzkarte** may be the best solution. It has eight strips, each valid for one day's travel on the network per person after validation (once) in the machines at the U-Bahn entrance or on a tram or bus. Information on the transport network and tickets may be obtained at the office on the Karlsplatz U-Bahn concourse, at Stephansplatz, the Westbahnhof and elsewhere.

Taxis

Taxis stand at ranks in the suburbs and Inner City (for example by Stephansdom) and at railway stations. Theoretically they should not be hailed in the street (but will often stop). A taxi summoned by telephone usually comes within five minutes anywhere except in the outlying suburbs. Radio taxis may be ordered on the following numbers: ☎ 40100, ☎ 60160 but there are many others in the phone-book. By Viennese standards, taxis are not all that expensive and are recommended for late night travelling (supplement payable).

Driving in Vienna

Driving in Vienna is not a rewarding experience. Viennese driving tends to be aggressive, self-righteous and not all that skilful. However, there are underground car parks at strategic points in the Inner City (e.g. at Freyung, Oper, Stephansdom), which motorists may have to use if staying in a hotel without own parking. Parking times are strictly limited in the centre and in parts of the suburbs (in so-called 'Blue Zones'). Permits purchased from *Tabaks* (tobacconists/newsagents) must be displayed. A concession allows a ten minute period of grace for loading or unloading before you get a ticket or are towed.

When driving, particular care should be taken with *trams*, which have right of way. You must stop for passengers boarding or alighting from trams in the street, unless there is a raised passenger platform (and even then caution is indicated). Care must also be taken with zebra crossings when turning right or left at junctions with traffic lights. Even if the light is green, you must wait for pedestrians crossing the street you *turn into*, until all pedestrians have crossed.

 # Where to stay

Hotel owners in Vienna often complain of unfilled beds, but this excess capacity mysteriously disappears if you actually try to book a room, at least at weekends or in the high season. Vienna gives good quality and reasonable value overall, especially when compared with the rip-off capitals of the world such as London or Tokyo. The prices quoted are usually inclusive of taxes and breakfast (but check). Beware of the classic telephone ploy, whereby a huge surcharge is added to calls made from your room (often there is a payphone in the lobby). Bookings, once accepted, are binding on *both* parties, even if not confirmed in writing. The Vienna Tourist Board issues a free list of Hotels and Pensions, which is obtainable at all tourist bureaux and at the National Tourist Offices abroad.

Booking accommodation

The Tourist Board in Vienna (Wien Tourismus) will make hotel reservations. Contact **Tourist-Info, Albertinaplatz 1**,Wien-Tourismus, A-1025 Wien. For further information ☎ 3 1 24 555. 📠 43 1 24 555 666. ✉ info@info.wien.at, or visit their website: 🖳 www.info.wien.at.

Listed below are some of the best-known and/or some of the best-loved places to stay in Vienna. The categories shown indicate price ranges from €€€ (luxury), €€ (medium-priced) to € (good value or cheap). The prices assume a double-bed with shower or bath and are *approximate only*; **always check the current price either with your travel agent or direct with the hotel**.

Luxury hotels from €200–€440

Ana Grand Hotel Wien (Kärntner Ring 9-13, ☎ 515 80-0. 📠 515 13-12) is the result of massive investment by *Japanese Airlines* and others before the Japanese economy went belly-up. State of the art, with attractive restaurants on the top floor.

Bristol (Kärntner Ring 1, ☎ 515 16. ▤ 515 165 50). Extremely elegant Ringstraßen hotel situated next to the Opera House. It was sufficiently accommodating to allow Leonard Bernstein to bring his piano with him. The city's best gourmet restaurant (*Korso*, p 25) is part of the hotel.

Im Palais Schwarzenberg (Schwarzenbergplatz 9, ☎ 798 45 15. ▤ 798 47 14). All that you would expect from a palace-cum-hotel owned by the scion of an ancient line of Central European aristocracy: discreet service, excellent food and period interiors.

Imperial (Kärntner Ring 16, ☎ 501 10. ▤ 501 104 10). The '*Staatshotel*' for visiting dignitaries, this was once the Ringstraßen palace of the Duke of Württemberg. Its café is favoured by '*Promis*' (prominent persons) for working breakfasts. *Imperialtorte* is a rival of *Sachertorte*.

Plaza Hilton Vienna (Schottenring 11, ☎ 313 90-0. ▤ 313 901 60). Much more attractive than the other Hilton in the city, this ultramodern hotel is decorated in a style reminiscent of the Wiener Werkstätte.

Sacher (Philharmonikerstraße 4, ☎ 514 56. ▤ 514 57-810). The most famous of Vienna's hotels (p 117) and not only because of *Sachertorte*. It is difficult to be objective about such a cult place, but prices at the middling to lower end of the luxury range seem reasonable for so much nostalgia and ambience.

Das Triest (Wiedner Hauptstraße 12, ☎ 589 18). An interesting, relative newcomer on the scene is this Conran-designed hotel which is stylishly modern, if somewhat puritan in style.

The major international chains are represented in Vienna by the *Inter-Continental* (Johannesgasse 28, ☎ 711 22- 126. ▤ 713 44 89), the *Vienna Marriott* (Parkring 12A, ☎ 515 18 0. ▤ 515 18-67 36), the *Hilton* (Am Stadtpark, ☎ 717 000) and some cheaper hotels away from the centre (*Ramada, Novotel*), oriented to the package tour market. Probably the nicest and certainly the most stylish of the upmarket chain hotels is the *Radisson SAS Palais Hotel* (Parkring 16, ☎ 515 17-0. ▤ 512 22 16).

Hotels with local flavour (€110–€260)

Altstadt Vienna (Kirchengasse 41, ☎ 526 33 99 0. ▤ 523 49 01). Antique and modern designer furnishings, a view over the roof of St Ulrich's church and a family atmosphere make this one of the more attractive of the relatively new Viennese hotels. It occupies the upper floors of an 18C house and is owned by a descendant of Grete Wiesenthal, the Isadora Duncan of *fin-de-siècle* Vienna.

Dorint Biedermeier Wien (Landstraßer Hauptstraße 28, ☎ 716 71 0. ▤ 716 71-503). Converted from a Biedermeier house, this is an extremely appealing hotel in a surprisingly quiet backwater, given its proximity to the traffic and shopping centres of Landstraßer Hauptstraße and Wien Mitte. Attractive original features in the interiors.

Gartenhotel Glanzing (Glanzinggasse 23, ☎ 470 42 72. ▤ 470 427 214). A 1920s villa that is rather far from the centre (a 7-minute walk to the bus stop), but by the same token quiet and with the bonus of a nice garden. Family-run, children welcome, bumper breakfasts a speciality.

Kaiserin Elisabeth (Weihburggasse 3, ☎ 515 26. ▤ 515 267). Biedermeier interiors, central position and reasonable prices considering the pleasant ambience.

König von Ungarn (Schulerstraße 10, ☎ 515 84. ▤ 515 848). Adjoining the **Figarohaus** (p 134), this 17C building retains its nostalgic charm, especially in the glassed-over inner courtyard with bar and seating area. First-class restaurant with Austrian cuisine attached (but under different management).

Hotel Römischer Kaiser (Annagasse 16, ☎ 512 77 51. 📠 512 7751-13). Striking Rococo interiors recall the heyday of this small town palace that once belonged to an adviser of Maria Theresia. Annagasse is picturesque and you are a few minutes' walk from the attractions of the city centre.

Hotel am Schubertring (Schubertring 11, ☎ 717 02 0. 📠 713 99 66). Much favoured by visiting musicians is this neo-Jugendstil decorated hotel, which is situated roughly equidistant from the main music venues. Very cosy, particularly the bar in the style of Adolf Loos. Also has apartment suites.

Pensions and cheaper hotels (€100–€200)

The classiest pensions are nudging the price levels of middle-range hotels, but most of those listed below will have rooms at reasonable prices.

Pension am Operneck (Kärntner Straße 47, ☎ 512 93 10. 📠 512 93 10-20). This tiny (six rooms) pension is for opera buffs who cannot bear to be more than a stone's throw from the opera house. Breakfast in bed. Early booking essential.

Jäger (Hernalser Hauptstraße 187, ☎ 486 66 20. 📠 486 66 20-8). Delightful family-run hotel of great comfort that makes up for being rather far out with charming service and pleasant garden. Tram 43 runs past the front door.

Pension Landhaus Fuhrgassl-Huber (Rathstraße 24, Neustift am Walde, ☎ 440 30 33. 📠 440 27 14). If you want to stay in a Heurigen village (p 200), this relatively new and rustically decorated pension with a courtyard for summer use is surely the nicest place you could find. It is at least 30 minutes from the city centre by bus and tram, and not that cheap, but its unrivalled charm compensates for any potential disadvantages.

Pension Nossek (Graben 17, ☎ 533 70 41. 📠 535 36 46). Very central, very elegant, some bedrooms overlooking the Graben. Bookings should be made well in advance.

Pension Pertschy (Habsburgergasse 5, ☎ 534 49. 📠 534 49-49). A favourite with old Vienna hands who like its friendly atmosphere and the location just off the Graben.

Hotel Wandl (Petersplatz 9, ☎ 534 55. 📠 534 55-77). Next to Peterskirche in the heart of the city in an historic building.

Seasonal hotels (€55–€75)

University hostels are turned into seasonal hotels during the academic summer holidays.

Academia (Pfeilgasse 3A, ☎ 401 76/55, 📠 401 76-20, which also reserves for the following two hostels: *Atlas* (Lerchenfelder Straße, 1–3, ☎ 521 78. 📠 401 76 20). *Avis* (Pfeilgasse 4, ☎ 401 74. 📠 401 76-20).

Accordia (Große Schiffgasse 12, ☎ 212 16 68. 📠 212 16 68-697).

Haus Döbling (Gymnasiumstraße 85, ☎ 369 55 89).

Rosen Hotels Austria (Linzer Straße 161, ☎ 911 49 10; information line).

Youth hostels

The *Österreichischer Jugendherbergsverband* is at Schottenring Nr 28 (☎ 533 53 53. ▤ 535 0861) and supplies information about the eight hostels in the city. Some of the latter are in fairly outlying districts.

Larger hostels are *Jugendgästehaus der Stadt Wien* (13th District, Schlossberggasse 8, ☎ 877 15 01. ▤ 879 79 51) and *Jugendgästehaus Wien Brigittenau* (20th District, Friedrich Engels-Platz 24, ☎ 332 82 94. ▤ 330 83 79).

Camping

For details of the five local camping sites, contact *Camping- und Caravaningclub Austria (CCA)* at Mariahilfer Straße 180, ☎ 891 21/0. ▤ 8912 1236.

Self-catering

Vienna City Apartments (Darwingasse 8/18 ☎ 0699/ 19 259 421. ▤ 957 56 44) can arrange self-catering.

Staying in private homes

Contact *Mitwohnzentrale, Odyssee Reisen GesmbH* (Laudongasse 8, A-1080 Vienna, ☎ 402 60 61. ▤ 402 60 62) for advice and assistance, or apply to an organisation in your country that arranges introductions for flat or house swaps.

 Eating and drinking

Vienna offers a wide choice of restaurants, cellars, cafés and night bars (known as '*Szene*' and often with some kind of music). As far as restaurants are concerned, the famous Wiener '*Beisl*' traditionally offered homely Viennese cooking at affordable prices. Unfortunately, many *Beisln* have gone up-market in an effort to milk the tourist trade, so the nomenclature is no longer a guarantee of good value. There is also a good selection of ethnic restaurants in the city, although Vienna is not much noted for first rate Indian and Chinese food (despite the proliferation of Chinese restaurants in the suburbs). Modestly priced food and wine can be found in the wine cellars, at most *Heurigen* (see p 200) and in cafés. At the bottom end of the scale come the self-service establishments, sandwich bars, fast food joints and the celebrated *Würstelstände*; the last named are huts dispensing fatty sausages, beer and soft drinks on the street.

A useful purchase is the annually updated complete guide to all Vienna's eateries (now 4000 and rising), *Wien, wie es isst...* ('Vienna, how it eats...', punning also on 'Vienna as it is'), published by Falter in German but relatively easy to decipher with details of type of food, location, price, opening hours, telephone numbers and whether credit cards are taken.

Typical Viennese dishes

Many places in the centre have menus in English, but interpretation of some primarily or typically Viennese dishes may be helpful for those eating in places less frequented by tourists.

Soups

Eierschwammerlsuppe, chanterelle soup
Frittatensuppe, clear broth with crêpes

Rollgerstelsuppe, pearl barley soup

Meat courses

Backhendl, chicken fried in breadcrumbs
Bauernschmaus, mixed meats with dumplings and sauerkraut
Beuschel, chopped lung in sauce
Blunzen, black pudding
Debreziner, paprika-spiced sausage
Faschiertes, minced meat
Fleischlaberl, rissoles
Grammelknödel, dumplings stuffed with pork scratchings
Selchfleischknödel, dumplings stuffed with smoked pork
Hirschragout, venison stew
Jungfernbraten, loin of pork
Kalbsvögerl, knuckle of veal
Karree, shoulder of pork (often smoked)
Kuttelfleck, tripe
Lendenbraten, roast sirloin

Lungenbraten, loin of pork
Krenfleisch, boiled pork with grated horseradish
Schöpsernes, mutton
Stelze, leg of veal or pork, roast, smoked or boiled
Tafelspitz, boiled beef, typically with horseradish, chives, apple sauce or other condiments (a Viennese speciality)
Vanillerostbraten, garlic-seasoned roast beef
Wiener Schnitzel, breaded veal or (usually) pork fillet; (a Viennese favourite, served with cold onion and potato salad)
Zwiebelrostbraten, roast or fried beef with crispy onions

Fish

Fogosch, pike-perch ('sander')
Forelle, trout

Karpf, carp
Lachs, salmon

Vegetables and pasta

Blaukraut, red cabbage
Bummerlsalat, iceberg lettuce
Bohnen, beans
Fisolen, runner beans
Jägersalat, salad of Chinese cabbage
Knödel, dumplings (made with flour, potatoes, bread or yeast)
Krautfleckerl, square pasta with seasoned cabbage

Nockerl, semolina dumplings
Paradeiser, tomatoes
Risipisi, rice with peas
Schinkenfleckerln, ham with square noodles
Semmelknödel, bread dumplings with parsley and onion
Serviettenknödel, as above, but with different seasoning

Some desserts

Auflauf, steamed or soufflé pudding
Buchteln (or Wuchteln), yeast dumplings
  with vanilla sauce or filled with jam
Germknödel, yeast dumpling
Gugelhupf, pound cake
Himbeergrotz, purée of fresh raspberries,
  (also made with other soft fruits;
  Grütze is the jellified juice)
Kaiserschmarrn, pancake with raisins
  and plum compote

Millirahmstrudel, strudel with sweet
  cheese filling and vanilla sauce, (also
  known as *Milchrahmstrudel*)
Mohr in Hemd, steamed pudding with
  chocolate and nuts
Palatschinken, pancakes
Powidl, plum sauce
Zwetschkenknödel, plum dumplings
Zwetschkenröster, plum compote

Restaurants

Price categories are indicated as €€€ (expensive or very expensive), €€ (moderately priced), and € (good value or cheap by Austrian standards). The following are recommended:

Viennese cuisine

Beim Czaak (Postgasse 15/Corner Fleischmarkt, ☎ 513 72 15; €€). Viennese cooking with a Czech accent (so some good dumplings available) in a traditional *Beisl* setting. Good atmosphere and friendly service.

Brezl-Gwölb (Ledererhof 9, ☎ 533 88 11; €€(€)). Ideal for a romantic evening out in an intimate setting, with Viennese specialities on offer including *Tafelspitz*. The summer garden is set against the last remains of the medieval city wall.

Eckel (Sieveringer Straße 46, ☎ 320 32 18; €€€) offers first rate cooking and attentive service. Good list of Austrian wines and knowledgeable sommelier.

Zum Herkner (Dornbacher Straße 123, ☎ 485 43 86; €€) is a favourite with the Viennese for its honest cooking and honest prices. Well worth the trek, but you must book.

Zur Goldenen Glocke (Schönbrunner Straße 8, corner Kettenbrückengasse, ☎ 587 57 67; €€) is especially pleasant in summer when you sit out in the courtyard.

Grünauer (Hermanngasse 32, ☎ 526 40 80; €€(€)). Hailed for its revival of traditional Viennese cooking (with a touch of 'Pannonia') and its excellent wine list. Must book.

Zur Tabakspfeife (Goldschmiedgasse 4, ☎ 533 72 86; €€) is very reasonable despite its touristy location and an ideal spot for a quiet lunch or earlyish evening meal.

Zum Schwarzen Kameel (Bognergasse 5, ☎ 533 89 67; €€€). The self-service part is cheaper, with legendary ham rolls, and is open until 11 p.m. The speciality is the lunch menu (warm food served only between 11.30 and 15.00), still among the best Viennese cooking in town, but with prices to match. Old world charm is evident in both the service and the Jugendstil decor of the restaurant's inner snug, for which you must book.

Immervoll (Weihburggasse 17, ☎ 513 52 88; €€). This trend-setting '*Neo-Beisl*' (which should mean the best of the old tradition enlivened with attractive new ideas) has some enthusiastic fans. The name means 'Always Full', which it may be over the lunch hours.

Kern's Beisel (Kleeblattgasse 4, ☎ 533 91 88. €€) has recently moved from decidedly modest to these definitely *gemütliche* premises and remains one of the best places for fairly priced and excellent Viennese cooking with impeccable service to match. It is crowded over the main lunch hour, but you can enjoy a glass of *Veltliner* at the bar while waiting for a table to become free. Closed at weekends.

Plachutta (Wollzeile 38, ☎ 512 15 77; €€€). For those who can't make the trek out to Hietzing for the famous *Tafelspitz* of the Hietzinger Bräu, the cadet line of HB's owners has opened this very smart establishment in the city. The style is ultra-professional, the atmosphere somewhat moneyed and trendy, but serious carnivores could hardly do better than here in the city centre.

The mecca for *Wiener Schnitzel* fans is *Figlmüller* (Wollzeile 5, in the alley, ☎ 512 61 77; €€), which is unbeatable for both the quality and size of its Schnitzels.

Excellent service and cooking with a regional flavour at *Zu den 3 Hacken* (Singerstraße 28, ☎ 512 58 95; €€€).

Schnattl (Lange Gasse 40, ☎ 405 34 00; €€). If you find yourself in the elegant Josefstadt, you could do worse than eat at this pleasant *Beisl* with Viennese and Austrian dishes and patrons from the theatrical world.

Luxury restaurants

At the following places you can expect to pay international gourmet prices (all €€€), but each offers something distinctive in terms of culinary expertise and/or ambience:

Korso bei der Oper (Mahlerstraße 2, ☎ 515 16- 546) is considered by many to be the best restaurant in Vienna. It offers unrivalled Viennese cuisine imaginatively interpreted, extended and enhanced by a perfectionist chef.

Altwienerhof (Herklotzgasse 6, ☎ 892 60 0). The Savoy-trained owner-chef produces marvellous French cooking and matches his artistry with a discriminating list of French wines and cheeses. Located near the Westbahnhof, which is not attractive, but still worth the trek.

Do & Co (Stephansplatz 12/Haas-Haus 7th Floor, ☎ 535 3969). Scores with the best views in Vienna, partly overlooking the cathedral. International and Viennese cooking, famously dynamic service, though cynics say that seems partly designed to turn over the tables quickly...

Restaurant Bauer (Sonnenfelsgasse 17, ☎ 512 9871) boasts one of the best cuisines in Vienna presided over by star-chef, Herbert Malek. A bonus is the excellent wine list and a wide selection of Schnaps and cigars. A good choice for that special evening out when you want to spoil yourself and be spoiled.

Steirereck (Rasumofskygasse 2, ☎ 713 31 68) offers the Austrian equivalent of *nouvelle cuisine* with a Styrian slant and is a favourite haunt of the diplomatic community. It is generally regarded as rivalling *Korso* for the laurels as the best restaurant in Vienna, some say in Austria. May be undergoing restoration for part of 2002.

Kervansaray-Hummerbar (Mahlerstraße 9, ☎ 512 88 43) is sumptuously Levantine on the ground floor, the lobster bar ('*Hummerbar*') on the first floor serving crustaceans, which, for obvious reasons are a rarity in Vienna.

The *Restaurant im Palais Schwarzenberg* (Schwarzenbergplatz 9, ☎ 798 45 15 600) is located in the Baroque palace of the same name (see p 20), which is now a hotel. Here you can dine in some splendour looking out over the Baroque park. Very elegant, very stylish, very expensive.

Le Siècle (Im Radisson SAS Palais-Hotel) (Parkring 16, ☎ 515 17-3440).

Probably the best of the international hotel restaurants offering inter alia 'fresh fish from river and sea'. A la carte and 'candle-lit' menu in the evenings. Closed in July and August.

Some restaurants with national cuisines
Italian
The choice is large, from noble restaurant to trendy or cheap and cheerful–Italian cooking has increasingly colonised Vienna. There are now innumerable pizza and pasta joints round the centre, but also some genuinely appealing establishments, as follows:

La Ninfea (Schauflergasse 6, ☎ 532 91 26; €€€) is a rather expensive but much applauded Italian restaurant, noted for a good list of Italian wines. *No* pizzas.
Cantinetta Antinori (Jasomirgottstraße 3-5, ☎ 533 77 22; €€€). This delivers all that the famous name promises in terms of Tuscan fare and superb wine. However book a table at the back of the restaurant for comfort and intimacy.
Novelli bacaro con cucina (Bräunerstraße 11, ☎ 513 42 00; €€€). Refined Italian cooking; restaurant situated in an old palais.
Il Centro (Graben 17, ☎ 533 50 92-13; €€). Trendy bar, café and small restaurant (on first floor) with Italian and international dishes and wines.

Indian
Restaurant Raagini (Franz-Josefs-Kai 49, ☎ 533 03 80; €€). Genuine charcoal grill dishes at reasonable prices.
Koh-i-noor (Marc-Aurel-Straße 8, ☎ 533 00 80; €€€). Expensive grill platters, curries, tandoori.

Hungarian
Ilona-Stüberl (Bräunerstraße 2, ☎ 533 90 29; €€). Hungarian, good value, enormous helpings, motherly service.

Balkan and Greek
Kornat (Marc-Aurel-Straße 8, ☎ 535 65 18; €€) will help you recall those sun-soaked holidays on the Dalmatian coast. Even their wines come from the offshore islands.
Orpheus (Spiegelgasse 10, ☎ 512 38 88; €€). Cretan specialities; their own imported oil and honey.

Chinese and Asian
East to West (Seilerstätte 14, ☎ 512 91 49; €€). Good selection of Asian dishes, including some from Manchuria and Mongolia, with emphasis otherwise on sweet 'n sour.

Japanese
Probably the second most persistent gastronomic invaders after the Italians, the Japanese have made *sushi* a must for image-conscious younger Viennese. There are numerous smaller or larger **sushi bars**–in the Naschmarkt, *Akakiko* at Heidenschuss 3 and Singerstraße 4, *Toko Ri* at Salztorgasse 4 and elsewhere.

EN (Werdertorgasse 8, ☎ 532 44 90; €€). Considered by aficionados to offer the best Japanese food in Vienna.
Yugetsu (Führichgasse 10, ☎ 512 27 20; €€€). On the upper floor, Teppan Yaki, on the ground floor, sushi with a special Sunday menu of the latter.

Cafés (Kaffeehäuser)

Although a coffee may seem expensive in a traditional Viennese café, you are also paying for the right to sit as long as you like in pleasant surroundings with newspapers supplied free. **Coffee** comes in many different forms, including espresso, *Wiener Mélange* (coffee with milk or whipped cream) *Grosser* (or *Kleiner*) *Braune*, coffee with a dash of milk, large or small.

Café food varies in quality and quantity, according to the pretensions of the establishment. Relatively expensive but above average for sophistication is the fashionable *Café Griensteidl* (Michaelerplatz 2), but economically priced and a favourite haunt of civil servants from nearby ministries on the Ring is the *Café Ministerium* at Georg-Coch-Platz 4. A major plus of many cafés is that they serve warm food at all hours, most of them opening as early as 07.00 or 08.00 (some even earlier) and closing at midnight (some in the early hours).

Distinguished traditional cafés include the *Bräunerhof* at Stallburggasse 2, *Diglas* at Wollzeile 10, *Hawelka* at Dorotheergasse 6 (the haunt of literati and Bohemians), *Landtmann* (Dr.-Karl-Lueger-Ring 4), which is very political, *Schwarzenberg* (Kärntner Ring 17) and *Tirolerhof* (Tegetthoffstraße 8). The last named was one of the few to develop a female clientele at the turn of the century and is still favoured by women. Its *Apfelstrudel* is unrivalled.

Konditoreien are another Viennese speciality, offering tea, coffee and a mouthwatering array of sticky cakes and pastries. The most famous is *Demel* (Kohlmarkt 14), although it is always bursting with tourists in season. A congenial establishment on the Graben is *Lehmann* (Graben 12), while the two *Heiner* (Kärntner Straße, 21–23, Wollzeile 9) are also pleasant, especially that on Wollzeile with its Biedermeier interior. Cognoscenti maintain that the best pastries can now be found at the relative newcomer to the city centre, *Kurcafé Konditorei Oberlaa* (Neuer Markt 16), which also does a good light lunch. Another branch has opened at Babenbergerstraße 15/Nibelungengasse. *Sluka* (Rathausplatz 8) under the arcades of the Rathaus is a comfortable and intimate café with excellent pastries.

Chocolates, Sachertorte

Those with a sweet tooth are well catered for in Vienna. The most prestigious purveyors of hand-made chocolates in the city are *Altmann & Kühne* at Graben 30, whose products are sold in decorated boxes imitating animals or furniture, which are themselves works of art. Less exclusive but greatly prized are the chocolate balls and coins known as *Mozart Kugeln* and *Mozart Taler*, which are widely available from confectioners and from quality grocers such as *Julius Meinl* on the Graben.

The famous *Sachertorte* is on sale at *Hotel Sacher* itself. A long-running dispute between Sacher and *Demel* as to who owned the rights to the recipe was settled some years ago with a typically Austrian compromise: Sacher alone can sell 'original Sachertorte', but Demel on the Kohlmarkt can also sell their own version, as long as they don't call it 'original'. Of course, this means that others can do the same: somewhat cheaper and perfectly good Sachertorte is sold, for example, by the *Aida* chain of *Konditoreien* (there is one on Stephansplatz).

Wine

Austrian wine is unjustly neglected and was even more unjustly penalised after the so-called 'glycol scandal' in the 1980s, at a time when German and Italian merchants were doing equally unscrupulous things on a bigger scale. Quality control is now probably the strictest in the world. The classic local grape is the *Grüner Veltliner* and generally the whites are more distinguished than the reds. *Wild* at Neuer Markt 10–11 is the city's gourmet grocer and stocks a vast number of quality wines and *Schnaps* in the cellars beneath the shop. Also worth visiting is the *Vinothek St Stephan* (Stephansplatz 6) while cognoscenti should pay a call to the restaurant and wine shop of *Unger und Klein* (Gölsdorfgasse 2, 1st District, ☎ 532 13 23). This is generally considered to be the wine buffs' mecca, its major strengths being in the selection of wines from Vienna, Styria, Lower Austria and Burgenland. The shop also sells *Schnaps* (fruit Schnaps are something of a cult in Austria) and wine accessories.

Wine cellars and wine-bars (€€)

The Baroque and medieval cellars under the Inner City serve Austrian wines by the glass, '*Achtel*' or '*Viertel*', one eighth and one quarter of a litre respectively. They also serve a limited menu of hot and cold food. Cellars are generally open from about 17.00 or 18.00 to midnight, although some of those that are in tourist areas (e.g. the *Augustinerkeller* beneath the Albertina) have restaurant opening hours. They are worth visiting as much for the surroundings and ambience as for the fare.

Popular wine cellars include the *Zwölf Apostel-Keller* (Sonnenfelsgasse 3, ☎ 512 67 77), which is a favourite with the young and has two layers of cellar, medieval and Baroque; the *Esterhazykeller* (Haarhof 1, ☎ 533 34 82), where the Esterhazys served the townsfolk with free wine during the Turkish siege of 1683; also the *Melker Stiftskeller* (Schottengasse 3, ☎ 533 55 30) and the *Augustiner-Keller* (Augustinerstraße 1, ☎ 533 10 26; open 11.00–midnight).

For those who just want to drop in for a glass of quality wine, there are an increasing number of pleasant wine-bars. One that has stood the test of time is *Vis à Vis* (opposite *Figlmüller* in the passage at Wollzeile 5). Top Austrian vintages are also on offer at *Vinissimo* (Windmühlgasse 20, off Mariahilferstraße). Spanish and Italian wines are the speciality of *Festival*, rather far out however at Döblinger Hauptstraße 6/Corner Glatzgasse (tram 37 from Schottentor); while those who insist on sticking with French wines may find a good selection of them at the bistro *Bordeaux* (Servitengasse 2).

Self-service restaurants

Two self-service chains can be recommended for convenience and quality: *Nordsee* (Kohlmarkt 6, Kärntner Straße 25 and elsewhere) has a wide range of fish dishes from plaice and chips to paella. The *Naschmarkt* (Schwarzenbergplatz 16 or Schottengasse 1) offers grills cooked to order, ready-to-eat hot dishes, salads and sandwiches at very reasonable prices. There is also a big selection of alcoholic and non-alcoholic drinks and the neo-Jugendstil interiors are pleasant places in which to linger after a few hours tramping the streets.

Sandwiches, snacks

Trzesniewski (Dorotheergasse 1) is Vienna's most famous sandwich bar, with many varieties of open sandwich (*Brötchen*) and wine or beer by the glass to wash them down. It has stiff competition around the centre, notably from *Superimbiss Duran* (Rotenturmstraße 11). Meaty snacks are available at many of the quality butchers (but usually have to be consumed standing up at a counter), while delicatessens such as **Wild** (Neuer Markt 10–11) and *Julius Meinl* (corner of the Graben and Kohlmarkt) serve pricey, but delicious, hot dishes and cold delicacies. The *Anker* chain of bakeries also serves oven-fresh snacks at the larger outlets, and coffee with filled rolls or pastries at almost all of them. Japanese **sushi bars** have proliferated, as also have stands selling **tramezzini** (e.g. in the Opern Passage). There are also several ethnic snack bars (*Pan e Wien* (Salesianergasse 25), *Köstli* (Karlsplatz Hauptpassage, Koje1) and *Olymp* (Liliengasse 3).

 # General information

Banking services
Banks are generally open Mon–Fri 08.00–12.30 and from 13.30–15.00 (17.30 on Thursdays). Major branches or headquarters of banks in the city centre do not close for the lunch break.

Major **credit and debit cards** are widely accepted in the inner city shops, restaurants and hotels. Some telephone kiosks (Wallnerstraße, Kärntner Straße and elsewhere in the centre) accept credit cards for international calls. Likewise the 'hole in the wall' Bankomat machines, which are steadily increasing in number, are available for cash withdrawals with credit or debit card.

Consulates
Australia: Mattiellistraße 2–4, ☎ 512 85 80.
Canada: Laurenzerberg 2, ☎ 531 38–30 00.
Ireland: Hilton-Center, 16th Floor, Landstraßer Hauptstraße 2A, ☎ 715 42 46.
New Zealand: Springsiedelgasse 28, ☎ 318 85 05.
South Africa: Sandgasse 33, ☎ 320 6493.
United Kingdom: Jaurèsgasse 10, ☎ 716 13-51 51.
United States: Gartenbaupromenade (Parkring) 2 (Marriott Hotel building), ☎ 313 39.

Emergency telephone numbers
Ambulance: ☎ 144
Befrienders: ☎ 713 33 74 (English spoken) (Seidlgasse 8. Stg 1).
Car Breakdown: (ÖAMTC) ☎ 120. (ARBÖ) ☎ 123. (Both 24-hours.)
Doctor on call (*Notarzt*): ☎ 141.
Dentist (nights and weekends, answer machine): ☎ 512 20 78.
Fire: ☎122.
Police: ☎133.
Vienna Hospitals Medical Emergency Service: ☎ 531 16.

Pharmacies
Pharmacies display the 24-hour duty rota that will indicate the nearest night dispensary, and are otherwise open during shopping hours (but with a longer 12.00–14.00 lunch break outside the city centre). On Saturdays they are open until midday.

There is also a recorded message (Apothekenbereitschaftsdienst ☎ 15 50) for advice. The Internationale Apotheke (Kärntner Ring 17, ☎ 512 28 25) has English-speaking staff. The emergency number for doctor on call (*Notarzt*) is ☎ 141, for an ambulance ☎ 144.

Personal safety

Vienna remains one of the world's safest cities, not least because Austria has so far eschewed the most ruthless policies of the New Right. Down-and-outs have increased in number, however, and the area of the Karlsplatz U-Bahn concourse is a meeting place for alcoholics and young drug-takers. The area around Mexikoplatz on the Danube bank to the northeast is a hive of black market and other dubious activity. It is best avoided. Travelling late at night is unlikely to be a problem, even for single women, and the new all-night bus service has made things safer. If in trouble see emergency telephone numbers, listed above.

Postal and telephone services

Opening hours for most post offices are as for shops, but the **Central Post Office** (*Hauptpostamt*) at Fleischmarkt 19 in the Inner City is open 24 hours. There are also 24-hour post offices at the Südbahnhof, Westbahnhof and Franz-Josefs-Bahnhof. Post Office information (Mon–Fri, 08.00–17.00; ☎ 51 551-0).

Many post offices also have **telephone kiosks** (ask at the counter for a line and pay afterwards). In the Inner City on Wallnerstraße, Kärntner Straße and elsewhere, there are telephones that accept major credit cards. Otherwise a local telephone card (*Telefonkarten*) may be purchased at the Tabak/Trafik newsagent outlets, which also sell stamps (*Briefmarken*). With privatisation and the introduction of competition, telephone prices have fallen steeply in recent years.

Dialling codes

The first zero is dropped from the local number when dialling Austria from abroad and vice versa.

To Austria

From Australia and New Zealand ☎ 001143
From the United Kingdom and Ireland ☎ 0043
From North America ☎ 001

From Austria

To Australia ☎ 0061
To New Zealand ☎ 0064
To North America ☎ 001
To Ireland ☎ 00353
To United Kingdom ☎ 0044

Newspapers

English language newspapers are available at kiosks around the city centre, as also at the Westbahnhof and Südbahnhof. The *Financial Times* and *Guardian* (Frankfurt editions) arrive in the morning, other papers at about 16.00. English Sunday papers are available only from Monday morning. American papers available include *USA Today*, the *Wall Street Journal* and *New York Herald Tribune*. The local paper in English, *Austria Today*, appears weekly.

Local customs

If you are invited to a Viennese household it is usual to take flowers for your hostess and a small gift for the host. At meals, never drink until the host has raised his glass and toasted the company ('*Prost!*').

Austrians are punctilious about greeting (*Grüß Gott!*—or *Guten Tag!* if you object to Christian monopoly of politeness). In particular, great importance is attached to shaking hands—always do so when meeting someone socially.

Public holidays

1 January (New Year's Day)	*Neues Jahr*
6 January (Epiphany, Twelfth Night)	*Dreikönigsfest*
Easter Monday	*Ostermontag*
1 May (Labour Day)	*Tag der Arbeit*
Ascension Day (6th Thursday after Easter)	*Christi Himmelfahrt*
Whit Monday (6th Monday after Easter)	*Pfingstmontag*
Corpus Christi (Thursday after Whitsun)	*Fronleichnam*
15 August (Feast of the Assumption of the Virgin)	*Maria Himmelfahrt*
26 October (Day of the Nation)	*Nationalfeiertag*
1 November (All Saints)	*Allerheiligen*
8 December (Feast of the Immaculate Conception)	*Maria Empfängnis*
24 December (Christmas Eve–an important family occasion for Austrians; everything, including public transport, closes down from midday)	*Heiliger Abend*
25 December (Christmas Day)	*Weihnachtstag / Christtag*
26 December (Boxing Day)	*Stephanitag / Stefanitag*

Religious services

Anglican: Christchurch, Jaurésgasse 17–19, ☎ 714 89 00.
Church of Jesus Christ and Latter Day Saints: Böcklinstraße 55, ☎ 367 5674.
International Baptist Church: Mollardgasse 35, ☎ 804 9259.
Jewish: Seitenstettengasse 4, ☎ 531 04-0.
Roman Catholic (in English and other languages): Contact Tourismus Pastoral, Stephansplatz 6, ☎ 515 52/3 75. Also occasional English Mass in the Augustinerkirche and the Votivkirche.
United Methodist Church: Sechshauser Straße 56, ☎ 893 69 89.

Tipping

The famed 'golden Viennese heart' is not very evident if you undertip. 10 per cent is adequate for most restaurant meals and it is customary to leave between 73 cents and 1 Euro for the cloakroom attendants at museums, a bit more at theatres and the opera. 10 per cent for taxis is sufficient.

Shopping

Opening hours Shops are generally open 09.00–18.00 (either 12.30 or 17.00 on Saturdays). Food shops may open up to one and a half hours earlier. It is at last permissible to open all day on Saturday and generally hours are being brought into line with most other EU countries.

Viennese specialities

The main shopping areas are the three sides of a rectangle in the Inner City formed by **Kärntner Straße, Graben** and **Kohlmarkt**, together with **Mariahilferstraße** in the 6th District, where the big stores are located.

The **Ringstraßen Galerien** (adjacent to Hotel Bristol on Kärntner Ring) is a newly opened shopping mall on two levels. It is well worth a visit, although the boutiques tend to be selling international wares. Many cafés and speciality eateries are also located here. Alternatively the determined shopper in search of good value (at least in local terms), can make the long trek out to the vast shopping mall of **Shopping City Süd** at Vösendorf (take the IKEA courtesy bus from the stop opposite the Opera House).

A useful list of suggested **presents** to take home from Vienna is obtainable at the information office on Albertinaplatz and elsewhere. It describes a range of **typically Viennese products** and the addresses of the shops where they can be bought, as well as charting the shops on an orientation map. However it inevitably concentrates on luxury items and antiques.

Porcelain, Viennese design, glassware, clothes

Augarten (Stock-im-Eisen-Platz 3–4) sells porcelain of the same name (although it may be cheaper if purchased at the factory itself, see p 189). *Backhausen* (Kärntner Straße 33) sells furnishing fabrics and some clothing items in patterns of the Wiener Werkstätte (Secession). *Lobmeyr* (Kärntner Straße 26) has been going since the 19C and offers exquisite Historicist and Jugendstil glassware. For gifts and ornaments with a Viennese flavour, the *Österreichische Werkstätten* (Kärntner Straße 6) has many attractive items.

Two shops selling **traditional Austrian styles of clothing** (*Tracht*) are *Resi Hammerer* (Kärntner Straße 29–31) and *Tostmann* (Schottengasse 3A). A specialist for the Salzburg loden coats is *Loden-Plankl* at Michaelerplatz 6.

Art and antiques

In the vicinity of the Dorotheum auction house in the Dorotheergasse (see p 121) are to be found many of Vienna's art dealers and antique shops. For a hefty price you can indulge a passion for Biedermeier furniture, 19C painting, or *fin-de-siècle* artefacts. Worth highlighting is *Herbert Asenbaum* (Kärntner Straße 28) for smaller antiques, such as silver or jewellery. The *Dorotheum* itself (Dorotheergasse 17) is the state auction house and is worth visiting to view its pre-auction displays. Although auction prices are sometimes quite reasonable, always remember that there will be a substantial addition of VAT and commission to the cost of your successful bid. Some objects can be purchased direct from the showrooms.

Serious antiques buyers might consider timing their visit to coincide with the annual mid-November **antiques fair**. This is held simultaneously in three locations: the Congress Hall of the Neue Hofburg, the Ferstel Palais and (adjacent to the latter) the Palais Harrach.

Bookshops

For the best selection of books on art and architecture in several languages, visit *Georg Prachner* (Kärntner Straße 30) or *Wolfrum* (Augustinerstraße 10). The latter also sells prints of old Vienna and posters of Viennese artists. Two exclusively English language bookshops are the *British Bookshop* (branches in Weihburggasse 24–26 and Mariahilferstraße 4, open Mon–Fri 09.30–18.30, Sat 09.30–17.00. ☎ 522 67 30) and *Shakespeare & Co* (Sterngasse 2).

Music shops

Opera and classical music buffs will find a good selection of CDs at *Gramola* (Kohlmarkt 5—bargains round the corner at Graben 16), and at *Arcadia Opera Shop* (Kärntner Straße 40 under the arcades of the Opera House itself). Other shops with a good classical selection are in the and Augustinerstraße. The *Virgin Megastore* on Mariahilfer Straße 37–9 sells the usual broad range of music but the classical section is limited.

Markets

The **Naschmarkt** (nearest U-Bahn: Kettenbrückengasse) is open Mon–Fri 06.00–18.30, Sat 06.00–14.00. This is Vienna's gourmet food market. On Saturday mornings there is also a **flea market** (*Flohmarkt*) at the western end, where small antiquities can occasionally be picked up at bargain prices.

In summer there are occasional markets elsewhere in the city, for example in the picturesque **Spittelberg** area, not far from the Volkstheater.

 # Entertainment

For precise details of current concerts, shows and their venues, see the monthly *Wien Programm*, obtainable from the Tourist Information Office at Albertinaplatz 1 and at booking agencies etc. elsewhere. (The *Programm* does not list cinemas, for which see the daily press.)

Vienna's **events listings** are also posted on ✉ **oeinfo@oewwien.via at**, the e-mail address for the Austrian tourist office (Osterreich Werbung /Urlaubsinformation Osterreich, Margarethenstrasse 1/Rilkeplatz 5, A-1040 Wien). The office is a short walk from Karlsplatz, Open Mon–Fri, 10.00–17.00 (to 18.00 Thur) ☎ 00 431 587 20 00. 📠 1 588 66 48.

Principal concert halls, opera houses and music venues

Bösendorfer Saal Graf-Starhemberg-Gasse 14.
Herbert von Karajan Centrum (Concerts, video archive), Kärntner Ring 4.
Konzerthaus (p 163), Lothringerstraße 20.

Musikvereinsgebäude (usually known as 'Musikverein'), (p 163–164), Dumbastraße 3/ Bösendorferstraße 12.
Raimund Theater (Musicals), Wallgasse 18.
Ronacher Theater (Musicals, variety) (p 132), Himmelpfortgasse 25.
Arnold Schönberg Center (Musical and other events), Palais Fanto, Zaunergasse 1-3
Staatsoper State Opera House, (usually known as the 'Oper') (p 153), Opernring 2.
Theater an der Wien (Musicals), Linke Wienzeile 6.
Wiener Kammeroper (Young ensemble, sometimes rareties), Fleischmarkt 24.
Wiener Volksoper (Opera, operetta), Währinger Straße 78.

Summer specials
Mozart operas are performed by the Wiener Kammeroper in the 'Roman Ruins' of the park at Schönbrunn (Schönbrunner Schloßpark, Schönbrunner Schloßstraße; ☎ 877 45 66 or see monthly *Wien Programm*).

Also at Schönbrunn, in the Schloßtheater, the same ensemble plays a festival of lighter music, the *Soirée bei Prinz Orlofsky* (Schönbrunner Schloßtheater, ☎ 894 6690-51, July and August only).

In the **Rathauspark**, before the City Hall, there are opera films on a big screen during the summer months (entrance free).

Son et Lumière takes place at the Schloß Belvedere, Prinz-Eugen-Straße 27; daily in summer from 21.30. See *Wien Programm* for booking details.

Tickets
Opera tickets (for both the Staatsoper and Volksoper) can be obtained from the **Bundestheaterkassen** at Goethegasse 1/Hanuschgasse 3 (just off Albertina-platz). Telephone reservations with credit cards: ☎ 513 1 513. Tickets are available about a month ahead of performance. Cheap standing places are available at the Opera House for those prepared to queue an hour or more ahead of that evening's performance. Other music tickets can be obtained direct at the venue or (at a price) through ticket agencies, or (at even greater price) through your hotel concierge. **Wien-Karte/Vienna Card** (p 17) offers reductions on some shows.

Principal theatres
Akademie Theater (second arm to Burgtheater), Lisztstraße 1.
Burgtheater (Still considered one of the best in the German-speaking world) (p 160), Dr.-Karl-Lueger-Ring 2.
Kammerspiele (mostly light comedy and farce), Rotenturmstraße 20.
Theater in der Josefstadt (popular programme and Viennese comedy; Nestroy, Raimund; p 184), Josefstädter Straße 26.
Volkstheater Neustiftgasse 1.

Performances in English
Vienna's English Theatre Josefsgasse 12.
International Theatre Porzellangasse 8/Müllnergasse.

Mime

Serapionstheater im Odeon, Taborstraße 10. One of the most sophisticated mime shows in Europe and highly recommended. However it may soon have to move from this venue.

Cabaret (in German)

Kabarett & Komödie am Naschmarkt Linke Wienzeile 4.
Kabarett Niedermair Lenaugasse 1A.
Spektakel Hamburgerstraße 14.
Theater Kabarett Simpl Wollzeile 36.

Cinema

The listings in the daily press indicate whether the film is in its original language with the rubric 'OF' (*Originalfassung*). Most foreign films are dubbed into German. Films in English (or other non-German languages) are regularly shown at the following venues:

Burg Kino (latest Hollywood films in the original versions), Opernring 19.
Artis Kinotreff (six rooms showing films exclusively in English), Schultergasse 5.
Filmcasino (serious European films) Margaretenstraße 78.
Haydn English Cinema (mainstream Hollywood and British films) Maria-hilferstraße 57.
Stadtkino (arthouse cinema showing original version films), Schwarzen-bergplatz 7.

Old films and retrospectives for film buffs

Österreichisches Filmmuseum (a small membership fee is payable), Augustinerstraße 1 (Albertina).
Votiv-Kino (three screens. 'Film-breakfast' on Sundays), Währinger Straße 12.

Sightseeing tours

Several firms offer sightseeing tours covering Vienna and further afield. Information can be obtained from the **Tourist Information** on Albertinaplatz or travel agencies. One company that is well established is *Vienna Sightseeing Tours / Wiener Rundfahrten* (Kärntner Straße 38, ☎ 515 14-225. ▤ 512 42 26). It offers a range of themed tours in the city, also to Salzburg, Prague, Budapest, etc. There is a service for groups and an expensive VIP service for individuals and small groups. They pick up from hotels, or you can join the tour at the Opera. A **boat tour** on the Danube Canal and the Danube itself is possible on the **MS 'Schlögen'**, leaving from Schwedenbrücke at 10.45 (also 14.45 in summer) and lasting three-and-a-quarter hours. The boat station by Schwedenbrücke is reached by U1 and U4 to Schwedenplatz.

Walking tours

Recommended are the guided walking tours covering various aspects of the city, such as the Vienna musical tradition, Freud's Vienna, the locations of *The Third Man* etc. (the choice is much wider if you can follow German). A list of walks can be obtained at **Tourist Information** offices and information can be obtained per ☎/▤ on 894 53 63, or 489 96 74.

Audio guides

A new initiative, these audio guides, like those in museums, may be hired for walks round the city. They are obtainable at some hotel reception desks, or **Intropa**, Karntner Straße 28 and the Tourist Information Centre on Albertinaplatz (☎ 729 7234).

 # Sport

Swimming and ice-skating are the most attractive physical pursuits on offer in Vienna. Some of the baths are of architectural interest, particularly the Amalienbad on Reumannplatz, a beautiful piece of Art Deco-influenced functionalism by Otto Nadel and Karl Schmallhofer (1926). Bicycling on the new Danube Island (Donauinsel) can also be a pleasant way of passing a summer's day.

Swimming baths
Opening times may change, but usually by extension.
Amalienbad Reumannplatz 23. (Open Tues–Sun 09.00–18.00, later (20.30) on Wed, Thur and Fri.)
Dianabad Obere Donaustraße 91–93. (Open Tues, Thur 06.30–21.00; Wed, Fri 09.00–21.00; Sat, Sun 07.00–18.00.)
Stadthalle Vogelweidplatz 14. (Open Mon, Wed, Fri 08.00–21.00; Tues, Thur 06.30–21.30; Sat, Sun 07.00–18.30.)
Thermalbad Oberlaa Kurbadstraße 10 (end stop for Tram 67). (Open Mon 09.00–21.00; Tues–Fri 09.00–22.00; Sat 09.00–21.00; Sun 08.00–22.00.) Luxurious facilities (hence a correspondingly high admission charge) include whirlpool, *Kneipp* cure, thermal pools, sauna, children's pool, hairdressers, chiropodist and restaurant.

Ice-skating
Wiener Eislaufverein Lothringerstraße 22. (Open late Oct–early Mar, Mon, Sat, Sun 09.00–20.00, Tues, Thur, Fri, 09.00–21.00, Wed, 09.00–22.00.)

Bicycle hire
Pedal Power Ausstellungsstraße 3, ☎ 729 72 34, 🖷 729 7235, in the Second District (open Mar–Oct from 08.00) offers a comprehensive service including delivery of bikes to your hotel and a selection of guided bicycle tours. Accessories such as helmets, ponchos etc. are extra, as is insurance, but the city map and suggested routes are thrown in for free.
Fahrrad- u. Inlineskaterverleih Copa-Cagrana Am Kaisermühlendamm 1 (east bank of the Neue Donau), ☎ 263 52 42, is handy for the bicyclists' paradise of the Donauinsel and includes in its range tandems, rickshaws, mopeds and bikes for the disabled.

Horse racing
Freudenau Rennbahnstraße (Freudenau) 65 (eastern end of Prater). U3 to Schlachthausgasse, then bus 77A. Flat racing and hurdling.

Krieau Nordportalstraße 247 (next to Messe Gelände, site of Trade Fairs). U1 to Praterstern, then Tram 21. Trotting races from September until June.

Tennis

Tennis courts tend to be rather far from the centre but those at the Arsenal are a bit more central: *Tennis Arsenal*, Arsenalstraße 3, ☎ 799 01 01. There are many others—look in the Yellow Pages (*Gelbe Seiten*) under *Tennishallen u -plätze* for the nearest indoor or outdoor courts in your area.

Fitness centres

A central fitness centre with plenty of facilities is: *John Harris Fitness* Nibelungengasse 7, ☎ 587 37 10 (close to Schillerplatz). A novelty here is the combination of language learning with exercise. There are very many others. Look in the Yellow Pages under *Fitneßcenter* for the one nearest you. There are also gyms for women, including one in the central Ringstraßen Galerien (*Femme*, ☎ 512 10 20).

 # Museums and galleries ~ a checklist

For **opening times** of individual museums and galleries, see the Guide. A few museums are not incorporated into the walks. In these cases, opening times are given here. Most galleries are **closed on Mondays** and smaller or local museums usually have a midday lunch break (12.15–13.00). An asterisk indicates a museum of particular charm or unusual content.

Admission charges are quite high in Vienna, and may well go higher as museums become semi-independent financial entities. Be warned that many museums do not accept credit cards. The **Wien-Karte/Vienna Card**, (currently around €16) is a useful combination card that entitles the holder to 72 hours of network travel on the underground, bus and tram, discounts on admission to a large number of performances, events and exhibitions, both permanent and temporary (these last may be charged extra to the regular admission fee). The card is available from Tourist Information and the Vienna Transport Information Offices.

Art History museums and galleries

*Academy of Fine Arts (Akademie der Bildenden Künste). Schillerplatz 3. ☎ 588 16/225 or 228. For information on guided tours ☎ ext. 230. ✉ GemGal@akbild.ac.at. Fine small art collection, originally accumulated as instructional material for the Academy. Collection includes the celebrated *Last Judgement* by Hieronymus Bosch (p 150).

Albertina (drawings, watercolours, graphics). Albertinaplatz 1, A-1010 Wien, ☎ 534 83-0, ✉ **www.albertina.at**. The world-famous collection of 60,000 drawings, one million graphics and a newly founded photographic department is due to reopen in March 2003. Parts of the palace not previously open to the public will be accessible in the new arrangement (p 119).

Museum of Art History (Kunsthistorisches Museum). Maria-Theresia-Platz. ☒ **www.khm.at**. World famous picture gallery and collection of antiquities drawing on centuries of Habsburg acquisitions (p 138).

Austrian Baroque Museum (Österreichisches Barockmuseum, Unteres Belvedere). In the Lower Belvedere, Rennweg 6A. Highlights are works by Georg Raphael Donner (p 172).

Austrian Gallery (Österreichische Galerie des 19. und 20. Jahrhunderts, Oberes Belvedere). In the Upper Belvedere, Prinz-Eugen-Straße 27. Major collection of Austrian 19C and 20C painting, including Klimt, Schiele, Kokoschka etc. (p 175).

Dali im 'Palais Surreal'. Palais Pallavicini, Josefsplatz 5, ☎ 512 25 49. Permanent display of over 200 artefacts by Salvador Dali, including lithographs, sculpture and Daum glasswork.

*KunstHaus Wien, Untere Weißgerberstraße 13. (Open daily from 10.00–19.00.) ☒ **www.kunsthauswien.com**. Exhibition on Friedensreich Hundertwasser, architect and artist (1928–2000) in the former *Thonet* factory. Multi-coloured Hundertwasser House is close by in Kegelasse.

Museum of Austrian Medieval Art (Museum mittelalterlicher österreichischer Kunst). In the Orangery (Belvedere) of the Lower Belvedere, Rennweg 6. Masterpieces of mostly sacred medieval art from all over Austria (p 174).

Museum of Modern Art (Museum moderner Kunst). In the new MuseumsQuartier ('MuQua'), (p 180).

*MuseumsQuartier ('MuQua') Museumsplatz 1. The new complex (p 180), adapted to house nine museums collectively in the former Baroque Court Stables and three modern buildings in the vast courtyard, became fully operational in the autumn of 2001:

- **ArchitecturZentrum Wien**
- **basis wien—Kunst, Information und Archiv**
- **Depot—Kunst und Diskussion**
- **Karst- und Höhlenkundliche Abteilung des Naturhistorischen Museums** (Spelaeology Department of the Natural History Museum)
- **Kunsthalle Wien im MuseumsQuartier**
- **Leopold Museum**
- **Museum Moderner Kunst (Museum of Modern Art)**
- **Zoom Kindermuseum (Children's Museum)**
- **Art Cult Center—Tabakmuseum (Tobacco Museum)**.

*Schottenstift Museum (Art Collection of the Benedictine Abbey of the Scots in Vienna), Freyung 6. Delightful small collection of chiefly Flemish masterpieces belonging to the Benedictine Monastery of the Scots. Highlight is the 15C winged altar of the 'Master of the Scots' showing early views of Vienna (p 97).

*Otto Wagner Villa (Ernst-Fuchs-Museum, Ben-Tiber-Villa von Otto Wagner), Hüttelbergstraße 26. (Open Mon–Fri, 10.00–16.00 but a telephone call advisable. Group visits ☎ 914 85 75, ▯ + 18). The Magical Realist painter, Ernst Fuchs, purchased this former family villa (1888) of Otto Wagner from the City of Vienna. He has restored the fabric and added his own colourful (but controversial) touches to interior and exterior decoration. Of the original ornament, note the magnificent coloured glass windows of Adolf Böhm (*Autumn Landscape of The Wienerwald*, 1900).

Applied and Decorative Arts museums

Austrian Museum of Applied Arts (Österreichisches Museum für angewandte Kunst, MAK). Stubenring 1, ■ **www.MAK.at**. Superb collection of Austrian and other artefacts displayed in clever contextual arrangements (p 155).

*Cathedral and Diocese Museum (Dom- und Diözesanmuseum). Stephansplatz 6. Religious and liturgical artworks of high quality and great historic interest adjacent to the Archbishop's Palace (p 108).

*Clock Museum (Uhrenmuseum der Stadt Wien). Schulhof 2. Enormous collection of early clocks in all shapes and forms (p 100).

*Doll and Toy Museum (Puppen- und Spielzeugmuseum). Schulhof 4 (First Floor). (Open Tues–Sun 10.00–18.00; p 101).

*Imperial Furniture Depository (Kaiserliches Hofmobiliendepot). Mariahilfer Straße 88, A-1070 Wien. U-Bahn to Zieglergasse, U3 to Zieglergasse. (Open Tues–Sun, 09.00–17.00. Information on ☎ 524 33 57-0. 📠 524 33 57-666). A welcome addition to Vienna's museum scene, the permanent collection displays furniture supplied to the imperial court through the ages. There are also periodic contemporary shows of various kinds (design, fashion, photography etc). Guided tours on application (also for children).

*Lobmeyr Exhibition Room (fine glass) Kärntner Straße 26. Open shop hours (p 123).

*Sacred and Secular Imperial Treasuries (Schatzkammer; Schweizerhof, Hofburg). Perhaps the most exciting museum in Vienna, with artefacts and treasures from the Carolingian age onwards (p 85).

*Treasury of the Teutonic Knights (Schatzkammer des Deutschen Ordens). Singerstraße 7. The treasures of the Teutonic knights (p 133).

Vienna Fashion Collection Museum (Modesammlung des Historischen Museums der Stadt Wien), Schloss Hetzendorf, Hetzendorfer Straße 79, 1120 Vienna, tram 62 from the Oper. Open for temporary exhibitions only (Tue–Sun, 09.00–12.00). A fascinating collection of fashion clothing through the ages. Bona fide researchers are also able to consult the remarkable library of 12,000 volumes and fashion journals dating from 1786, plus photographs and etchings (☎ 80 21 657 to arrange an appointment).

History, Ethnology, Music, Natural History, Transport, Technology

Museum of Austrian Folklore (Museum für österreichische Volkskunde). Laudongasse 17–19 (Palais Schönborn). A museum gradually awakening from decades of slumber. It now has more challenging temporary exhibitions (p 185).

*Austrian Resistance Archive (Archiv des österreichischen Widerstands). Wipplingerstraße 6-8 (First Floor). (Open Mon, Wed, Thur 09.00–17.00, ☎ 53 436-01779) (p 113).

*Capuchin (Imperial) Crypt (Kapuzinergruft). Tegetthoffstraße 2. An obligatory visit for all those fascinated by the necrological rites and funerary monuments of the Habsburgs (p 122).

Carriage Museum (Wagenburg). Schloß Schönbrunn, Schönbrunner Schloßstraße 47 (p 192).

Ephesos Museum. Neue Burg (Hofburg). ■ **www.ethno-museum.ac.at**. Greek and Roman antiquities from 19C Austrian archaeological excavations in Ephesus and Samothrace (p 90).

Ethnology Museum (Völkerkunde Museum). Neue Burg (Hofburg). (Open Mon, Wed–Sun 10.00–16.00.) The museum includes oriental, African, Polynesian, Australasian and Eskimo artefacts (p 91).

Haus der Musik Wien, Seilerstatte 30, A-1010 Wien. (Open daily 10.00–22.00.) ☎ 516 48 51. ✉ cantino@weinzirl.at ⌨ **www.haus-der-musik-wien.at.** Music can be heard, seen and felt, and the history of music explored on the seven floors of this 'house of music'. Opportunities for interactive musical play. Café-restaurant *Cantino im Haus der Musik Wien*. Also shop selling musical items, souvenirs etc. (p 131).

*Hermesvilla. Lainzer Tor, Lainzer Tiergarten, (Bus 60A). Late 18C country villa of Empress Elisabeth; also temporary exhibitions. (Open Wed–Sun 09.00–16.30; p 197.)

Historical Museum of the City of Vienna (Historisches Museum der Stadt Wien). Karlsplatz. Vienna's development from pre-history to the present (p 169).

Imperial Apartments (Kaiserappartements). Reichstor (Hofburg—'In der Burg') (p 83). The Emperor's dreary apartments. Strictly for Habsburg devotees.

*Jewish Museum (Jüdisches Museum der Stadt Wien). Dorotheergasse 11. (Open Sun–Fri, 10.00–18.00, Thur to 20.00.) ⌨ www.jmw.at. Permanent display of religious objects, viewable storage area and archives, plus a café and bookshop (p 121).

Museum Judenplatz. Judenplatz 8 (open Sun–Thur, 10.00–18.00, Fri, 10.00–14.00). Museum of Medieval Jewish Life, remains of the medieval synagogue, adjacent to Rachel Whiteread's Shoah Memorial (p 113).

Lipizzaner Museum (Museum of the Lipizzaner Horses), Stallburg/Hofburg. Reitschulgasse 2. New museum devoted to the beautiful white horses of the Spanish Riding School (p 90).

*Museum of Military History (Heeresgeschichtliches Museum), Arsenal. Gegastraße Objekt 18. Austria at war in pictures, uniforms and weapons (p 179).

Natural History Museum (Naturhistorisches Museum), Maria-Theresia-Platz. ⌨ **www.nhm.at.** Star attraction is the 25,000 year old Willendorf Venus (thought to be a fertility symbol) but there is much else also of interest (p 137).

*Neidhart Frescoes (Neidhart-Fresken). Tuchlauben 19. Medieval frescoes of episodes from the poetry of the Minnesänger Neidhart von Reuental (pre-1200–1250). The frescoes are later creations, c 1400. (Open Tues–Sun 09.00–12.00; pp 113–114.)

Roman Ruins of dwelling houses (Römische Ruinen unter dem Hohen Markt). Hoher Markt 3. (Open Tues–Sun 09.00–12.15, 13.00–16.30.) Officers' quarters with remains of hypocaust heating system (p 109).

Schloß Schönbrunn. Schönbrunner Schloßstraße 47. Nikolaus Pacassi's unsuccessful attempt to rival Versailles. Kilometres of Rococo interiors and a lovely park (p 191).

*Technical Museum (Technisches Museum für Industrie und Gewerbe). Mariahilfer Straße 212, ☎ 89 998-6000, ⌨ **www.tmw.ac.at.** Recently reopened after complete refurbishment, a stimulating presentation of Austrian achievements in the progress and history of technology (p 195).

*Tramway Museum (Wiener Straßenbahnmuseum). Erdbergstraße 109. (Open May–Oct, Sat, Sun, hols, 09.00–16.00.) Rides on the Oldtimer Trams start from Karlsplatz: details on rides from the Vienna Public Transport Information Office in the U-Bahn concourse at Karlsplatz, ☎ 985 4553.

Court Weapons Collection and Armoury (Hofjagd und Rüstkammer, Hofburg). Unique suits of armour and weaponry collected on a historical basis by a Habsburg obsessed with such things (p 90).

Social History, Medicine, the Arts

*****Alte Backstube** (historic bakery). Lange Gasse 34 (p 184).

*****Burial Museum** (Bestattungsmuseum), Goldeggasse 19. (Open Mon–Fri 12.00–15.00, by appointment ☎ 501 95-4227). Very unusual undertaker's museum that is most revealing about the Viennese attitude to death (p 179).

*****Crime Museum** (Kriminalmuseum). Große Sperlgasse 24. Much what you would expect, with horrors aplenty (p 188).

Freud Museum, Berggasse 19. ▨ **www.Freud.to.or.at**. The great man's consulting rooms and some items that belonged to him (however the famous couch is in London) (p 188).

*****Josephinum**, Währinger Straße 25/1. Named after Joseph II. Wax figures by Tuscan sculptors for apprentice military surgeons. Fascinating, gruesome (p 186).

*****Museum for Pathological Anatomy** ('Narrenturm' or 'Fools Tower'). Spitalgasse 2 (in the grounds of the Allgemeinen Krankenhaus). (Open Wed 15.00–18.00, Thur 08.00–11.00.) ▨ **www.pathomus.ac.at**. Even more gruesome than the Josephinum with all manner of human deformations etc. on display (p 186).

Collection of Old Musical Instruments (Sammlung alter Musikinstrumente). Neue Burg (Hofburg). Many beautiful and delicate pieces, plus some with historical associations (p 91).

Theatre Museum in Palais Lobkowitz. Lobkowitzplatz 2. A trot through Viennese (and Austrian) theatre history in a beautiful palais where Beethoven once played (p 121).

Tobacco Museum (Art Cult Center—Tabakmuseum—now part of the MuseumsQuartier). Mariahilfer Straße 2, Klosterhof (p 182).

Memorial Rooms

Gustinus Ambrosi Museum. Augarten/Scherzergasse 1A. (Open Tues–Sun, 10.00–17.00). Life and work of this modern sculptor (1893–1975) (p 190).

Beethoven Memorial Rooms:

Eroica House. Döblinger Hauptstraße 92. (Open Tues–Sun 09.00–12.15, 13.00–16.30.)

Pasqualati House. Mölkerbastei 8. Beethoven rooms and museum dedicated to Austria's greatest writer of prose fiction, Adalbert Stifter. (Open Tues–Sun 09.00–12.15, 13.00–16.30).

Beethoven House, Probusgasse 6. Where Beethoven wrote the Heiligenstädter Testament. (Open Tues–Sun 09.00–12.15, 13.00–16.30.)

Johannes Brahms Memorial Room. See Haydn Museum below.

Franz Grillparzer Memorial Room. Johannesgasse 6. (Open Mon–Fri, 08.30–14.30.) Original office furniture of Austria's greatest playwright, who was also a (moderately) diligent official. (See also Historical Museum of the City of Vienna, p 132).

Haydn Museum. Haydngasse 19. Includes a room devoted to Johannes Brahms. (Open Tues–Sun, 09.00–12.15, 13.00–16.30.)

Franz Kafka Memorial Room, in the former Hofman Sanatorium, Kierlinger Hauptstraße 187, Kierling by Klosterneuburg. The room where Kafka spent his dying days. (Open Mon–Sat 08.00–12.00, 14.00–17.00; obtain key in the house.)

Lehár Schlößl (Schikaneder Schlößl), Hackhofergasse 18. Lehár bought the Baroque house originally belonging to the impresario and librettist of the *Magic Flute* in 1932. Groups may visit by appointment, ☎ 31 85 416.

Mozart Memorial Rooms ('Figarohaus'). Schulerstraße 8, entrance at Domgasse 5. Mozart lived here between 1784 and 1787, during which time he wrote *The Marriage of Figaro*. (Open Tues–Sun 09.00–18.00.)

Schubert Museum (Schuberthaus). Nußdorferstraße 54. (Open Tues–Sun 09.00–12.15, 13.00–16.30.)

Schubert's Death Chamber. Kettenbrückengasse 6. (Open Tues–Sun, 10.00–12.15, 13.00–16.30.)

Arnold Schönberg Center, Palais Fanto. Schwarzenbergplatz 6. Entrance Zaunergasse 1–3. ☎ 712 18 88/▤. 712 18 88 88. (Open Mon–Fri, 10.00–18.00 during exhibitions, otherwise to scholars on application.) Archive and temporary exhibitions on the composer's life and work.

Adalbert Stifter Museum. See Pasqualati House, above.

Johann Strauß House. Praterstraße 54. Strauß wrote the *Blue Danube Waltz* here. (Open Tues–Sun 09.00–12.15, 13.00–16.30.)

Otto Wagner House(Otto-Wagner-Archiv, Akademie der Bildenden Künste). Döblergasse 4. One of the homes of the leading Secession architect. (Open Mon–Fri 09.00–12.00, but in July and August by arrangement only, ☎ 93 22 33.)

Memorial Rooms of the Austrian Theatre Museum. Hanuschgasse 3. (Open Tues–Fri 10.00–12.00 and 13.00–16.00, Sat, Sun, 13.00–16.00.) Rooms dedicated to leading figures of the Austrian theatre, including the critic Hermann Bahr, the operetta composer, Emmerich Kálmán, the actor and director, Max Reinhardt, and others. Also examples of the stage designs by the sculptor Fritz Wotruba.

District museums
Many of Vienna's 23 districts have their own local museums, which could be of interest to those with a penchant for local detail. Look in the telephone book under '*Bezirksmuseen*' for their addresses and call them up to ascertain their (often irregular) opening hours. The **Bezirksmuseum for the Inner City** is located in the Alten Rathaus at Wipplingerstraße 8.

Major public exhibition halls for temporary shows
Hermesvilla, see *History Museums* (p 196).
Kunstforum der Bank Austria. Freyung 8.
Kunsthaus Wien, see *Art History, Museums and Galleries*.
Kunsthalle Wien, now in the MuseumsQuartier.
Künstlerhaus. Karlsplatz 5 (p 164).
Palais Harrach. Freyung 3 (temporary exhibits from the collection of the Kunsthistorischen Museum; p 98).
Secession, Friedrichstraße 12 (p 166).

The monthly *Wien Programm* will indicate what shows are running at the above venues.

Arts Festivals in Vienna

Winterträume (Winter Dreams). Concert cycle in the Musikverein featuring the Wiener Philharmoniker and other great orchestras, conductors and performers. Mid-February. Tickets ☎ (43-1) 505 81 90. 🗏 505 81 90-94.

Osterklang (The Sound of Easter). Sacred music at Easter in the Musikverein and St Stephen's. Tickets ☎ (43-1) 427 17. 🗏 4000-99-8410. 🖾 **tickets@osterklang.at**.

Frühlingsfestival (Spring Music Festival, held in April). Another cycle with big names in the Musikverein. Tickets as for **Winterträume**.

Wiener Festwochen (Vienna Festival Weeks). Theatre, opera, dance. Mid-May to mid-June. Tickets and information ☎ (43-1) 589 22-0. 🗏 589 22-49. 🖾 **kartenbuero@festwochen.at**.

Im Puls Tanz (Contemporary Dance). July-August. Tickets: ☎ (43-1) 523 55 58. 🗏 523 16 839. 🖾 **office@tanzwochen.at**.

Jazz Fest Wien (Vienna Jazz Festival). June–July. Tickets ☎ (43-1) 319 06 06. 🗏 319 05 49. 🖾 3190606@allevent.com.

KlangBogen (Summer Music Festival). Opera, orchestral and chamber music. July–August. Tickets ☎ (43-1) 427 17. 🗏 4000 99 8410. 🖾 **tickets@klangbogen.at**.

Rathausplatz Music Film Festival. Opera and classical music films shown in the evenings on a giant screen in front of the city hall. July and August. No charge, but arrive early to get a seat.

Viennale Wiener Filmfestwochen (Vienna Film Festival). Two weeks in October of minority and commercial film screenings. ☎ (43-1) 526 59 47. 🗏 523 41 72.

Wien modern (Festival of Modern Music) in the Konzerthaus. October and November. Tickets ☎ (43-1) 712 12 11. 🗏 712 28 72. 🖾 **ticket@konzerthaus.at**.

In addition to all the above there are both seasonal and year-round popular concerts extracting every ounce of musical and touristic potential from the works of Mozart and Strauss. Some of these concerts feature players in contemporary costume. Venues (apart from the mainline concert halls) include the Hofburg, Palais Palffy, the Orangery at Schönbrunn, Palais Liechtenstein, Palais Ferstel (in the former Stock Exchange), the Altes Rathaus and the Deutsch Ordenshaus. Brochures may be picked up at the **Tourist Information** on Albertinaplatz. Tickets for several of these performances can be obtained through hotel concierges, as well as the usual ticket agencies, or by telephone, fax or e-mail at the numbers given in the brochures.

BACKGROUND INFORMATION

History of Vienna

Pre-History and the Roman Period

The site of what is now Vienna entered history with twin functions—the one strategic, the other commercial—and these have determined most of its subsequent development. As early as the Bronze and Iron Age culture of Hallstatt (9C–5C BC), the important amber trade route, running from the Baltic littoral to Aquilea on the Adriatic, crossed the River Danube at this point. Traffic in the reverse direction brought luxury artefacts and precious metals northwards through the Alpine pass known as the '*schräger Durchgang*'. It was natural for a settlement to grow up at the nodal point where the north–south flow of goods was intersected by the east–west traffic on the 'dustless highway' of the great river.

The strategic importance of this intersection was not lost on the Celts, who built a fortress on the rocky outcrop later named the Leopoldsberg after a Babenberg duke. From this vantage point they could observe and control the river traffic below. Pliny the Elder describes their stronghold, together with its area of influence stretching into the *Wiener Becken* (basin of the River Wien), as being on the edge of the *deserta Boiorum*: that is, the area formerly belonging to the Boier Celts, a tribe decimated by Dacians from the east around 50 BC. The vacuum resulting from this defeat was filled by the neighbouring power of Noricum, an aristocratic Illyro-Celtic civilisation which covered much of modern Austria, and which had grown extremely wealthy from its iron exports. To the northeast were warlike Germanic tribes that were later to give the Romans endless trouble.

That the local Celtic civilisation had been relatively advanced is suggested both in evidence of their viticulture and the numerous shards dug up by archaeologists over the years. Many of the latter came to light when the panoramic **Höhenstraße** was built as a job creation scheme under the clerico-Fascist dictatorship of the 1930s. When the Romans arrived around 15 BC, the Celts were removed from their hilltop strongholds on to the plain, and were gradually absorbed into Roman civilisation. The region's centre now shifted towards the east, and the settlement known as Vindobona became part of the administrative province of Pannonia.

Vindobona—a name derived from the Vinid tribe of Celts—became the second most important military garrison of Pannonia after neighbouring Carnuntum, a few miles downstream on the Danube. The *urbs quadrata*, for which the original model, here as elsewhere, was the ancient centre of Rome, was situated on the plateau commanding the main arm of the river, an area which is now the First District of Vienna. The military camp was strongly built on a site with natural protection on three sides: streams bounded it in the southeast and northwest, while to the northeast was a precipitous drop to the river-flat (now the Danube Canal). The **Hoher Markt** is in the middle of this area,

Salzgries follows the northeasterly perimeter, the **Tiefer Graben** the north-westerly, **Naglergasse** the southwesterly and **Rotenturmstraße** the southeasterly one. Part of the southwestern periphery had no natural protection and was dug out with three lines of ditches, as is recalled in the name **Graben**, today a focal point for the life of the city's *beau monde*.

Vindobona remained insignificant until the era of **Trajan** (emperor AD 98–AD 117), who turned it into a powerful military base and stationed the 13th Legion here. By the time the 10th Legion arrived in 114, the camp's walls were 2m thick and 6m high, and it could accommodate 6000 men. The soldiers of the 'House Legion' of Vindobona exploited the warm springs along the Danube and founded the spa at **Baden bei Wien**, thus initiating a tradition that reached its apotheosis in the Biedermeier period, when the patronage of Emperor Franz made the place fashionable with well-to-do officials.

Other ameliorations to the rigours endured at the furthest limits of civilisation were available just outside the camp in the service facilities known as *canabae*. In 1990 excavations began in the **Michaelerplatz** in front of the Hofburg, once the terminus of a Roman street running from the Porta Decumana, the camp's southwestern gate. Archaeologists have uncovered a 'recreation area' for the military, dating to the 2nd and 3C AD. Part of this seems to have been a brothel.

The Romans were constantly obliged to fend off incursions from barbarians to the east and north. In 169–171, a coalition of the two fiercest Germanic tribes, the Markomanni and the Quadi, broke through the defensive line of fortresses along the Danube known as the *limes*; their forces penetrated as far as Italy itself, before the Romans rallied under Marcus Aurelius. The latter's victories were consolidated by one of Rome's greatest generals, Septimius Severus, whose rise to power began in 193 when the garrison at Carnuntum proclaimed him emperor.

In the following century Roman power gradually declined, although this period witnessed the reorganisation of local viticulture under Probus (Roman general, then emperor 276 AD–282 AD), and the building of the first Christian church in Vindobona on the site later occupied by the **Peterskirche**. However, the onset of the *Völkerwanderung* from the early 5C brought waves of Goths, Vandals, Ostrogoths and other nomadic peoples crashing against the defences of the Roman Empire. Vindobona's *de iure* departure from Roman hegemony took place in 433, when the Eastern Emperor, Theodosius II, signed it away to the Huns. Out of the smoke-filled gloom of burning towns and ravaged crops that hung like a pall over the ruins of collapsing empire in the 5C, one striking figure emerges: Flavius Severinus, a Roman consul who converted to Christianity. As the troops fled, leaving civilian populations to their fate, Severinus is reported to have been tireless in his negotiation with the invaders to save what human life he could, if not goods and chattels. In the annals of the Church he appears as **St Severin**, who proclaimed the gospel along the Danube from Vindobona to Passau and died (482) in a monastery at Favianae (Mautern, Lower Austria). The last Roman troops to leave the Danube region in 488 carried Severin's remains with them over the Alps, so that he should be laid to rest on Latin soil. It is said that the village of Heiligenstadt, in Vienna's 19th district (originally *heilige Stätte*, i.e. *sanctus locus*), was so named by Severin's converts.

From Charlemagne to the Babenbergs, 'Ostmark' to 'Ostarrichi'

Charlemagne

The Dark Ages is normally taken to cover the period from 378 (when the Goths defeated the Emperor Valens at Adrianople) to Christmas Day, 800, when **Charlemagne** was crowned as 'Roman Emperor' by Pope Leo III. During the early period of Carolingian hegemony in the late 8C, the former settlement of Vindobona, now called **Vindomina**, sometimes Vedunia, was focused on the triangle comprising the former Berghof (near the corner of Hoher Markt and Marc-Aurel Straße), the Ruprechtskirche and the Peterskirche. Of the Berghof nothing remains, but a long inscription on the wall of a neighbouring building recalls that it was traditionally regarded as the oldest house in Vienna, the erstwhile seat of the post-Roman governors and the law court.

With the partition of Charlemagne's empire after his death in 814, its eastern outposts were exposed to the increasingly destructive attacks of the Hungarians, who settled definitively in the Carpathian Basin in 896. By then, the Vienna area was subject to both Slav and German (Bavarian) influence. Ancient local place-names reflect this early racial duality: Döbling, Währing, Rodaun and Lainz are said to be of Slav origin, while Ottakring, Hietzing and Sievering suggest Bavarian provenance.

The Babenbergs

In 955 the German king, **Otto the Great**, dealt a crushing blow to the Hungarians at the Battle of Lechfeld, an event often taken to mark the birth of the geo-political concept of Austria. It was a few years, however, before German hegemony over the whole area was assured with the establishment by Otto II of the **Babenberg Margrave** (976); a reference to the lands described as Ostarrichi occurs for the first time in a document stipulating the rights devolved to the Babenberg family in perpetuity. The former Eastern March (Ostmark) of Charlemagne thus became a largely autonomous buffer region controlled by the first of Austria's two great dynasties; it was to rule for 270 years.

The Babenbergs, described by the *fin de siècle* writer, Hermann Bahr, as an 'austere, sly and cautious stock', gradually moved their centre of operations along the Danube basin: from Melk to Tulln, to Klosterneuburg and finally to the place already described as **Wenia** in a document of 881. The new—and final—nomenclature for Vienna is probably a corruption of *vedunja*, a word of Illyro-Celtic origin meaning woodland stream. The stream referred to is the *Wienfluß* (River Wien), an undistinguished and much built-over rivulet that trickles or floods from the Wienerwald according to season, and now flows into the Danube Canal.

The pious Babenbergs (especially **Leopold III**, later canonised), were energetic founders of monasteries (Melk, Heiligenkreuz, Klosterneuburg and others); several dukes were ardent crusaders and almost all showed themselves to be able administrators. For Vienna, the most fateful year of Babenberg rule was 1156, when **Heinrich II** 'Jasomirgott' (so named after his favourite exclamation: 'Yes, so help me God!') set up his residence in the area of the First District still known as Am Hof (i.e. at the Court). Hardly less significant was the granting of the *Privilegium minus* by the **Emperor Friedrich Barbarossa** the following year, which elevated the Babenberg possessions to a dukedom. Under Heinrich's successors, Leopold V and Friedrich I, Vienna experienced an economic and cultural golden age. The glittering ducal residence attracted celebrated *minnesänger*, such as Walther von der Vogelweide, who wrote elegant verse in the courtly love tradition; it was a time when, as the author (Jans Enikel) of the 13C *Book of Princes* nostalgically recalled:

> *At the court was joy and honour,*
> *Ladies wooed in knightly manner;*
> *Sorrow each man kept at bay,*
> *Naught but pleasure, night and day.*

From this and similar accounts it can be seen that the later Babenbergs were lavish investors and even more lavish spenders (Styria, with its mines, was added to their patrimony in 1192). Under **Leopold V**, also in 1192, they received an unexpected financial windfall of dubious legitimacy through the imprisonment and ransoming of Richard Coeur-de-Lion. During the **Third Crusade**, the English king had quarrelled with Duke Leopold at the Siege of Acre; but he was also wanted by the German Emperor, who suspected him of having plotted the assassination of his relative and personal appointee as King of Jerusalem, Konrad of Monferat. The 150,000 silver marks agreed for Richard's release from the Danubian castle of Dürnstein has been calculated at an astronomic one and a half billion pounds at today's values. Leopold spent his share of the proceeds on building **Wiener Neustadt** (later the retreat of more than one Habsburg ruler when Vienna was in revolt), and strengthening the defences of Hainburg, Enns and Vienna. The **Graben**, with its adjacent network of streets, and probably also the **Hoher Markt** were laid out at this time.

The Babenbergs astutely played a mediatory role in the long drawn-out **investiture dispute** between pope and emperor in the 11th and early 12C. Notwithstanding their sympathy for the position of the papacy and their evident piety, there was friction locally between the dukes and the over-mighty bishops of Passau. By a compromise reached with the bishops in 1137 (the Treaty of Mautern), the **Peterskirche** was yielded to the Passau diocese and the building of a new parish church for Vienna was begun outside the city boundaries. This eventually became the mighty **Stephansdom** (St Stephen's Cathedral), the focal point for the city and its inhabitants in the Middle Ages, as it still is today. In the treaty, Vienna is for the first time described as *civitas*, implying civic status.

In the 12C the **religious life** of Vienna expanded with an influx of contemplative and caritas orders, whose institutions moulded the face of the medieval city and whose presence strongly influenced its culture and society. (Even today, the church is the second largest individual property owner after the city council.) In the wake of flourishing religion came hordes of clerics, not all of them very respectable, if the contemporary term of abuse *Lotterpfaffen* (slovenly priests) is anything to go by. They worked in administration, as diplomats, as tutors and even as physicians.

The city's **economic expansion** was reflected in the colonies of merchants, whose activities or provenance are reflected in surviving street names (e.g. Wallnerstraße, a corruption of the word *welsch*, referring to Latins from France or Italy). The cloth traders were particularly influential and formed a pressure group that eventually developed into a guild. **Tuchlauben** in the city centre recalls where cloth from Western Europe was offered for sale.

Vienna also had to import most of its craftsmen at this time, as is indicated by a ducal proclamation of 1208, which bestowed special privileges on Flemish dyers (hence Färbergasse). The Viennese themselves were awarded what was virtually a licence to print money when **Leopold VI** instituted the staple right in 1221. Foreign merchants had to sell their goods to locals within two months of landing them: the latter then sold them on (chiefly to Hungary) at a huge mark-up. Goods still unsold as the deadline approached were often disposed of in a fire sale, failing which they had to be re-exported on payment of high duty. Vienna's favoured geographical position evidently enabled it to enforce such practices, even though the Hungarian king later called an (unsuccessful) summit (1335) with his Bohemian and Polish counterparts to discuss ways of circumventing the Viennese monopoly.

Financial and trading activity brought with it another ingredient of Viennese culture which recurrently gave rise to tension, envy, and officially inspired hatred. Early **Jewish settlers** enjoyed the personal protection of the rulers and the first director of the mint under Leopold V was a Jew named Schlom, who seems to have had equal rights with other citizens and to have had Christian servants. Schlom's murder in 1196 in a dispute over property (he owned four houses) was, however, symptomatic of the dangers to which Jews were exposed, since the church also legitimised their persecution and (on occasion) their liquidation. **Friedrich II** regulated Jewish privileges and terms of business in 1244, his proposals serving as a model for several other rulers. High rates of interest were allowed to the Jewish money-lenders, which naturally increased the feeling against them. Christians were obliged to avail themselves of the money-lenders' services because of the canonical prohibition on usury.

Segregation of Jews and Christians was demanded by the church; a special council held in St Stephen's in March 1267 during the **interregnum** of Ottokar of Bohemia attempted (inter alia) to correct the king's regrettable lack of animus against Jewish residents. It ordered that Jews should be completely quarantined from the Christian population, wear horned hats and be barred from the city's inns and baths. The Jews' only protection from Christian vengeance (officially justified by the church's claim that the entire race was to be held responsible in perpetuity for the death of Christ), was the patronage of the ruler of the day, which in turn might be conditional on his need of credit. Unsurprisingly, therefore, Jewish habitations were clustered near the ducal court (Am Hof), in an area that gradually developed into a ghetto.

The last Babenberg, **Friedrich II**, '**der Streitbare**' (the warlike'), was killed in 1246 in a battle against the Hungarians. At the time of his death Vienna was a thriving economic centre with a fairly autonomous **city council**. The latter consisted of 24 senior members and 100 representatives elected directly by knights and merchants, who qualified for citizenship by virtue of property ownership. Prosperous Vienna also had a reputation for 'Phaeacianism', a word originally coined by Tannhäuser and recalling the pleasure-loving people of Scheria in Homer's *Odyssey*. The poet complained that his money melted away in expenditure on beautiful women, '*leckerbissen*' (fine pastries), and twice-weekly baths (probably a euphemism for brothels). The reputation for licentiousness was one that the city would never quite shake off: it was to be regarded as axiomatic in the 19C, just as it was in the Middle Ages.

From Rudolf I of Habsburg to the Reformation

Přemysl Ottokar II of Bohemia

When the Babenberg line died out, the Austrian lands were for a while left rudderless. The power vacuum was filled by the Bohemian Prince Ottokar, who bolstered his claim to the dukedom by marrying the late Friedrich II of Babenberg's sister, Margaret, in 1252. The bride was 47—an old lady by medieval standards—and the groom, at 22, less than half her age. A year earlier, the Austrian Estates (their minds concentrated by bribes and the presence of a huge army) had elected Ottokar as their ruler and in 1253 he succeeded his father as King of Bohemia.

Notwithstanding subsequent Habsburg propaganda to the contrary, Ottokar seems to have been an able, if tough, overlord who endowed his lands with sound administration and raised the standard of living through the further encouragement of trade. Vienna prospered under his rule and steadfastly supported him against German attempts to reassert control. It was Ottokar who founded the **Bürgerspital** (Community Hospital—actually concerned with poor relief) c 1255 and who helped the city to recover from devastation by fire in 1258 and 1262 by easing taxes and arranging the delivery of building materials. In anticipation of attack by imperial forces, he built a fortress (1275) on a site later taken over by the Habsburgs and extended over the years into the huge and rambling **Hofburg**.

Rudolf I of Habsburg

The turning point for Ottokar, however, came with his failed attempt to be elected Holy Roman Emperor in 1273. The successful candidate was a relatively obscure count from southwest Germany named Rudolf von Habsburg. His line came from Alsace, but the title was taken from a possession on the banks of the Aar, halfway between Basle and Zürich, in an area that was later to become part of the independent Swiss Confederation. On the rocky prominence of the Wülpersberg was situated the family's romantically named Habichtsburg (Hawk-Castle), which thus became associated with the most spectacularly successful dynasty in history.

After five years of biding his time, Rudolf moved to wrest the Austrian territories from Bohemian control. At the last moment he was joined by the Hungarian cavalry of **Ladislas**, the half-Cumanian (and half-mad) King of Hungary; the latter's intervention may well have been decisive in bringing about the defeat of Ottokar at Dürnkrut (1278) on the **Marchfeld**, a plain northeast of Vienna that takes its name from the River March (now the border with Slovakia). Ottokar was killed during the battle, possibly assassinated by one of his own nobles.

The victory on the Marchfeld marked the beginning of 640 years of Habsburg hegemony over Austria. In the 19C, the great Austrian dramatist, Franz Grillparzer, was to celebrate this historic event in terms extremely flattering to the ruling house in his play *König Ottokars Glück und Ende* (*The Rise and Fall of King Ottokar*). In a famous passage, Ottokar von Horneck celebrates the downfall of an overweeningly ambitious but charismatic opponent of the Habsburgs in words that conjure a patriotic myth of Austria similar to the 'scept'red isle' and 'other Eden' apotheosised by John of Gaunt in Shakespeare's *Richard II*.

Nevertheless the initial phase of Habsburg rule was not auspicious. The arrogant behaviour of Rudolf's Swabian knights did not endear them or the new ruler to his subjects. When Rudolf's son, **Albrecht**, was installed as regent in 1281, his abolition of the staple right and removal of the clergy's tax exemptions led to outright rebellion in 1288. In February 1298 Albrecht held a **Fürstentag**, a congress of princes intended to promote his claim to the German throne. This was even less popular with the Viennese, who had to accommodate the invitees and their entourages; the most unruly of the latter were the Cumanians from the Great Hungarian Plain, who stabled their horses in dwelling houses and flung themselves on the local women.

Albrecht II

After a period of considerable confusion and unrest, **Albrecht II** ruled what were now the Habsburg Hereditary Lands from 1330 to 1358. He was the first of the dynasty to devote himself exclusively and single-mindedly to his Austrian territories, to which was added **Carinthia** in 1335. During his reign the so-called Albertine Choir of **Stephansdom** was begun, part of the latter's transformation into a graceful, Gothic hall-church.

Vienna was now on the brink of a great flowering of Gothic architecture; but despite the prosperity generated by the building boom, Albrecht's resources were strained by a succession of natural disasters—earthquakes, fires and especially the **Black Death**. The new strain of the disease had originated in Italy (the plague described by Boccaccio in *The Decameron*), and spread rapidly throughout Europe. Vienna is said to have buried as many as 1200 people in a single day of 1349. The fear engendered by this horrific visitation not only stimulated attacks on the Jews (who were accused of poisoning wells), but also encouraged religious fanaticism. Vienna was invaded by sinister processions of flagellants, brutish, half-naked figures wearing black hoods with eye-slits and wielding spiked scourges.

Albrecht himself was no stranger to suffering: the origin of his nickname 'the Lame' was made abundantly clear when his body was exhumed in 1985 and he was found to have suffered from cripplingly painful polyarthritis. His other nickname was 'the Wise', and it was his prudent management of affairs that laid the basis for the achievements of his more illustrious successor, Duke Rudolf IV '*der Stifter*' (the Founder).

Rudolf IV

Rudolf IV founded the **University** of Vienna in 1365 (although the Pope would not at first grant it the all-important Faculty of Theology). At the beginning of March 1359 he turned the first sod for the foundations of the south tower of **Stephansdom**, thus initiating the single most ambitious piece of architecture ever undertaken in Vienna. Like many other Habsburg projects, however, it was destined to remain incomplete.

Rudolf was a forceful young ruler (he was only 26 when he died in 1365), and evidently not afraid to promulgate necessary measures that cannot have been popular: a 10 per cent tax was levied on wine in taverns and the restrictive practices of the guilds were curtailed (in Vienna even the beggars had their own guild). He was also notorious for his forgery of the *Privilegium maius*, which purported to be an extension of the genuine *Privilegium minus* granted to the Babenbergs by Friedrich Barbarossa. The Duke employed a clutch of industrious scholars for the fabrication of evidence that traced imperial grants of succession to the Austrian rulers as far back as Julius Caesar and Nero. The Holy Roman Emperor, Karl IV, asked the poet Petrarch to determine the authenticity of these audacious claims, the latter producing a crisply written report that ended with the words, 'he who fabricated [the documents] is an arrant nave; and he who believes them is an ass'.

Building activity in Vienna led to increasing prosperity and to more economic power and political influence for non-aristocratic groups. Craftsmen in particular benefited from a reform of the City Council's voting system in 1396, which no doubt reflected their burgeoning numbers (by the end of the following century no fewer than 91 crafts and branches thereof are recorded as taking part in a funeral cavalcade). Rich burghers extended their power through the office of **mayor**, an example being **Konrad Vorlauf** (1406–08), who possessed at least three properties and a vineyard. However, he overreached himself by taking sides in the struggle for power of the joint-regents, Duke Ernst and Duke Leopold, following the death of Albrecht IV in 1404. After the warring Habsburg brothers were reconciled, Vorlauf was executed on the pig market (now Lobkowitzplatz), the first of three Viennese mayors to suffer a similar fate.

Albrecht V

The early 15C was a violent and turbulent epoch in Central Europe. The Habsburgs were threatened by neighbouring powers and by the spreading influence of the **Hussites** in Bohemia, who challenged the abuses and corruption of the church. Albrecht V (1404–1439) took energetic measures to bolster his position by bringing the protection of the 'true religion' into his own hands at a time when no fewer than three 'anti-popes' were impotently threatening each other. All university teachers and priests were required to abjure Hussite heresies under oath (if necessary under torture). He also initiated a **pogrom** against the Jews in 1420–21, a popular move with the Viennese who were then suffering an economic downturn, and who thereby acquired Jewish property for nothing. Rich Jews were tortured until they revealed where their treasures were hidden; thereafter they and their families were burned alive on the Erdberg. The chief motive for this act of Christian barbarism was to raise money for the struggle against the Hussites.

Friedrich III

Friedrich III, who succeeded Albrecht in 1439, was of a less violent temperament. Contemporaries referred to him as the *Erzschlafmütze* (The Arch-Nightcap), because of his alleged somnolence (in fact he suffered from low blood pressure). He left his mark on the dynasty by introducing the titles 'Archduke' and 'Archduchess' for all members of the imperial family, and eventually consolidated his power by outliving his rivals. Notwithstanding the vaingloriousness of his personal device AEIOU (variously interpreted as *Austriae est imperare omni universo*, in German *Alles Erdreich ist Österreich untertan*—the whole world is subject to Austria—or *Austria erit in orbe ultima*—Austria will outlive all other powers), Friedrich was at first politically weak and beset by difficulties.

In 1462 he was besieged in the Hofburg (though admittedly by a rival Habsburg), and had to be rescued by the Hussite King of Bohemia, George of Podiebrad. Legend has it that the city council took pity on Friedrich's little son, the future Emperor Maximilian, and smuggled food for him into the Burg. This particular conflict claimed another mayoral victim in **Wolfgang Holzer**, who changed his allegiance once too often between Friedrich and his brother, Duke Albrecht VI. After the cessation of hostilities, he was sentenced to be quartered alive on Am Hof.

Friedrich's achievements were not insignificant. They included stabilising the currency and having Vienna raised to a bishopric in 1469. He was the last of the Holy Roman Emperors to be crowned by the Pope in Rome (1452) and was able to exploit his support of the papacy in its dispute with the Council of Basle to establish Catholic orders in Austria and advance the canonisation of Leopold III of Babenberg.

Maximilian I

However, it was his son, Maximilian I, who laid the foundation for worldwide Habsburg power by means of his adroit marriage-bed diplomacy. Maximilian's son, Philip, was married to the daughter of the King of Spain and he himself had married Maria of Burgundy in 1477. In July 1515 a double marriage was held in St Stephen's: the Jagellonian heir to the united thrones of Bohemia and Hungary, Lajos II, was married to Philip's daughter, the ten-year-old Maria. Lajos's sister, the 12-year-old Anna, married Maximilian's grandson, Ferdinand. This put the seal on a process of territorial accumulation that had already been encapsulated in a contemporary aphorism adapted from Ovid: *Bella gerant alii, tu, felix Austria nube!* (Let others make war; you, fortunate Austria, marry!) The saying was extremely apt: Karl V (1519–58) was to be heir to an empire that was simply too large for a single person to rule—one on which 'the sun never set'.

Maximilian was a Renaissance man of parts known as 'the last knight' because of his anachronistic love of jousting. Although he set up his court in Innsbruck, he did not entirely neglect Vienna. In 1498 he founded a **Knabenchor** (forerunners of the Vienna Boys' Choir), and he also encouraged leading humanist scholars such as Conrad Celtis and Johannes Cuspinian to teach at Vienna University.

Ferdinand I

In contrast, Maximilian's grandson, **Karl V**, visited Vienna only once and in 1521 transferred the Austrian possessions of the Habsburgs to his brother, **Ferdinand I**. The latter was at once confronted with an uprising of the Viennese led by their able mayor, **Dr Martin Siebenbürger.** Although the latter attempted to negotiate with Ferdinand for more civic autonomy, he and five colleagues were brought to trial in Wiener Neustadt and executed. In 1526 Ferdinand went further, removing all the city's freedoms and privileges and placing it directly under the control of an imperial administrator.

Three years later, the oppressed city was faced with a siege by the Turkish army under **Suleiman II**. It was ably defended by Count Salm, although at a cost of 1500 casualties. Following this shock, Vienna was girdled with a star-shaped **fortification** (*tracé italien*) built by Italian engineers on the familiar Renaissance model, and destined to remain in place until 1857. The relative paucity of Renaissance architecture in Vienna is probably due to the fact that construction of this fortification absorbed so much of available funds. However, the oldest extant part of the Hofburg, the **Schweizerhof** and the **Schweizertor**, as well as the **Stallburg**, all date to this period.

Ferdinand needed to erect spiritual defences as much as military ones: the **Reformation** had already percolated to Vienna by the time he arrived and the aristocracy was going over to the new faith in droves. The Catholic church was in an abject state of corruption; Ferdinand's own commission reported that there were thirteen monks, two nuns, six women and eight children living in convivial, but hardly monastic harmony in the monastery of Klosterneuburg. By that time (1561) it is estimated that four-fifths of the population of Vienna were Protestant and ten of its 13 parishes lacked priests.

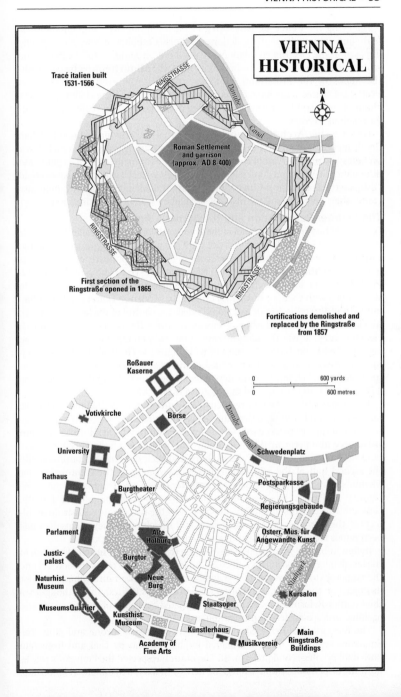

VIENNA HISTORICAL

N

Tracé italien built
1531–1566

RINGSTRASSE

Danube Canal

Roman Settlement
and garrison
(approx. AD 8–400)

RINGSTRASSE

First section of the
Ringstraße opened in 1865

RINGSTRASSE

Fortifications demolished and
replaced by the Ringstraße
from 1857

Roßauer
Kaserne

Votivkirche

Börse

0 — 600 yards
0 — 600 metres

University

Schwedenplatz

Danube Canal

Rathaus

Burgtheater

Postsparkasse

Regierungsgebäude

Parlament

Alte
Hofburg

Österr. Mus. für
Angewandte Kunst

Justiz-
palast

Burgtor

Stadtpark

Naturhist.
Museum

Neue
Burg

Kursalon

MuseumsQuartier

Staatsoper

Kunsthist.
Museum

Künstlerhaus

Main
Ringstraße
Buildings

Academy of
Fine Arts

Musikverein

Following the **Peace of Augsburg** (1555), the nobility could choose their faith and impose it on their followers. Since Catholicism was theoretically imposed in the city, the population streamed out on Sundays to worship at the seats of the Protestant nobility. In the city itself, the **Minoritenkirche** came into the hands of the Protestants in 1569, and by 1576 even the Mayor was Protestant. Three years later, citizens assembled in front of the Hofburg set up a chant of 'we want the gospel' and handed over a petition (in reality a demand) for religious freedom.

However, the **Archduke Ernst** (Governor of Austria since Rudolf II had finally moved his court to Prague in 1583) proved strong enough to crack down on heresy by making Catholicism a condition of citizenship, as well as enforcing attendance at Mass and confession. The days when fiery Lutheran pastors could castigate the Pope as anti-Christ, and Protestant noblemen could with impunity canter their horses round the aisles of St Stephen's, were now numbered.

The Counter-Reformation and the Baroque Age

Ferdinand I had fired the first shot in the Counter-Reformation by calling the Jesuits to Vienna in 1551; however it was not until the mid-17C that ground lost to the Protestants could systematically be recovered. The battle for hearts and minds was joined by **Archbishop** (later Cardinal) **Khlesl** (1553–1630), himself the son of a Protestant baker, who launched the so-called '**Klosteroffensive**', whereby Austria was flooded with Catholic orders. As Chancellor of Vienna University, Khlesl had purged it of Protestantism (it was placed under the control of the Jesuits in 1622); as Vicar-General for the Bishop of Passau he swept the Lower Austrian church clean of heresy. It was the *Klosteroffensive* that really changed the face of Vienna; between 1614 and 1638—for most of which time the Thirty Years War was raging—no fewer than nine orders settled in the city, many of them building their monasteries and churches in the new, sensual Baroque style. By the middle of the 17C, it could justly be observed that '*Österreich*' was '*Klösterreich*'.

The monks and nuns who streamed into Vienna were often Italian—preferable for the court and church to Germans, since their inability to speak the language meant that they were less easily infected with Protestant ideas. However, **Italian influence** also permeated the city culture in other ways: Italian architects had built the Renaissance part of the Hofburg and their dominance continued into the second half of the 17C, when they received most of the commissions for Vienna's sacred and profane Baroque **architecture**. Only towards the end of the century was the architectural hegemony of Ferrabosco, the Carlone dynasty, Galli-Bibiena, Martinelli and Tencala broken by the two greatest Austrian architects of the Baroque, Fischer von Erlach and Hildebrandt; they themselves had been pupils respectively of Bernini and Carlo Fontana.

Italian influence was also pervasive in the **theatre** and in **music**, above all in the lavish operatic spectacles laid on by the Jesuits (to instil religious fervour) and the Emperor (to inspire awe of the dynasty). While Protestantism had relied for its impact on the spoken and written word (*Kultur des Wortes*), the Catholicism of the Counter-Reformation was largely propagated by means of theatrical art and architecture, spectacle and music (*Kultur der Sinne*).

The Baroque Age heralded a new solidarity between throne and altar. The Emperor considered himself ordained for his position by God and from him flowed all privileges and preferment. The church respected the Emperor's role as bulwark of orthodoxy and scourge of heresy. In such a symbiotic relationship, however, the balance of power was always delicate: strong-minded priests might well see it as their prerogative to remind the ruler of the obligations attaching to his unique role. Cardinal Khlesl, for instance, put pressure on the **Archduke Matthias** to unseat the latter's elder brother, Emperor **Rudolf II**, whose rather lax rule from Prague exhibited a lamentably conciliatory spirit in matters of religion. As the son of **Maximilian II** (1564–76), whose attitudes were so liberal that he was suspected of being a secret Protestant, Matthias was less motivated by religious intolerance than by dynastic considerations and disappointment in his inheritance. His success in deposing his brother in 1608 was actually achieved with the assistance of the Protestant nobility.

Ferdinand II

The final, doomed assault of Protestantism was provoked by the heavy-handed approach of Matthias's pietistic successor, **Ferdinand II**: in 1618 his councillors were thrown from the windows of the Hradcin (the famous '**defenestration of Prague**'), and the following year Protestant nobles demanding religious freedom besieged him in the Vienna Hofburg. Only with the **Battle of the White Mountain** (1620), when Protestant Bohemia was utterly routed, did the tide finally begin to turn in favour of Catholicism in Austria and Bohemia, although Vienna was twice threatened in 1645 by Swedish armies in the ensuing Thirty Years War.

By 1629, Ferdinand was strong enough to issue his **Edict of Restitution**, returning to the Catholic church all of the 1555 properties expropriated by Protestants. By the beginning of the reign of **Leopold I** (1657–1705), the Counter-Reformation was triumphant in the Habsburg Empire: the Protestant nobles gave grudging allegiance, the peasants were savagely subdued and the mostly Lutheran entrepreneurial classes had been driven out from the cities. Thereafter, advancement was only possible through absolute religious conformity and civil obedience; the result was that 'the smallest office at court seemed more attractive than a high office in the city council', an attitude that was to have long-lasting implications for the culture and society of Vienna.

The Golden Apple of Christendom

Leopold had originally been intended for the church, and in adult life he was surrounded by mumbling confessors and ruthless prelates. Notable among the latter was **Bishop Kollonitsch** (1631–1707), whose father had commanded the fortress at Komárom (Hungary), and who dedicated himself with military zeal to the extirpation of any remaining Protestants, of Jews (who had drifted back to Vienna after their expulsion in the 15C), and of any kind of opposition to imperial absolutism. With the aid of Leopold's bigoted Spanish wife, Kollonitsch persuaded the Emperor to expel the Jews from the Unteren Werd in Vienna in 1670, the area being renamed the **Leopoldstadt**. Unfortunately, this decree brought about an economic crisis and rich Jews had to be invited back to help rescue the city's finances.

Leopold's reckless extravagance had anyway made him heavily dependent on Jewish financiers, the most famous (or notorious) of whom was **Samuel Oppenheimer**. The dramatic collapse of the latter's business was hastened by an (officially inspired?) riot in 1700, during which, most conveniently for the court, all his business papers and lists of debtors were burned. (The crash temporarily bankrupted the state.)

Leopold spent lavishly on building (notably the **Leopoldinische Trakt** of the Hofburg) and on fabulous operatic spectacles. A performance of *Il Pomo d'Oro*, to celebrate the emperor's marriage to the Spanish Infanta, cost 100,000 gulden to stage; earlier in the same year (1667), a *Roßballett* (equine ballet) had featured ships floating on artificial lakes, horses and carriages suspended in mid-air and 80,000 fireworks to illuminate models of mounts Etna and Parnassus. The value of the stolen plates alone was put at 9000 gulden. Such shows were not only useful as propaganda; they also accorded with the theologically based Baroque idea of *spectaculum mundi*—the world as theatre, where every man played out the role allotted to him. Even the much more cost-conscious Maria Theresia was later to remark, 'There must be spectacles: without them one cannot live in the royal seat'.

Funds of such magnitude would have been better spent preparing to resist the Turkish armies, a point that occurred to a Swabian monk calling himself **Abraham a Sancta Clara**, who electrified the Viennese with his preaching in the 1670s. In his sermons, he castigated his audience mercilessly for their heedless self-indulgence, but also offered them scapegoats for their sufferings—Protestants, Turks and of course Jews. The plague of 1679 supplied him with ideal conditions for Savonarola-like denunciations: in a famous diatribe, '*Merck's Wien!*' (Take Heed Vienna!), he built up a harrowing picture of a city where death was omnipresent—'in the Street of the Lords (Herrengasse), Death is the master; in Chorister Street (Singerstraße), Death has sung many a requiem; Death has made of the Graben a burial ground'. One of his sermons features a drunken bagpipe player named Augustin, who became a symbol of Viennese survival skills and was subsequently immortalised in the **ballad of Lieber Augustin**. Stumbling home from the tavern, Augustin falls into a pit of plague corpses; blissfully unaware of the grim nature of his sleeping quarters, he snoozes the night away in a prophylactic haze of alcohol, rising next morning to continue his riotous living.

Scarcely had the plague receded than an even greater menace appeared on the horizon. In the early summer of 1683, a huge Ottoman army under **Kara Mustafa** approached through the Balkans, gathering contingents from vassal states as it advanced. When the first reports of it reached the city, 3000 of the more prosperous Viennese fled to the west, and the Emperor Leopold himself left for Passau on 7 July. From there he set about rousing the conscience of Christendom, and an army was hastily put together, nominally under the command of the King of Poland, **Jan Sobieski**. Its military strategist, however, was **Duke Karl of Lorraine**, among whose commanders was an ambitious 20-year-old named **Eugene of Savoy**, who subsequently became the most successful general the Habsburgs ever employed. The city held out valiantly under **Count Starhemberg**, although a final assault by the Turks near today's Burgtheater very nearly succeeded. That same evening the arrival of the imperial armies was heralded by rockets soaring into the night sky over the Kahlenberg. On 12 September, the Turks were put to flight; and on the 14th the Emperor triumphantly arrived to attend a *Te Deum* in St Stephen's.

Vienna as 'Residenzstadt'

With Vienna secured from further Turkish attack, its role as the 'Residenzstadt' of the dynasty was confirmed. The nobility, clergy and court personnel—many of the latter foreigners—enjoyed economic and social privileges, while the Viennese burghers were relatively disadvantaged. By 1730, under Karl VI, some

The Indigo Love of Reading Fund
provides books for learning
in high-needs schools.

Every child
deserves a chance.

How can you help?
Add a donation to
your next purchase.

Together, we can reach
our fundraising goal of
$1.5 million.

25 per cent of the city's population depended directly or indirectly on the court payroll and were quartered in the Inner City. In the faubourgs lived the artisans, large numbers of whom had been attracted to Vienna as a result of the building boom of the Baroque Age.

The early 18C saw some of the greatest **construction projects** in Vienna's history. The hero of the Turkish Wars, **Prince Eugene of Savoy**, spent the rewards heaped on him by a grateful emperor on the **Belvedere Palace** and a winter palace in the Himmelpfortgasse. He employed the greatest architects of his day, Johann Bernhard Fischer von Erlach and Lukas von Hildebrandt, who were also given commissions by other nobles competing with the emperor in Baroque splendour.

Karl VI, who succeeded the short-lived Josef I in 1711, spent untold sums on ambitious projects such as **Klosterneuburg**, where he intended to create an Austrian Escorial, on the **Hofbibliothek**, the **Spanish Riding School** and the **Karlskirche** (the last three being works of the Fischer von Erlachs, father and son). Even so, he found it hard to compete with the conspicuous display of the aristocracy: Montesquieu remarked that the latter lived better than their ruler (although Lady Mary Wortley Montagu complained that their palaces looked cramped in the Inner City). However, there was also an economic motive behind the pouring of capital into real estate: it was safer to invest the huge surpluses accruing through the 'robot' (obligatory labour) system of secondary serfdom in this way, than to risk losing such wealth in uncertain capitalistic ventures on the margins of developed Europe.

Maria Theresia

When Maria Theresia succeeded her father in 1740, savings in state expenditure and **reform** of government administration had become imperative. At the same time her position was under threat from France, Bavaria and Prussia, whose rulers were determined to ignore the **Pragmatic Sanction** (1713), by which Karl had tried to guarantee the succession in the female line. Even more urgent, therefore, was the need for reform of the army, the chaotic state of the Habsburg forces having become one of the wonders of the civilised world.

With the help of well-chosen advisers (all of them drawn from other parts of the Habsburg realms) and the financial skills of her husband, **Franz Stephan of Lorraine**, Maria Theresia succeeded in putting the imperial finances in order and beating off repeated attempts to dismantle her empire in the **Seven Years War** with Prussia (1756–63). A general income tax was introduced which neither the nobility nor the church could evade; this was followed by reforms establishing primary and improving secondary education; the administration of justice was rationalised and certain civil rights defined in the **Codex Theresianus** (1776). Efficiency measures in Vienna included the registration of citizens, a census (1754) and the numbering of houses in order to facilitate conscription (1770).

Maria Theresia understood the Viennese well, remarking that 'they would do anything if talked to kindly and shown affection'. At **Schönbrunn**, the palace originally planned under Leopold, but only completed by Maria Theresia's court architect, the imperial life-style was familial, unaffected, verging on the bourgeois. Conversation was in '*Schönbrunnerisch*' (Viennese dialect laced with French idioms) and the monarch's 12 surviving children (of 16 births) were accustomed to make their own entertainment. Her blind spots arose from a limited education and religious influence: practising Jews were not to be admitted into her presence and negotiations with a Jewish financier once took place with the latter separated by a screen from the royal person. It also took six years of persuasion by her enlightened minister, **Joseph von Sonnenfels**, before she conceded that torture was not the ideal nor the only method for establishing the guilt of suspects.

Moreover, in spite of her best efforts, the absolutist institutions remained barnacled with monopolies, sinecures and place-mongers. Herr von Faninal in Richard Strauss's opera *Der Rosenkavalier* is a devastating portrait of the type of person (a military contractor) who did well out of the system: he owns 12 rent houses in the suburb of Wieden, a substantial town palace and a brand new patent of nobility. Even at court it proved impossible to manage with less than 1500 chamberlains, whose duties ranged from fetching the imperial glass of milk each day from the dairy at Schönbrunn, to bringing snow into the city for the little Archdukes and Archduchesses to sledge on.

It was no wonder that a chronic shortage of accommodation developed in the Inner City: householders were obliged to surrender ground floors for billeting court employees; retail shops were forbidden in order to make space for living quarters, and were replaced by hordes of pedlars visiting the city daily; such craftsmen as could find space were compelled to ply their trades in tiny airless attics.

Joseph II

From 1765, when Franz Stephan died, Maria Theresia ruled jointly with her son Joseph until her death in 1780. Strongly influenced by the ideas of the French **Enlightenment**, Joseph wished to carry reform further and enact it more quickly than his mother. His intention was reform from above—'everything *for* the people, nothing *through* the people' in the well-known phrase. The Viennese benefited from his decision to allow the public into the Prater, the Augarten and the Imperial Picture Gallery at the Belvedere (Prince Eugene's palace having passed into imperial possession).

Joseph was a constitutionalist who delighted to see laws and rights codified in minute detail; yet he failed to resolve the conflict between natural rights, as posited by his spiritual mentors of the Enlightenment, and the royal prerogative of absolutism. The latter he did not hesitate to use, even against so formidable a vested interest as the church, which owned three-eighths of the land when he came to the throne. He reduced the 2000 **monasteries** by approximately 17 per cent, closing down those which fitted the Gibbonian description of 'wealthy and useless'. Secularised buildings were turned into barracks, military depots, hospitals and hostels for workers. The 60 million gulden in cash he collected from rich foundations, he applied to building parish churches (no one was to be more than one hour's walk from mass), and to training priests for an active mission. The monasteries that were spared were those engaged in charitable or educational work.

The Emperor's most lasting and valuable measure was the **Edict of Tolerance** (1781), which reversed centuries of Habsburg persecution of Protestants and Jews. The former were able to set up two churches in Vienna, although the façade had to be inconspicuous and bell-towers were prohibited. Jews were now to be admitted to schools, the university, the civil service (theoretically) and the professions. The aim was assimilation, not the encouragement of a parallel culture; the ghettoes were opened up and those of Joseph's Jewish subjects who refused to take a German name were arbitrarily allotted one by the authorities (for example Grün, Gelb, Schwarz, Weiss—or joke-names like Mandelbaum or Rosenzweig). Synagogues were still forbidden, however, as was the appointment of a rabbi; furthermore a 'tolerance tax' ensured that only richer Jews could afford to live in the *Residenzstadt*.

Joseph II's legacy in Vienna includes the **Josephinum**, an academy for training military surgeons, and the **Vienna General Hospital** with its Narrenturm ('Fools' Tower') for confining lunatics. His reign also overlaps with perhaps the greatest period of Viennese music, whose masters included **Gluck**, **Haydn** and **Mozart**. The fortunes of the latter two in Vienna were mixed—Haydn enjoyed his greatest successes in London, Mozart in Prague. Nevertheless, Mozart's mentor did find secure employment as Prince Esterházy's Kapellmeister, while *The Marriage of Figaro* (premiered at the Hoftheater in 1786) received so many encores that the Emperor was obliged to issue an order restricting the latter to arias only; the Viennese, however, with their obsession for novelty, soon lost interest in the piece, and Mozart's star began to wane thereafter. He did score one more triumph with *The Magic Flute* (1791), whose success owed a good deal to Emanuel Schikaneder's brilliant showmanship. The public (as opposed to official arbiters of taste) took this story spiced with irreverence to their hearts, not least because its juxtaposition of sly humour (Papageno) with pretentious bombast (Sarastro) was in a tradition they understood and loved.

Mozart died 22 months after his lukewarm patron, Joseph II, the self-styled 'servant of the people'. The composer had defied the norms of Baroque patronage, but died with huge debts, although these were incurred more through extravagance than neglect.

The Emperor had demolished long-standing shibboleths, believing that the application of rational measures would create an ordered state of happy, obedient citizens. On his deathbed he had second thoughts and rescinded almost all his most radical decrees. Frederick II of Prussia provided a fitting epitaph for him, remarking that he 'always took the second step before the first'.

Biedermeier Vienna

After the brief reign of **Leopold II** (1790–92), a protagonist of the Enlightenment like his brother Joseph, reactionary government was established under **Franz II**, the last Holy Roman Emperor (1792–1835). The latter suffered the indignity of seeing Vienna twice occupied by French troops—in 1805 and 1809. Foreseeing the inevitable, Franz took the title of Franz I of Austria, after **Napoleon** was crowned as Emperor of the French. A proclamation, issued from the balcony of the Jesuit church Am Hof on 6 August 1806, announced the extinction of the nearly 900-year-old Holy Roman Empire, for which the House of Habsburg had supplied emperors continuously (except between 1740 and 1745) since the mid-15C.

A further indignity was the opportunist marriage arranged by Franz's shrewd Foreign Minister, Prince **Metternich**, between Napoleon and the Emperor's eldest daughter, Marie Louise. After Napoleon had finally been defeated, it was again Metternich who presided over the **Congress of Vienna** (1814–15), attended by representatives of 200 states, cities and dominions. The deliberations of the Congress and the subsequent decrees of congresses at Karlsbad, Troppau, Laibach and Verona, re-established the conservative order in Europe after the Napoleonic Wars.

Between 1815 and the outbreak of revolution in 1848, Metternich administered the Empire as a police state, in which checks on individual initiative and censorship were pervasive, although there were ways round the latter. At the same time, the Emperor posed as the father of his people, regularly receiving petitions and living a life of bourgeois rectitude. This somewhat paradoxical interlude is known either as the *Vormärz* (i.e. the period leading up to the March Revolution of 1848), or as the age of **Biedermeier**. The word is derived from the name of a gently satirised figure invented for a Munich magazine, an obedient and somewhat complacent citizen, whose solution to repression in the public and political sphere is to embrace a life of 'inner emigration' and 'happiness in a quiet corner'.

The term **Biedermeier** also extends to the arts in Central Europe at this time. In Vienna, craftsmen like **Josef Danhauser** produced solidly comfortable and elegant furniture, while painters like **Ferdinand Waldmüller** portrayed the domestic idyll of the Biedermeier bourgeoisie. The architect **Josef Kornhäusel** erected sober neo-Classical edifices in Vienna and Baden bei Wien, the latter a suburban spa made fashionable by imperial patronage. Censorship failed to quell the Viennese passion for theatre, where actor-playwrights such as **Ferdinand Raimund** (1790–1836), and especially **Johann Nestroy** (1801–1862), smuggled subversive material into their performances by improvising on stage. The great **Franz Grillparzer** (who was also a civil servant) celebrated the Habsburg myth in his historical dramas, but agonised in private over the oppressive nature of the regime.

The most conspicuous expression of Biedermeier values is to be found in **Adalbert Stifter's** strange, utopian novel *Der Nachsommer* (Indian Summer), which is full of yearning for a life filled with stability, peace and harmony. In the same way, the music of **Franz Schubert** seems to epitomize an age when romantic sensibility creatively conflicts with restraints that are externally determined, but also self-imposed. Schubert greatly admired **Beethoven**, who lived in Vienna for 35 years, and whose *Fidelio* was premiered in the Theater an der Wien in 1805 before an audience packed with French officers of the occupation force. However, in contrast to Beethoven's articulation of the universal themes of freedom and human dignity, much of Schubert's art is distinctively Viennese, evoking intensely intimate feelings of joy, melancholy and yearning, particularly in his 600 beautifully crafted songs. These were played to an appreciative audience at soirées known as *Schubertiades*, a regular feature of the composer's mildly Bohemian existence. Although Schubert had aristocratic patrons, he was composing in an age when the emergent bourgeoisie were already becoming their own cultural sponsors: the **Society of the Friends of Music** was founded in 1814, the **Konservatorium** in 1822 and the subsequently famous **Wiener Philharmoniker** in 1842. (Nevertheless they required imperial approval.)

Revolution

Under the surface calm of the Biedermeier age, frustrations were building up, both among the exploited workers trapped in the miserable conditions produced by the first phase of industrialisation, and among the middle-class, chafing under petty and often pointless restrictions which even threatened technological progress. When a run of bad harvests and food shortages coincided with rising unemployment, the scene was set for revolution. On 13 March 1848, the Lower Austrian Diet met in the Herrengasse and addressed a petition to Franz's successor, the simple-minded **Ferdinand I of Austria**, demanding civil rights and press freedom. Shortly afterwards, a demonstration of students and members of the Diet was fired on by Italian troops commanded by one of the more stupid

Archdukes. In the violence that followed, intellectuals and the bourgeoisie fought in the Academic Legion and the National Guard, while workers conducted their own campaign.

Playwrights Raimund and Nestroy

The playwrights Ferdinand Raimund (real name 'Raimann') and Johann Nestroy are the two most beloved figures in the history of Viennese theatre, and their works, written partly in Viennese dialect, complemented their contrasting personalities. Both were artistically active through the period of Metternich's oppressive regime, although only Nestroy lived to see the Revolution of 1848 that ended it—a revolution in which he took part, if not valiantly, at least with a display of characteristic self-irony. Their plays, which included set-piece musical numbers, provided an outlet both for the escapism and the irreverence of audiences who were treated like children by a paranoid regime and its censors. One way of circumventing the censor was to improvise pointed allusions and wisecracks during performance, and Nestroy was particularly adept at this.

Raimund, as author and leading actor in his own comic roles, came from, and enlarged on, a tradition of fairy tale and magic that mixed Baroque illusion with melancholy and humour. He unlocked the casket of dreams for his public, who could vicariously enjoy sudden access to wealth and power in the fantasies he so expertly spun for them. One of his best known works has been translated into English as *The Spendthrift* and relates how the eponymous hero is saved from his otherwise fatal weakness by the good offices of a benign fairy. Raimund himself was not so fortunate: chronically depressed like many great comics and perennially unhappy in his relationship with women, he died of a botched suicide attempt after being bitten by a dog that he wrongly assumed had rabies.

Nestroy was a more robust character and his works had correspondingly more satirical bite. Influenced partly by French vaudeville and contemporary English and German comedy, he held up a mirror to his age, lacing his pieces with irreverent topical allusion, parody, and satirical dissection of contemporary society. He wrote and performed in some eighty plays and was a genius of aphorism and neologisms (which earned him the admiration of the linguistic purist, Karl Kraus). However this has made him somewhat inaccessible to non-German speakers, even to non-Viennese. In the English-speaking world, only the Broadway hit *Hello, Dolly* has a distant Nestroy ancestry, being based on Thornton Wilder's adaptation of *Einen Jux will er sich machen* (He Loves to Play Pranks). As Paul Hofmann puts it: '[Nestroy] portrayed the Viennese society of his day: the greedy speculators, scheming widows, smug shopkeepers, sly servants, pompous officials, languid bourgeois girls and their romantic suitors, the sales clerk who wants to get some fun while the boss is out of town and ... the outcasts and vagrants.'

2001 was the bicentenary of Nestroy's birth and a large programme of performance and symposia held in Vienna further raised his cultural profile. No doubt he would have observed such goings on with his customary irony, perhaps using it as a peg for one of his aphorisms, for example: 'What has posterity ever done for me? Nothing! OK, so that's what I'll do for it...'

The differing aims of the participants was a principal cause of the failure of the revolution in Vienna. In any case, it turned out that the dynasty was not the focus of revolutionary hatred (Ferdinand was popular), and even the government might have been tolerated without Metternich. According to an ancient Viennese tradition, the Jews were seen as those most immediately responsible for such ills as high prices and unemployment, and anti-semitic riots also broke out elsewhere in the Empire. With Italy, Hungary and even Prague in revolt, the old order was rocked. However, after some notable successes by the Hungarians, the rebellion was put down by overwhelmingly superior forces (in the case of Hungary, with the help of a Russian army).

The events of 1848 did result in the temporary removal of Metternich, who fled to England, and the deposition of Ferdinand, who was replaced by his nephew, the 18-year-old **Franz Joseph I**. Under the influence of his strong-minded mother and hard-line advisers, Franz Joseph began his reign with savage repression. He withdrew most of the concessions to democracy that his uncle had been compelled to make and ordered executions of 13 Hungarian generals. His unpopularity among the educated classes was by no means diminished by the retrograde **Concordat** with the papacy in 1855, which restored the right of the church to interfere directly in social matters and education. Only after his marriage to the beautiful Elisabeth of Bavaria in 1854 did his standing begin to improve.

As far as Vienna was concerned, Franz Joseph's most notable act was to order the demolition of the bastions of the city in 1857, a decision that inaugurated the era of economic and political Liberalism known as the **Gründerzeit** (Founders' Period). The main architectural legacy of the Gründerzeit is the **Ringstraße**, a boulevard that follows the contour of the old city fortifications, and along which arose the great representative buildings of a newly self-confident and prosperous élite drawn from the entrepreneurial middle class.

Franz Joseph and the Ringstraßen era

The impulse, but not the model, for laying out a new area of Vienna on a grand scale may have come from Haussmann's ambitious replanning of Paris. The Viennese project was ingeniously financed by selling off to developers those plots of land not required for public buildings. The purchasers then built palaces containing grandiose apartments for the wealthy. Tax concessions and a time limit on building permits aimed (with some success) to prevent land speculation. The monumental architecture of the constituted a symbolic expression of Liberal values. Theophil Hansen's classical **Parliament** (1883) recalled the cradle of democracy in Athens; Friedrich Schmidt's **City Hall** (Rathaus) (1883) evoked the independent trading cities of free burghers in the Middle Ages; the neo-Renaissance **University** (1884), designed by Heinrich Ferstel, saluted the humanist learning of the Italian Renaissance.

The *Gründerzeit* was a time of ostentation and conspicuous consumption, the dark side of which was the exploitation of a large working-class population housed in insanitary '*Mietskasernen*' ('rent barracks') in the Viennese suburbs. While fortunes were being made, however, the Empire was growing weaker. The unsuccessful war in Italy led, it seemed inexorably, to the completion of the Risorgimento (the unification of all Italy under the Savoy monarchy); contemporaneously, the Habsburgs lost their influence in Germany after a catastrophic defeat by the Prussians at Sadowa (Königgrätz—1866). In 1867 Franz Joseph was forced into the *Ausgleich* (Compromise) with Hungary, that created a constitutional oddity known as the **Austro-Hungarian Empire**, or **Dual Monarchy**. Under this arrangement, foreign policy, defence, the army and finance were regarded as matters of joint administration, while domestic affairs were dealt with by each country's parliament individually.

This solution temporarily appeased the Hungarians, but in the long run it created as many problems as it solved. Rising Czech nationalism made Bohemia, with its strong economy, ever more restive under Austrian hegemony; at the same time, the Slavs, Rumanians and others who suffered under heavy-handed Hungarian rule became increasingly discontented. Even so, the contemptuous term *Völkerkerker* (prison of nations), that achieved some currency as a description of Franz Joseph's empire, was a caricature of Habsburg rule that had many features worthy of respect. These included constitutional rule and economic progress.

The Great Crash and the end of the nineteenth century

In 1873 a **World Exhibition** was held in the Prater. Modelled on similar events which had been staged in London and Paris, it was intended not only to display the material achievements of the empire, but also to give visible expression to Liberalism's belief in progress and in the expanding horizons of the future. Unfortunately, events conspired to give this self-confidence a hollow ring: an outbreak of cholera proved a powerful deterrent to visitors (Franz Joseph nobly visited 48 times with guests); worse still, the self-congratulation of Liberal capitalism turned to dismay when the stock market crashed one week after the opening. The aftermath of the crash revealed the slough of corruption in a city where political and economic power was narrowly based in the hands of a self-interested clique voted in by 3.3 per cent of the population. Two days after the crash, the journalist Ferdinand Kürnberger wrote: 'Since yesterday, a thief is once again called a thief and no longer a baron. Never has such a beautiful storm cleansed such stinking air.'

Nevertheless, the state finances were able to ride out the storm and important infrastructural projects were continued in the 1870s. These included the building of **aqueducts** supplying Alpine water, the opening of the **Central Cemetery** and much-needed regulation of the **Danube**. Liberals were able to maintain their power in the City Council until the 1890s, but the widening of the franchise (1885) to include those who paid as little as five gulden in tax eroded their power base. The champion of these '*Fünfguldenmänner*' was a charismatic local politician of humble origins named **Karl Lueger**. Fifteen years later he was finally confirmed as mayor, his four previous election victories having been set aside by Franz Joseph: the Emperor feared (inter alia) that Lueger's attacks on the Jews could lead to a flight of Jewish capital (some of it to Budapest) and the collapse of the city's already precarious finances.

Lueger's populism and anti-semitism exploited the resentment felt by the small traders and petit bourgeois against the rich and often corrupt Liberal establishment, many of whose members were indeed assimilated Jews. Between 1897 and 1910, he pursued a policy of **municipalisation** that removed utilities from rapacious private companies (the worst was the English Imperial Continental Gas Association), and built up a comprehensive network of services. These included new schools, shelters for the aged and the homeless, an employment bureau, municipal undertakers, communal insurance and a savings bank.

He was also a proto-Green, ordaining that 'where there is room for a tree in Vienna, I wish that one be planted'.

Lueger's brand of 'Christian Social' politics did produce major policy achievements. However, it left largely untouched the desperate situation of the worker masses, who found a standard-bearer in the Jewish doctor, **Viktor Adler**. Adler's experiences of dealing with the poor in his professional capacity convinced him that they needed effective political representation even more than they needed medical help. His decision to found a **Social Democratic Party** committed to social justice cost him several periods of gaol. He bore these stoically however, memorably describing the somewhat bumbling repression of the late Habsburg régime as 'absolutism mitigated by muddle'. His party, an alliance of moderate Socialists with radical Marxists, became the largest political grouping after the introduction of **universal male suffrage** in 1907.

Culture in 19C Vienna

The period of Liberal hegemony in the City Council (1861–95) is associated with a somewhat decadent hedonism, distinguishing features of which were operettas, Strauß waltzes and the overripe painting of Hans Makart. Crowds thronging the dance-halls and cafés apparently paid scarce attention to the news of Sadowa in 1866; the financial crash of 1873 was celebrated to the gleeful strains of a *Krachpolka*, as banks imploded and the figure for suicides mounted. While **Johann Strauß Senior** had supported the authorities in 1848 and composed his celebrated *Radetzky March* to honour the man who had subdued the Italian Revolt, his son had stood on the side of the rebels, and was now the idol of an age deluged in champagne and bad debts. '*Glücklich ist wer vergißt, was doch nicht zu ändern ist*' (Happy is he who forgets what anyway cannot be altered) are much quoted lines from his operetta *Die Fledermaus* (1874), and they could be the motto of the age.

The Viennese love of spectacle was also gratified by **Makart**, the hugely successful history painter, whose sententious works were acted out as tableaux in fashionable society. In 1875, his mega-canvas of *Karl V's Entry into Antwerp* was admired by 34,000 visitors and four years later he organised a Wagnerian pageant on the Ringstraße to mark the silver wedding anniversary of Franz Joseph and Elisabeth. Dressed in a suit of black silk and riding a white horse, Makart himself led the procession of 43 groups of artisans, whose exquisite historical costumes he had designed with no expense spared.

In the 1890s, a reaction set in against increasingly vacuous Historicism and the general conservatism of the art scene. It culminated in the foundation of the **Vienna Secession** (1898), with **Gustav Klimt** at its head. Adopting the slogan 'to every age its art, to art its freedom', the Secessionists opened up the claustrophobic Viennese art world to the stimulation of contemporary foreign painting and sculpture. They built their own exhibition hall, founded an influential journal (*Ver Sacrum*) and staged 23 exhibitions in seven years. Their influence on the applied arts can be seen from the foundation of the **Wiener Werkstätte** by Josef Hoffmann in 1903.

There was also a new spirit in architecture: **Otto Wagner**, who had begun his career building in the style of Historicism, became the most influential of the architects who turned their backs on the now rather debased replication of neo-Renaissance or neo-Baroque. As leader of a pioneering city-planning commission, he designed the 36 stations of a new urban transit railway; other important projects for the municipality followed, including his two most celebrated works, the post-office savings bank and the church for the municipal asylum.

At the turn of the century, Vienna's 'culture of the senses' was complemented by a new flowering of the 'culture of the word'. **Hermann Bahr** and his associates in the **Jung Wien** movement campaigned to sweep away the dead hand of tradition in the arts and championed the new, whether it was foreign and shocking, such as the theatre of Strindberg and Ibsen, or home-grown and disturbing to Viennese sensibilities, such as the music of Mahler and Schoenberg. **Gustav Mahler** himself revolutionised performances at the Viennese opera, demanding greater discipline and commitment from performers and audience alike. His own music, filled with the emotionalism and tortured feeling of late Romanticism, was little appreciated by conservative Viennese audiences, whose taste was for the emollience of **Brahms**. The latter lived happily in the city from 1869 to 1897, for most of that time conducting an unprincipled campaign against the saintly **Anton Bruckner** (whose crime, in the eyes of the Brahms faction, was that he had been adopted as their totem by the Wagnerians).

The Bohemian element in turn of the century Vienna revolved around the **literary cafés**, where men like Bahr, **Hugo von Hofmannsthal**, **Peter Altenberg** and **Karl Kraus** held court, and the 'Feuilletonists' scribbled their witty cultural essays for the daily press. Feuds and intrigue were endemic to this milieu; its greatest polemicist was Karl Kraus, who founded a journal (*Die Fackel*) entirely written by himself, in which he attacked the corruption of the press, the imbecilities of politicians, the posturing of Hermann Bahr and the pseudo-science peddled by Freud.

Sigmund Freud's *Interpretation of Dreams* appeared in 1900 in an edition of 600 copies (it took seven years to sell out). The founder of psychoanalysis was viewed with some reserve by the Viennese medical establishment, which somewhat presciently distrusted the psychoanalytic movement's cultist character. Perhaps, also, many were unhappy about his claimed revelations of what lay beneath society's veneer of civilisation. Similar revelations, however, were made by the brilliant **Arthur Schnitzler**, whose novels and plays illuminated the desperation at the heart of a world where the brief solace of sexual satisfaction seemed only to intensify individual isolation and heighten a sense of impending doom. Freud described Schnitzler as his 'double', discovering through intuition and insight what he himself could only retrieve through laborious investigation.

The First Republic

With the outbreak of the First World War in 1914, the days of Vienna as a uniquely creative and culturally febrile environment were numbered. The last flowering of a literature inspired by the empire was to take place in retrospect—Robert Musil's masterpiece on a society in decline, *The Man Without Qualities*, was written in the 1930s, and **Joseph Roth** mythologised the dying days of Habsburg rule in a series of novels written about the same time. The world memorialised by Roth came to an end when the ancient Franz Joseph finally expired at Schönbrunn in 1916. His successor, **Karl I**, was swept away in the aftermath of a defeat that saw the empire dissolved and the setting up of the tiny, bankrupt, First Republic of Austria. The latter was cut off from most of its traditional sources of raw materials; whole industries that had been linked to structures now in the hostile successor states simply collapsed.

Vienna, disparagingly described as Austria's *Wasserkopf* (hydrocephalus), was full of unemployable Austrian officials who had lost their jobs in the administration of the former imperial territories (although the city's total population fell by over 400,000). The solution to economic catastrophe and diplomatic isolation wanted by most Austrians was the incorporation of the country into Germany; it was an aim shared across the political spectrum from German nationalists on the right to Marxists and Socialists on the left, although the motives of each group differed. The merging of Austria with Germany was, however, forbidden by the victorious powers.

Vienna was the stronghold of the Social Democrats, whose power and autonomy were enhanced by the elevation of the city in 1922 to the status of Federal State (Land). '*Rotes Wien*' (**Red Vienna**), as it was called, introduced a remarkable programme of welfare (especially for young mothers and children), that dovetailed with reforms carried through by the Social Democrat Minister for Social Provision in the National Government. Social security insurance, paid holidays and an eight-hour working day were made obligatory. The most spectacular of Red Vienna's achievements was the building programme: **Adolf Loos** was one of several distinguished architects who worked for the city council, although his designs for settlements were too revolutionary for a conservative and cost-conscious housing department. Otto Wagner's disciples were more successful, erecting huge blocks of flats to standard designs and sizes, the famous **Gemeindebauten**. The programme was financed by a tax on home occupancy, charged at a sharply progressive rate, and a payroll levy. The rich were ruthlessly squeezed—82 per cent of taxed households contributed a mere 22 per cent of the tax.

Vienna's Socialist régime, which consciously promoted *Arbeiterkultur* (worker culture) and offended Catholic sensibilities by measures such as building a crematorium at the Central Cemetery, was greatly mistrusted by the right, represented politically by the Christian Social Party. The latter ruled in most other areas of the country and was led by an ascetic priest, **Ignaz Seipel**, who became Chancellor in 1922. Seipel succeeded in obtaining much needed credits for the Republic through the **Geneva Agreements**; the latter paved the way for the introduction (in 1924) of a new currency, which effectively ended hyper-inflation overnight (10,000 old Kronen were rebased as one new Schilling).

Despite the considerable achievements of both Seipel and Red Vienna, tension between left and right continued to grow, with both sides arming their supporters (the Christian Socials formed the *Heimwehr* and the Social Democrats the *Schutzbund*). In 1927, a **riot** after a miscarriage of justice led to the burning of the Palace of Justice in Vienna by Socialist demonstrators, 85 of whom were killed by police.

Seipel's successor, **Engelbert Dollfuß**, suspended parliament on a technicality in 1933 and destroyed the administrative independence of Vienna. A clerico-Fascist dictatorship or *Ständestaat* (Corporative State) was set up, underpinned by a political movement known as the Fatherland Front. **Civil war** broke out in 1934, in the course of which Vienna's most spectacular *Gemeindebau*, the huge Karl-Marx-Hof in the 19th District, was bombarded by government artillery. Dollfuß's forces easily subdued the ill-prepared *Schutzbund*, but the Chancellor himself was assassinated in an attempted Nazi putsch on 25 July 1934.

The Anschluß and the Second World War

The new Chancellor was an ineffectual lawyer named **Kurt von Schuschnigg**. Summoned by **Hitler** to Berchtesgaden in February 1938, Schuschnigg was subjected to several hours of ranting monologue, during which the *Führer* observed that 'the whole history of Austria was nothing but an uninterrupted act of high treason.' The days of the Republic were clearly numbered. On 11 March, Hitler decided to forestall a referendum called to decide over the question of Austrian independence, and ordered his troops to occupy Austrian territory. On 15 March, an ecstatic crowd of 250,000 people acclaimed their fellow-countryman when he appeared on the balcony of the Neue Hofburg in Vienna to announce the '*Anschluß*' ('joining') of Austria to the German Reich.

The majority of Austrians (excluding Jews) were at this time delighted with Hitler and even more delighted to be part of 'Greater Germany'. The Social Democrats' leader, **Karl Renner**, had always been in favour of incorporating Austria into Germany and now wrote a newspaper article describing the 20 years of the First Republic as a 'wrong turning'. The church hastened to accommodate the Nazis, recommending a 'yes' vote in the referendum on the *Anschluß*, which produced 99.6 per cent in favour (it was rigged, but scarcely needed to be). Hitler sentimentally proclaimed Vienna 'a gem' which he would place in a setting worthy of it, entrusting it to the care of the entire German Reich. The reality was to prove rather different: Austria was degraded to provincial status (latterly the Alpen-und-Donau-Reichsgau), whose function was to supply materials for the war effort and cannon fodder for the German army.

About two thirds of Vienna's 180,000 Jews escaped or bought their freedom from **Adolf Eichmann's** Orwellianly named 'Central Office for Jewish Emigration' at No. 22 Prinz-Eugen-Straße. One of these was Sigmund Freud, who left Vienna with his family on 4 June, 1938, after paying a large sum described as 'Tax on Fleeing the Reich'. On 9 November came the **Reichskristallnacht**, when synagogues were burned, shops plundered and Jews murdered in the streets. Over the next four years, the remaining Jews (over 60,000) were shipped to the concentration camps to be worked to death or slaughtered. By September 1942, Eichmann (who, incidentally, was brought up in Linz) could proudly announce that Vienna was 'Jew-free'.

If the war brought only privations, '**liberation**' by the Russians in 1945 was little improvement. Primitive, undisciplined Red Army soldiers indulged in an orgy of rape and looting. To add insult to injury, a bombastic monument to the liberators was immediately erected on Schwarzenbergplatz. Vienna was subsequently placed under four-power control that lasted ten years—the 'four men in a jeep' period, so vividly evoked in Graham Greene's screenplay for *The Third Man*. Although still subject to monitoring by the Allied Council, a grand coalition government led by the Socialist Karl Renner and the Conservative Leopold Figl gave Austria a semblance of independent government.

The Staatsvertrag (1955) and the Second Republic

The **Marshall Plan** helped the country to recover economically but independence had to wait until after Stalin's death in 1953. Negotiations with the Russians took place in an attempt to implement the allies' **Moscow Declaration** (1943), which had promised the reconstitution of Austria after the war. The success of these talks paved the way for the **Staatsvertrag** (State

Treaty), signed in the Belvedere by representatives of the four powers and the Austrian government on 15 May 1955.

The Second Republic immediately pledged itself to neutrality (in effect a condition of the Russians removing their troops) and set about building a diplomatic and economic role for itself as mediator between east and west. In Vienna, a new era symbolically began when the rebuilding of the bombed opera house was completed: it had closed on 30 June 1944, with a performance of *Götterdämmerung*, and reopened on 5 November 1955, with *Fidelio*. In the meantime, the Stephansdom (which had burned out in the closing days of the war) had been repaired with contributions from all over Austria. Much of the residential housing stock, 20 per cent of which had been lost through war damage, was also replaced, although the quality of the new buildings was well below traditional Viennese standards.

Most of Austria's leading politicians of the post-war period had suffered together in Nazi imprisonment or worked together in exile. Determined to avoid the mistakes of the 1930s, they developed an informal system for balancing the interests of capital and labour, known as **Sozialpartnerschaft** (Social Partnership), which laid the foundations for remarkable prosperity from the 1960s onwards. Vienna has remained under Socialist control, the Mayor being a powerful and significant figure in his double capacity as the capital's chief executive and Governor of a *Land*.

On the whole, the trust placed in the Viennese Socialists has been honoured: the needs of modernisation, expansion and development have been balanced against the requirements of conservation better than in most other cities. In 1978 the first phase of the **U-Bahn** was completed, and extensions to the network are still being made. The housing problem has been tackled by means of subsidised **housing associations** (control of which, in true Austrian style, is divided between the conservative People's Party and the Socialist Party); grants also assisted people willing to invest in the city's aging housing stock. Pressure on accommodation remained, although it was for long somewhat ameliorated by the fact that the population declined steadily to 1.6 million by 1985. Numbers have since begun to rise again, and attempts to loosen up the housing market, without disturbing the protection that many Viennese tenants have enjoyed since a rent-freeze in 1917, have only resulted in the free rents exploding and all manner of chicanery.

Since the late 1950s, Vienna has once again become an international city. The International Atomic Energy Agency was established here in 1957, to be followed, ten years later, by the United Nations Industrial Development Organisation. During the chancellorship (1970–83) of Austria's greatest post-war leader, the Socialist **Bruno Kreisky**, Vienna was the venue for a number of important multi-lateral or bi-lateral negotiations. It has hosted sessions of the Conference for Security and Co-operation in Europe, and the participating countries of OPEC also meet here. However, the lavishly paid officials and diplomats who staff these and other organisations remain somewhat marginal to Viennese life; more visible are the large numbers of Turkish, Serbian, Croatian and Bosnian *Gastarbeiter*, who are vital to the economy of the city, particularly in service industries and construction.

Seventy per cent of Austria's imported labour force is concentrated in the capital, where different ethnic groups have set up their own communities and services. Sadly, many of these migrants are exploited by racketeering landlords; at the same time, those who decide (or are encouraged) to work illegally in the black economy live a precarious existence under threat of discovery and possible deportation. According to estimates in the early 1990s, there were 300,000 foreigners in Vienna (excluding members of the Diplomatic Corps) and perhaps another 60,000 living unregistered. Altogether, non-Austrians may constitute up to 16 per cent of the city's population.

Vienna has traditionally been a city of immigration, so these figures do not represent a startlingly new phenomenon. In the 19C, most immigrants came to settle and their children became Viennese, as a glance at the phone-book will confirm. In the 20C, the aim of many short-term foreign workers was often to accumulate capital and start a business back home. The war in former Yugoslavia has frustrated that goal in many cases, and it remains to be seen how many refugees in the 21C become long-term residents.

Vienna in the New Millennium

A government minister recently observed that 'Austrians are in favour of change, as long as everything stays just as it was.' Although there is some truth in this, entry into the European Union in 1995 has forced the pace of economic change in the country, leading to more competition in business and a modest upswing in an economy already very strongly based. Austria has also signed up for the Euro.

Perhaps even more threatening to traditional ways of doing things, and specifically to the *Sozialpartnerschaft* mentioned above, was the formation of a right-wing coalition in 2000 between the ÖVP and the FPÖ, although the oppositional **Social Democrats (SPÖ)** remained the largest single party. There was an international outcry against the anti-immigrant comments and apparently exculpatory attitude towards old Nazis on the part of Jörg Haider, former leader of the **Freedom Party (FPÖ)**—now the **People's Party**'s (**ÖVP**'s) partner in government—and illegal and hypocritical 'sanctions' were imposed against Austria by her European partners. Since Austria is virtually devoid of racial violence (one racial terrorist in thirty years), the full scale of this hypocrisy rapidly became obvious to the electorates in whose name it had been applied. The European Union hastily devised a face-saving formula of 'three wise men' who solemnly inspected Austria's government and came to the only possible conclusion, namely that the government was just as democratic as any other in the EU (they might have added, considerably more democratic than some). The Centre Right coalition has been taking some unpopular, but probably necessary, economic decisions and the Freedom Party has been losing in the polls as a result of having to shoulder responsibility in government instead of making wild promises from the side-lines. Certainly the consensual 'Social Partnership' is under pressure, but in many respects it has served Austria well and is more likely to re-emerge in a more modern guise than disappear completely.

Meanwhile, and irrespective of international *Spesenritter* (riders of the international gravy train) and the large *Gastarbeiter* community, Vienna remains *sui generis*. The Vienna of the *Beisl* (restaurant with home cooking), of the *Heurige* (wine tavern on the edge of the Wienerwald), of the Sunday morning concerts for season ticket holders of the Wiener Philharmoniker, of the intrigue-ridden Burgtheater and Oper, continues imperturbably on its way. *Wien bleibt Wien* as the saying goes, 'Vienna will always be Vienna'.

Important dates in Viennese history

AD	
8	'Vindobona' becomes part of Roman province of Pannonia.
400	Last mention of Vindobona in annals of the Roman Empire.
400–791	Era of the Great Migrations (*Völkerwanderung*).
791	Vienna included in Charlemagne's 'Ostmark'.
955	Defeat of Hungarians by the German King, Otto I the Great, at the Battle of Lechfeld.
976	First mention of Babenbergs as local Margraves.
996	First documentary reference to '*Ostarrichi*' (Austria).
1137	Contract between the Babenbergs and the Bishop of Passau refers to Vienna as '*civitas*'.
1147	St Stephen's Church (Stephansdom) consecrated.
1155	Heinrich II founds the *Schottenstift* in Vienna.
1156	Vienna becomes the ducal residence of the Babenbergs.
1192	Imprisonment of Richard Coeur-de-Lion by Duke Leopold V.
1221	Leopold VI grants civic rights to the Viennese.
1246	The Babenberg line dies out.
1251	Premysl Ottokar II referred to as Austrian Duke.
1276	Rudolf of Habsburg occupies Vienna.
1278	Battle of Dürnkrut; death of Ottokar II.
1326	One of the worst of many fires in medieval Vienna.
1349	Plague epidemic; inhabitants reduced by two thirds.
1359	Rudolf IV begins the extension of St Stephen's.
1365	Foundation of University of Vienna.
1408	Mayor Konrad Vorlauf beheaded.
1421	Pogrom: 210 Jews burned alive, the rest expelled ('*Wiener Geserah*').
1469	Vienna made a bishopric.
1485–90	Matthias Corvinus of Hungary occupies Vienna.
1497	Spanish Empire inherited by Habsburgs through marriage.
1498	Maximilian I founds Hofburgkapelle and *Knabenchor*.
1515	Double marriage, in St Stephen's, of Maximilian's grandchildren will eventually secure Bohemian and Hungarian thrones.
1517	Lutheranism rapidly gains ground in Vienna.
1521	House of Habsburg divided into Spanish and German lines.
1522	Dr Martin Siebenbürger and leading citizens executed.
1526	Ferdinand I removes Vienna's administrative autonomy.
1529	First Turkish siege of Vienna.
1531–66	*Tracé italien* defences built around the city.
1546	*History of Vienna* published by Wolfgang Lazius.
1547	Wolfgang Schmeltzl celebrates Vienna in noble verse.
1551	Ferdinand I invites the Jesuits to Vienna.
1566	First registration of houses: 1065 recorded.
1577	Protestant worship forbidden.
1619	Ferdinand II besieged in the Hofburg by Protestants.
1622	Jesuits gain control of Vienna University.
1645	Swedish army threatens Vienna in Thirty Years War.
1679	Plague: Abraham a Sancta Clara preaching in the city.
1683	Second and final, unsuccessful Turkish siege.
1697–1717	Turkish wars of Prince Eugene of Savoy.
1704	Linienwall defence built to protect the suburbs against marauding Hungarian forces.
1713	Last major plague epidemic.

1714–23	Construction of Schloß Belvedere by Hildebrandt.
1716–39	Building of Karlskirche by Fischer von Erlach, father and son.
1744–49	Nikolaus Pacassi alters and completes Schönbrunn.
1766	Prater opened to the public by Joseph II.
1770	Houses in Vienna are given numbers.
1781	Joseph II issues his Tolerance Patent.
1784	The Vienna General Hospital is opened.
1791	*The Magic Flute* is played at the Theater auf der Wien.
1792	Beethoven settles in Vienna.
1805	Napoleon occupies Vienna (and again in 1809).
1811	Austrian state declared bankrupt.
1814	Founding of the Society of the Friends of Music.
1814–15	Congress of Vienna.
1830	Serious flooding of the Danube.
1842	First concert by the Wiener Philharmoniker.
1845	First gas installations in the city.
1848	Revolution in Vienna and elsewhere in the Empire.
1857	Franz Joseph orders the city bastions to be demolished. Ringstraße initiated.
1861	Liberals take control of the City Council.
1862	Johannes Brahms settles in Vienna.
1865	First section of the Ringstraße opened.
1873	World Exhibition in the Prater. Outbreak of cholera and stockmarket crash.
1875	Regulation of the Danube completed.
1877	First use of electric lamps in a Viennese theatre.
1888–89	Social Democratic Party founded by Viktor Adler.
1889	Crown Prince Rudolf commits suicide at Mayerling.
1890	First May Day parade of workers in the Prater.
1890–92	Linienwall razed. Population now 1,365,000.
1893	Christian Social Party formed.
1895–1902	Stadtbahn planned by Otto Wagner.
1897	Secession founded.
1897–1910	Dr Karl Lueger the Christian Social Mayor.
1900	Sigmund Freud's *Interpretation of Dreams* published.
1902	Electricity generator for the city begins functioning.
1907	Introduction of universal male suffrage.
1914–18	First World War.
1919	Treaty of St Germain fixes borders of Austria.
1919	Social Democrats take control of Vienna Council.
1922	Vienna becomes one of the Federal States of Austria.
1927	Burning of the Palace of Justice in riots.
1930	The largest *Gemeindebau* (Karl-Marx-Hof) completed.
1934	February: Civil War in which the left are defeated.
1934	July: Chancellor Dollfuß assassinated by Nazi thugs.
1938	Hitler invades Austria. *Anschluß* with Germany.
1939–45	Second World War.
1943	Moscow Declaration of Allied Powers promises that Austria will be reconstituted after the war.
1945–55	Vienna under Four Power control.
1945–66	Coalition governments of the Austrian People's Party with the Socialist Party of Austria.
1948	Austria begins to benefit from the Marshall Plan.
1955	Austrian State Treaty (*Staatsvertrag*) signed.
1957	International Atomic Energy Organisation set up in Vienna.
1967	United Nations Industrial Development Organisation (UNIDO) establishes its headquarters in Vienna.

1970	Bruno Kreisky becomes Chancellor.
1978	First phase of U-Bahn network completed.
1979	Vienna International Centre opened.
1981	Corruption trial concerning new General Hospital (AKH).
1995	Austria joins the European Union on 1 January.
2000	Centre-Right coalition of People's Party and Freedom Party formed. Countries of the European Union apply diplomatic sanctions, which are lifted after a report on democracy in Austria by 'Three Wise Men'. Sacred cows (Social Partnership, neutrality) and taboos (membership of NATO) begin to be questioned.
2001	New MuseumsQuartier is ceremonially opened in the former Court Stables, the result of ten years discussion, argument and ultimately compromise. It realises (albeit in a completely different concept) the 19C dream of Gottfried Semper to make a huge (and originally imperial) forum for art and museums stretching from the Hofburg to the far side of the Ringstraße.

Chronological table of Austrian rulers

House of Babenberg (Margraves)

976–94	Leopold (or Liutpold) I
994–1018	Heinrich I
1018–55	Adalbert
1055–75	Ernst
1075–95	Leopold II
1095–1136	Leopold III (canonised 1485)
1136–41	Leopold IV
	(**Dukes** from 1156)
1141–77	Heinrich II ('Jasomirgott')
1177–94	Leopold V ('the Virtuous')
1195–98	Friedrich I
1198–1230	Leopold VI
1230–46	Friedrich II ('the Warlike)'
1246–73	**Interregnum**: Marguerite of Babenberg, widow of Friedrich II, married Premysl Ottakar II of Bohemia in 1251, the latter taking possession of the dukedom, and subsequently losing it to Rudolf of Habsburg after Rudolf was elected German king.

House of Habsburg

1273–91	Rudolf of Habsburg
1291–1308	Albrecht I, elected King of Germany in 1298
1308–30	Friedrich I ('the Handsome'), King of Germany from 1314 as Friedrich III
1330–58	Albrecht II
1358–65	Rudolf IV ('the Founder')
1365–95	Albrecht III, who divided the Habsburg possessions with his brother, Leopold III
1395–1404	Albrecht IV
1404–11	Dynastic struggle between Habsburgs. Tutelary regime with Albrecht V as ward, first of Duke Wilhelm, then of Duke Leopold IV.
1411–39	Albrecht V, from 1438 Emperor Albrecht II of Germany
1439–57	Ladislas ('the Posthumous'), King of Bohemia and Hungary (Ward of Friedrich V of Styria, see below, and never ruled)

1457–93	Friedrich of Styria (as Friedrich IV, German King from 1442, as Friedrich III, Holy Roman Emperor from 1452)
1493–1519	Maximilian I
1519–21	Karl V, who in 1521 transferred the German possessions of the Habsburgs to his brother Ferdinand
1521–64	Ferdinand I, Emperor from 1556 on abdication of Karl V
1564–76	Maximilian II
1576–1612	Rudolf II (who ruled from Prague)
1612–19	Matthias
1619–37	Ferdinand II
1637–57	Ferdinand III
1658–1705	Leopold I
1705–11	Joseph I
1711–40	Karl VI
1740–80	Maria Theresia (ruled, until his death in 1765, with her consort, Franz Stephan III of Lorraine, as Franz I Stephan, Holy Roman Emperor from 1745)
1780–90	Joseph II (who had ruled jointly with his mother from 1765)
1790–92	Leopold II
1792–1835	Franz II (from 1804, Emperor Franz I of Austria, anticipating the demise of the Holy Roman Empire in 1806)
1835–48	Ferdinand I (of Austria), known as 'the Benevolent'
1848–1916	Franz Joseph I
1916–18	Karl I

Austrian Chancellors

FIRST REPUBLIC

1918–20	Karl Renner	1933	Introduction of the *Ständestaat* ('corporative state')
1920–21	Michael Mayr		
1921–22	Johann Schober		
1922–24	Ignaz Seipel	1932–34	Engelbert Dollfuß
1924–26	Rudolf Ramek	1934–38	Kurt Schuschnigg
1926–29	Ignaz Seipel	1938	Nazi take-over. *Anschluß* with the Third Reich
1929	Ernst Streeruwitz		
1929–30	Johann Schober		
1930	Carl Vaugoin	1938–45	Nazi regime
1930–31	Otto Ender	1945	Provisional government under Karl Renner
1931–32	Karl Buresch		

SECOND REPUBLIC

1945–53	Leopold Figl	1983–86	Fred Sinowatz
1953–61	Julius Raab	1986–97	Franz Vranitzky
1961–64	Alfons Gorbach	1997–2000	Viktor Klima
1964–70	Josef Klaus	2000–	Wolfgang Schüssel
1970–83	Bruno Kreisky		

Federal Presidents

FIRST REPUBLIC

1920–28	Michael Hainisch	1928–38	Wilhelm Miklas

SECOND REPUBLIC

1945–50	Karl Renner	1974–86	Rudolf Kirchschläger
1951–57	Theodor Körner		
1957–65	Adolf Schärf	1986–92	Kurt Waldheim
1965–74	Franz Jonas	1992–	Thomas Klestil

Further reading

This list includes a number of volumes that are out of print and must be sought in libraries.

Books published locally

History and Culture
A Brief Survey of Austrian History, Richard Rickett (Georg Prachner Verlag).
Music and Musicians in Vienna, Richard Rickett (Georg Prachner Verlag).
Vienna—The Past in the Present, Inge Lehne and Lonnie Johnson (Österreichischer Bundesverlag).
A Concise Cultural History of Vienna, Martina Pippal (C.H. Beck).
Otto Wagner and the New Face of Vienna, Dr. M.P.A. Sheaffer (Compress Verlag, Wien).
Vienna 1900: Architecture and Painting, Christian M. Nebehay (Verlag Christian Brandstätter).

Published in the UK and/or USA

History and the Viennese
The City and the Crown: Vienna and the Imperial Court, 1600–1740, John Spielman (Purdue University Press).
Daily Life in the Vienna of Mozart and Schubert, Marcel Brion (Weidenfeld and Nicholson).
Vienna, Ilsa Barea (Pimlico).
The Viennese: Splendor, Twilight and Exile, Paul Hofmann (Doubleday).
The Habsburg Twilight: Tales from Old Vienna, Sarah Gainham (Weidenfeld and Nicolson).
A Nervous Splendour—Vienna 1888/1889, Frederic Morton (Penguin).
Thunder at Twilight: Vienna 1913–14, Frederic Morton (MacMillan, NY).
Hitler's Vienna, Brigitte Hamann (Bertelsmann).
The World of Yesterday, Stefan Zweig (University of Nebraska Press).
Vienna: The Image of a City in Decline, Edward Crankshaw (Macmillan).
Red Vienna: Experiment in Working Class Culture, 1919–1934, Helmut Gruber (Oxford University Press).
Last Waltz in Vienna: The Destruction of a Family, 1842–1942, George Clare (Holt Rinehart and Winston).

Cultural Studies
Time and Order in Metropolitan Vienna, Robert Rotenburg (Smithsonian Institute Press).
The City as a Work of Art: London, Paris, Vienna, Donald J. Olsen (Yale University Press).
Vienna 1900: From Altenberg to Wittgenstein, Ed. E. Timms & R. Robertson (Columbia University Press).
Wittgenstein's Vienna, Allan Janik and Stephen Toulmin (Simon and Schuster).
Vienna and the Jews, 1867–1938, Stephen Beller (Cambridge University Press).
The Jews of Vienna, 1867–1914: Assimilation and Identity, Marsha Rozenblit (State University Press of New York).

The Jews of Vienna in the Age of Franz Joseph, Robert S. Wistrich (Oxford University Press).

Freud, Peter Gay (Oxford University Press).

Fin-de-Siècle Vienna: Politics and Culture, Carl E. Schorske (Alfred A. Knopf).

Karl Kraus, Apocalyptic Satirist, Edward Timms (Yale University Press).

The Austrian Mind, William M. Johnston (University of California Press).

Art and Society: The New Art Movement in Vienna, 1897–1914, James Shedel (SPOSS, Palo Alto CA).

Robert Musil and the Crisis of European Culture, 1880–1942, David S. Luft (University of California Press).

Music

Vienna: A Guide to its Music and Musicians, Franz Endler (Timber Press, NY).

Wien: Eine Musikgeschichte, Henry Louis de La Grange (Insel Verlag, originally published as *Vienne, une histoire musicale* by Librairie Arthème Fayard).

Musical Life in Biedermeier Vienna, Alice M. Hanson (Cambridge University Press).

The Classical Style: Haydn, Mozart, Beethoven, Charles Rosen (Faber).

Haydn: His Life and Work, H.C. Robbins Landon and D. Wyn Jones (Thames and Hudson).

Mozart in Vienna, Volkmar Braunbehrens (Harper Perennial).

Mozart, Wolfgang Hildesheimer (J.M. Dent).

Mozart: A Cultural Biography, Robert W. Gutman (Secker & Warburg).

Mozart's Letters, Mozart's Life: Selected Letters, Robert Spaethling (Faber).

Memoirs of Lorenzo Da Ponte (Review Books N.Y.).

Schubert: A Documentary Biography, Otto Erich Deutsch (J.M. Dent).

Johannes Brahms, his Works and Personality, Hans Gál (Alfred Knopf).

Bruckner Remembered, Stephen Johnson (Faber).

Mahler Remembered, Norman Lebrecht (Faber).

Schoenberg: A Critical Biography, Willi Reich (Da Capo Press).

The Fine Arts

The Sacred Spring: Arts in Vienna 1898–1918, Nicolas Powell (Studio Vista).

Art in Vienna: 1898–1918, Peter Vergo (Phaidon).

Viennese Painting at the Turn of the Century, Ilona Sármány-Parsons (Corvina, Budapest).

Austrian Expressionism: The Formative Years, Patrick Werkner (SPOSS, Palo Alto, CA).

Gustav Klimt, Alessandra Comini (Thames and Hudson).

Gustav Klimt, Frank Whitford (Thames and Hudson).

Gustav Klimt, Ilona Sármány-Parsons (Bonfini Press/Crown).

Egon Schiele, Frank Whitford (Thames and Hudson).

Topographical, Descriptive, Architecture

Vienna—A Travellers' Companion, selected and introduced by John Lehmann and Richard Bassett (Constable).

Vienna: Bridge between Two Cultures, Elisabeth Lichtenberger (Belhaven Press).

Vienna, 1850–1930: Architecture, Peter Haiko (Rizzoli, NY).

Introductory Criticism

Major Figures of Turn-of-the-Century Austrian Literature, Ed. Donald Daviau (Ariadne Press, Riverside CA).

Major Figures of Modern Austrian Literature, Ed. Donald Daviau (Ariadne Press, Riverside CA).

Major Figures of the Austrian Interwar Years 1918–1938, Ed. Donald Daviau (Ariadne Press, Riverside CA).

Major Figures of Contemporary Austrian Literature, Ed. Donald Daviau (Peter Lang, NY).

Literature with a Viennese Setting

Radetzky March, Joseph Roth (Penguin).

The Emperor's Tomb, Joseph Roth (Chatto & Windus /Hogarth Press).

Vienna 1900: Games with Love and Death, Arthur Schnitzler (Penguin).

No Compromise: Selected Writings of Karl Kraus, Ed. Frederick Ungar (Frederick Ungar Publishing, NY).

The Vienna Coffeehouse Wits, 1890–1938, Ed. Harold B. Segel (Purdue University Press).

The Man Without Qualities, Robert Musil (Picador/Vintage).

Man of Straw, Heinrich Mann (Penguin).

The Tongue Set Free (Vol 1 of Autobiography), Elias Canetti (Picador).

The Torch in My Ear (Vol 2 of Autobiography), Elias Canetti (Picador).

The Demons (3 Vols), Heimito von Doderer (Quartet).

The Third Man, Graham Greene (Bodley Head).

The Piano Teacher, Elfriede Jellinek (Serpent's Tail).

Wonderful Wonderful Times, Elfriede Jellinek (Serpent's Tail).

Austria and Austrians: Background, History and Rulers

The Holy Roman Empire, Friedrich Heer (Phoenix).

History of the Habsburg Empire, 1526–1918, Robert A. Kann (University of California Press).

The Austrians, Gordon Brook-Shepherd (HarperCollins).

Maria Theresa, Edward Crankshaw (Constable).

Metternich, Alan Palmer (Phoenix).

Napoleon and Marie Louise: The Second Empress, Alan Palmer (Constable).

Francis Joseph, Steven Beller (Longman).

Twilight of the Habsburgs, Alan Palmer (Phoenix).

The Fall of the House of Habsburg, Edward Crankshaw (Macmillan).

Sissy, Brigitte Hamann [on Empress Elisabeth] (Taschen, America).

To read on the aeroplane: *The Xenophobe's Guide to the Austrians*, Louis James (Oval Publishing).

Two websites may be of interest to travellers before or after their journey: ▨ **www.cs.umn.edu** the Center for Austrian Studies website at the University of Minnesota contains a massive amount of information on academic activity in the field, together with extensive book reviews and useful links. The site specifically for Habsburg studies is also of interest: ▨ **www2.h-net.msu.edu**.

THE GUIDE

Inner City walks

In the following walks, the many historic sights of Vienna have been grouped in ways that allow you to quarter the city systematically, starting and ending at a convenient traffic connection. Fortunately for the tourist, Vienna's originally medieval core, the **Innere Stadt** (Inner City) is compact enough to cover on foot. It is enclosed by the **Ringstraße**, built in the mid-19C, itself a showcase of the architecture of Historicism. Two sights are considered important enough to warrant a 'walk' of their own: the vast Hofburg complex (see under Museums and galleries for museums within the complex) that incorporates seven centuries of dynastic history and cumulative building, and the **Stephansdom** (St Stephen's Cathedral), traditionally the focal point of the city.

1 • The Hofburg

The Hofburg is reached by taking the U3 to Herrengasse, from where it is a short walk to the Michaelertor on Michaelerplatz.

History

The Babenberg dynasty (976–1246) had set up their court in the area still known as 'Am Hof' (p 99) in 1156, but nothing remains of their residence. Their Habsburg successors chose the **Burg**, a fortress already partially built by the charismatic Bohemian king, Ottokar II, in 1275. This first fortress occupied the site of the subsequent **Schweizertrakt** of the Hofburg. Ottokar's successor, Rudolf I of Habsburg, lived in the Burg for three years after defeating his rival at the Battle of Dürnkrut on the Marchfeld in 1278. It was enlarged twice in the mid-15C under Friedrich III, but major alterations did not occur until the reign of Ferdinand I (1521–64). In the 16C, two free-standing Renaissance parts were added the **Stallburg** (1558) and the **Amalienburg** (1575), the latter acquiring its name in the 18C, when the widow of Josef I lived here. The **Schweizerhof** was first joined to the Amalienburg under Leopold I in the 1660s by means of a Baroque wing, the **Leopoldinischer Trakt**. The wing burned down in 1668, was rebuilt and acquired its present aspect under Maria Theresia (1740–80). It was also in the time of Maria Theresia that the Schweizerhof and Schweizertor acquired their names from the Swiss guards quartered here.

During the reign of her father, Karl VI (1711–40), some of the finest Baroque architecture of the Hofburg was built by Johann Bernhard Fischer von Erlach and his son, Joseph Emanuel (for example, the **Hofbibliothek** and **Winterreitschule**). The Fischer von Erlachs and Lukas von Hildebrandt also designed the missing part of the rectangle opposite the Leopoldinischen Trakt, a wing to be occupied by the officials of the Holy Roman Empire (**Reichskanzleitrakt**, 1723–30). However, the rectangle was not fully completed until the 19C, when the **Michaelertrakt** (1893, adapted from the Fischer von Erlach design by Ferdinand Kirschner) was constructed, with access to the Michaelerplatz. Its spectacular ceremonial gateway is topped by a green and gilded cupola.

Franz Joseph's reign also saw the completion of what is now the Congress Centre on the southwest side and the vast **Neue Hofburg** along the southern rim of the Heldenplatz. If Gottfried Semper's plan had been followed, this would have been matched by a wing on the opposite side of the square, and both would have been linked across the Ringstraße to the great museums (see below and p 181). The Hofburg thus represents seven centuries of cumulative building. Like all the great Habsburg projects, political and architectural, it remained unfinished.

- **Opening times** vary from one part of the Hofburg to another.

Innerer Burghof housing the entrance (**Kaisertor**) to the **Imperial Tableware and Silver Treasury** (Hoftafel- und Silberkammer) and **Kaiserappartements**. Daily 09.00–17.00, last admissions 16.30.

Burgkapelle (entrance via Schweizerhof). Jan–end June, mid-Sept–end Dec, Mon–Thur 11.00–15.00; Fri 11.00–13.00. Tours: 14.30, 15.30. Sung mass by the **Vienna Boys' Choir**, 3 Jan–27 June, 12–26 Dec, every Sunday incl. 25 Dec at 09.15. Tickets available at the Burgkapelle box office (Hofburg, Schweizerhof) on the Friday preceding the performance, 11.00–13.00 and 15.00–17.00. Faxed applications on ⌨ 533 9927-75. Information on ☎ 533 99 27. The chapel is closed in July and August.

Weltliche und Geistliche Schatzkammer (Secular and Sacred Treasury), Schweizerhof. Wed–Mon 10.00–18.00. Last admissions 17.30.

Schmetterlinghaus (Butterfly House), Burggarten. April–Oct, Mon–Fri 10.00–17.00; Sat, Sun, Hols 10.00–18.30. Nov–March, daily 10.00–16.00.

Globenmuseum, Nationalbibliothek, Neue Burg. Cartographic collection. Mon–Wed and Fri, 11.00–12.00, Thur 14.00–15.00.

Prunksaal (Ceremonial Hall), Nationalbibliothek, Neue Burg. May–Oct, Mon–Wed, Fri and Sat 10.00–16.00, Thur 10.00–19.00, Sun and Hols 10.00–14.00. Nov–Apr, Mon–Sat 10.00–14.00.

Papyrusmuseum Nationalbibliothek, Neue Burg. Mon 09.00–18.45 and Tue–Fri, 09.00–13.00.

Esperanto Museum Balthyanystiege, Hofburg. Mon and Fri 10.00–16.00, Wed 10.00–18.00.

Spanish Riding School. Performances are held in the Winter Riding School, Josefsplatz.

- **morning training** Tue–Fri 09.40–12.30. Tickets are available on the day at the door (Josefsplatz Tor 2) and from ticket agencies.
- the **standard shows** take place May–Jun, Sept–Oct, Nov on Sun at 10.45 (Gala), occasionally Wed at 19.00 (or as otherwise posted).
- the **alternative programme** of the 'Classical Art of Riding with Music' takes place Apr–Jun, Sept–Nov, Sat at 10.00 (or as otherwise posted). Tickets are available from travel agents and booking agents, or by post but to be sure of a seat it is best to book at least a month in advance. Address:

Spanische Reitschule, Hofburg, Michaelerplatz 1, A-1010 Wien. ☎ 533 9031. ▤ 535 01-86.

Lipizzaner Museum, Stallburg. Daily 09.00–18.00.

Ephesos Museum, Neue Burg. Mon, Wed–Sun 10.00–18.00.

Hofjagd und Rüstkammer (Weapons Museum), Neue Burg. Mon, Wed–Sun 10.00–18.00.

Sammlung Alter Musikinstrumente (Musical Instruments Museum), Neue Burg. Mon, Wed–Sun 10.00–18.00.

Museum für Völkerkunde (Ethnology Museum), Nueu Burg. Mon, Wed–Sun 10.00–18.00.

On either side of the **Michaelertor**, facing onto Michaelerplatz, note the sculptured fountains of Rudolf Weyr and Edmund Hellmer: bombastic neo-Baroque representations of *Power at Sea* and *Power on Land*, they were completed only a few years before the Habsburgs were to lose both. The other sculptures are genuine Baroque works by Lorenzo Mattielli and depict the *Labours of Hercules*. To your left, on the external wall, you will see a plaque recalling the old **Burgtheater**. It stood here until the construction of the great new theatre on the Ringstraße in 1888. Built under Maria Theresia, it was declared the National Theatre by Joseph II. Attending the Burgtheater's 1782 première of Mozart's *Die Entführung aus dem Serail*, the Emperor famously complained that the opera had 'very many notes'. (The composer, unfazed by this imperial insight, replied spiritedly: 'Exactly the necessary number, your Majesty'.)

Mozart in Vienna

Mozart first performed in Vienna as an infant prodigy in 1762, when the family appeared before Maria Theresia at Schönbrunn. There followed a further, hugely successful tour taking in many of the German courts, as well as Paris, London, The Hague and Geneva; he went on to appear in all the great music centres of Italy. However, being a *Wunderkind* was little better than being the flavour of the month; there was always another other up-and-coming or briefly fashionable phenomenon for aristocratic audiences to prattle about. So Mozart needed his modest salary of 150 Gulden per year that he was eventually awarded in 1772 as Konzertmeister to Salzburg's Archbishop Colloredo after three years' unpaid work in the job. Nine years later, Mozart was literally kicked out of this post (for insolence) when the Archbishop and his entourage were on a visit to Vienna. After his marriage to Constanze Weber (a furious Leopold Mozart boycotted his son's wedding), Mozart initially did well in Vienna; his father, visiting him 18 months later, was mollified to find him apparently prosperous and well respected by the Emperor. 'I tell you before God', Haydn told Leopold, 'that your son is the greatest composer that I know in person or by reputation.'

Mozart earned money from concerts (as composer and performer), from teaching the piano and from an increasing flow of royalties as well as the occasional imperial fee. However he was extravagant and liable to get financially overstretched. His first great success in Vienna was *The Marriage of Figaro* (1786) on the potentially hazardous subject of the humiliation of a misbehaving aristocrat. Yet it was in tune with the principles of an enlightened emperor who had been known to punish errant nobles by putting them

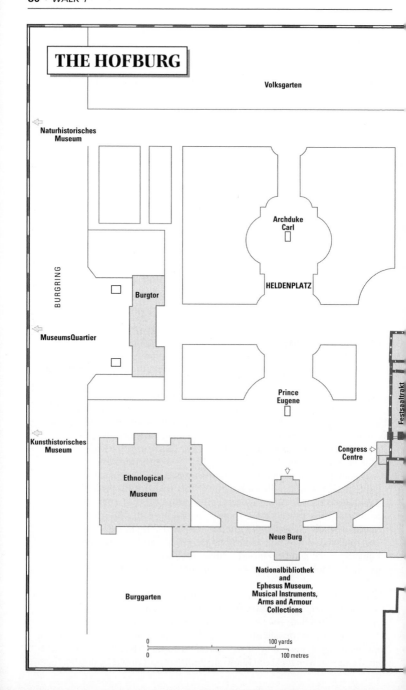

THE HOFBURG

Volksgarten

Naturhistorisches
Museum

BURGRING

Burgtor

Archduke
Carl

HELDENPLATZ

MuseumsQuartier

Prince
Eugene

Kunsthistorisches
Museum

Festsaaltrakt

Congress
Centre

Ethnological
Museum

Neue Burg

Burggarten

Nationalbibliothek
and
Ephesus Museum,
Musical Instruments,
Arms and Armour
Collections

0   100 yards
0   100 metres

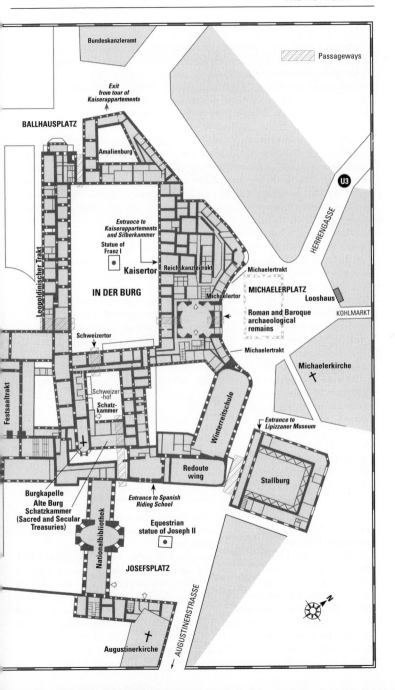

to street cleaning. Mozart's partnership with the librettist Lorenzo da Ponte continued with *Don Giovanni* (1787) and *Così fan tutte* (1790). However, Joseph II's death in the same year spelled the end of imperial commissions. Mozart was cold-shouldered at the coronation of Leopold II in Frankfurt and turned down an offer of 2500 Gulden for performances in London. But *Don Giovanni* had been a huge hit in Prague and *Die Zauberflöte* (*The Magic Flute*) was to be an equally great success with the Viennese.

Mozart was earning well—more than 2000 Gulden in the year of his death—but was overworking and anxious about the health of his wife, who was taking long cures in Baden bei Wien. He had been promised the well-paid and relatively undemanding post of Kapellmeister at St Stephen's on the death of the ailing incumbent, but it was Mozart himself who fell ill, just after starting work on a Requiem for an anonymous patron. The composer died of rheumatic fever in the night of the 4th–5th December 1791, aged just 35.

Most of the romantic fabrications about Mozart's life and death (that he was a misunderstood genius who died in bitter poverty and neglect) are the products of 19C hagiography. He did leave debts of 1000 Gulden, but Constanze soon paid them off with benefit concerts. In any case he had an offer of a generous retainer from a Hungarian nobleman just before his death, and an even better offer from a Dutch music lover arrived just after it. He was buried—like everybody else at that time—according to the puritan-ical Josephin ordinances in an unmarked grave; it was hardly surprising that mourners did not make the long trek from St Stephen's to Sankt Marx ceme-tery as dusk was falling and in freezing December weather. Also the tale that Mozart was poisoned by Salieri is pure invention.

Mozart was evidently a colourful character—his taste for scatological jokes in his letters and his occasionally reckless behaviour in regard to his potential patrons is evidence of that. On the other hand, so far from dying in poverty, riches beckoned in Vienna, despite his tendency to live beyond his means. The lovingly nurtured picture of a martyred aethereal being is eye-wash. Emanuel Schikaneder, his librettist for *Die Zauberflöte*, respected Mozart's musical genius, but liked to take the bumptious composer down a peg or two: 'My Magic Flute was so nice,' he once remarked, 'but that fellow Mozart spoiled it all with his music...'

Another première took place at the Burgtheater under Franz I, that of Haydn's glorious melody, later the imperial anthem, with words by Leopold Haschka's, unfortunately better known to foreigners as *Deutschland über Alles*.

Inside the domed hall of the cupola, you will notice niche sculptures which symbolise the mottoes of four Habsburg rulers (Karl VI, Maria Theresia, Joseph II and Franz Joseph I). Continue through the arch and turn right (30m) for the entrance to the **Silberkammer** (Silver and Porcelain Collection of the Court) and the **Kaiserappartements** (Imperial Apartments), the latter being situated in the Reichskanzleitrakt and the Amalienburg. (Access is also possible from the Michaelertor itself.) In the lobby leading to the ticket office, there is an interest-ing model of the Hofburg and the Kaiser Forum, as envisaged, but only partially realised, in the plans of Semper and Hasenauer (see above and p 137). As the exit from the Kaiserappartements takes us to another part of the Hofburg, it is advisable to visit the court tableware collection first.

Hoftafel- und Silberkammer

The **Imperial Tableware and Silver Treasury museum** (Hoftafel- und Silberkammer), to give it its full name, adjoins the lobby. Gold, silver and porcelain used for imperial banquets are now optimally displayed in this unusual, small museum. The porcelain includes Sèvres, Meissen and home-produced items from the Vienna porcelain manufactory, which still exists. Despite its high quality, the latter undertaking has had a chequered history. Although Joseph II had rescued it from bankruptcy with state money in 1780, it declined in the 19C and had to close in 1864. It was refounded by the municipality in 1924 and set up in the Augarten, where it remains. The series with painted views displayed here dates to 1820.

Another local product is the Historicist glass service by the Viennese firm of *Lobmeyr* (those who want to see more of the exquisitely ornate neo-Renaissance and neo-Baroque Lobmeyr glass should visit the shop at Kärntner Straße 26). Other highlights of this museum are a gilt silver service by Guillaume Biennais, whose plate decoration was inspired by the work of David; and a vast 33 metre-long **centrepiece** of gilded bronze made in Milan in the early 19C. The heavy formal service, dating from Franz Joseph's rule, was used for state receptions until recently. However, the cost of replacing a single plate runs into tens of thousands of schillings, so the responsible Ministry commissioned a modern replacement. Following an old Viennese tradition, this 'economy measure' turned out to be more costly than the problem it was designed to solve.

The Kaiserappartements

The 20 rooms of the neo-Rococo Kaiserappartements are more of historic than aesthetic interest, and one can only wonder at Emperor Franz Joseph's willingness to reside in what looks like a series of opulent but characterless railway compartments. However, the three pictures in the **Audienzsaal** (audience chamber) by the Biedermeier painter, Johann Peter Krafft, are noteworthy examples of public relations on behalf of Franz I; the scenes were carefully chosen by Empress Caroline to win sympathy for the 'bourgeois' monarch, who nevertheless presided over a police state. The first scene shows his return to Vienna in 1809 after defeat by Napoleon, the second, his triumphal entry to the city (1814) after Napoleon's defeat, and the third, his first carriage excursion (1826) after a serious illness. This room also has portraits of Franz I, of Ferdinand I and of Franz Joseph (the last-named is seen in middle age and as an 85-year-old).

In the adjoining **Audienzzimmer** is the high desk where Franz Joseph stood to receive petitions, a ritual he punctiliously observed until his death. You will see from the book that one of the visitors is coming to thank the Emperor 'for being elevated to the nobility'. Franz Joseph was generous in awarding patents of nobility to successful entrepreneurs, many of them Jewish. This provoked bitterness among the old aristocracy, who referred to the Emperor slightingly as a *Seeadler* (a pun on the German for sea-eagle—twin eagles being the Habsburg emblem—and the idea that he only needed to see [*sehen*] somebody to ennoble [*adeln*] him).

Franz Joseph's Bedroom contains his bathtub (his dominating mother, the Archduchess Sophie, resisted civilised plumbing in the imperial quarters till the end of her days). Frederic Morton, in his book *A Nervous Splendour*, describes the Emperor's punishing routine: he rose at 4 a.m. and was sponged by a footman at the washstand by the flickering light of a candle. At 4.20 his valet arrived with his uniform. After a cup of coffee and a crescent roll, he was at his desk in the neighbouring room by 5 o'clock, while 'his cities snored from the Swiss to the Turkish border'. In the **Grand Salon** (tenth room) are portraits of Franz Joseph and Empress Elisabeth by Franz Winterhalter, the most assiduous and obsequious of 19C royal portraitists.

After the **Cabinet Room**—with pictures on the wall of Field Marshal Radetzky's victories in Italy—we pass through Franz Joseph's study, where there is a bust of the Field Marshal. (In old age, Radetzky was given a suite of rooms in the Schweizertrakt of the Hofburg; the young emperor deeply admired the man who had done so much to save his throne in 1848, even if he subsequently forgot the lessons of Radetzky's army reforms.) The informal portrait of Elisabeth in the study is again by Winterhalter.

A left turn brings us into the **Amalienburg** (Amalia Wing) and the **Empress Elisabeth's Bedroom**, followed by her dressing room with its exercise equipment. Elisabeth had a regime scarcely less spartan than that of her husband, taking a plunge in a copper bath of cold water at 5 a.m. each morning. She was an early aerobic fanatic and a keen horsewoman—in her suite are pictures of her favourite horses, and a scene of her riding in the English countryside.

The **Apartments of Tsar Alexander I** (1777–1825) so called because he used them during the Congress of Vienna (1814–15) include the **Red Salon** with Gobelin tapestries from designs by Boucher (a gift from Marie Antoinette to her brother, Joseph II). The last room is the **State Banqueting Hall**, with a long table laid as for a state occasion. Naturally, the Emperor was always served first; he was not interested in food, however, and usually disposed of a few morsels before rising to leave—a move which signalled the end of the banquet, even if guests at the lower end of the table had scarcely received their portions. It is said that Sacher's Hotel had a flourishing trade from famished dignitaries rushing over from the Hofburg on banquet days.

In der Burg

You leave the Imperial Apartments by a door leading onto the Ballhausplatz. Turn right and follow the Burg back round to the Michaelertor. Passing under the cupola, you find yourself once again in the rectangular **central courtyard** (In der Burg), once the site of tournaments, festivities and executions. Ahead of you, on the southwestern side of the rectangle is the **Leopoldinischer Trakt**, which joins the outer line of the Old Burg (the **Schweizerhof** and **Schweizertor**) at the southern end. In front of this was once the ditch defending Ottokar and Rudolf of Habsburg's early (1270s) fortress. The Leopoldine Wing is now the **Präsidentschaftskanzlei** (Offices of the Austrian President) and incorporates the former apartments of Maria Theresia and her son, Joseph II (the President actually works in Joseph II's study).

In the middle of the courtyard is a **monument to Franz I** by Pompeo Marchesi (1846), commissioned by Franz's son, Ferdinand 'der Gütige' ('the benevolent'—a euphemism for his simple-mindedness). He is represented, as was then the fashion, in the guise of a Roman emperor, complete with laurel crown, sceptre and toga. The Latin inscription on the front is a quotation from his will,

('My love is for my peoples'), while that on the rear extols his virtues. The four female figures of the plinth symbolise Faith, Peace, Strength and Justice.

The Renaissance **Schweizertor (Swiss Gate)** is surmounted by the Habsburg coat of arms and a Latin inscription to Ferdinand I, listing his titles and king-ships, followed by the date MDLII (1552). The rollers for a drawbridge chain can still be seen.

Passing through the Schweizertor, you come upon a **fountain** on the left, the only memorial in the Hofburg to Karl V, briefly the ruler of the combined Spanish and Austrian Empires 'on which the sun never set', and which he divided with his brother Ferdinand in 1521. The **Schweizerhof** is the oldest part of the Burg, flanked to the east and southeast by the Schatzkammer (see below) and the Burgkapelle in the south.

The Burgkapelle

Originally built by Friedrich III between 1447 and 1449, the Burgkapelle's Gothic features have been partially masked by subsequent alterations in the Baroque period and further 'neo-Gothicising' carried out by Louis von Montoyer in 1802. The 13 carved figures (of the originally 14 'Holy Helpers' in the interior are now attributed to Nicolas Gerhaert van Leyden, the creator of Friedrich III's magnificent tomb in Stephansdom. On the left-hand side altar is a late Gothic statue of the Madonna; the little crucifix on the tabernacle is the one to which Ferdinand prayed for assistance when the Hofburg was besieged by angry Protestants in 1619 (p 55).

The Wiener Sängerknaben (Vienna Boys' Choir)

Between September and June, the Vienna Boys' Choir performs a sung Mass on Sundays at 09.15, accompanied by members of the male chorus and orchestra of the Staatsoper. The choir was founded in 1498 by Maximilian I and numbers among its distinguished former members Joseph Haydn, Franz Schubert and Clemens Krauß. The total choir numbers 100, divided into four groups of 25, one or two of which is always on tour abroad. Participation involves a complete musical and general education in the Augarten college of the Sängerknaben, and is very prestigious: according to a Viennese saying, all ambitious boys want to be a *Sängerknabe* in their youth and a Lipizzaner when they grow up.

Weltliche und Geistliche Schatzkammer

Under the stairway to the Burgkapelle, you will see the entrance to the **Secular and Sacred Treasury** one of the most spectacular museums in Europe. It was originally assembled by Ferdinand I (1521–64) and placed on the ground floor of the Hofburg by Karl VI in 1712.

Room 1 displays the so-called 'hereditary homage' of the Austrian Archduchies (orders, insignia, staffs of office, etc.). **Rooms 2–4** cover aspects of the ritual legitimisation of the Austrian Empire, brought into being by Franz I in 1804. **Room 5** contains Napoleonica, notably the silver gilt cradle made for the Duc de Reichstadt, the ill-starred son of Franz I's daughter, Marie Louise, the latter having been forced to marry Napoleon by Metternich. **Room 6** contains baptismal objects and gowns, **Room 7** gemstones and jewellery.

In **Room 8** ('Inalienable Heirlooms' of the Habsburgs) are two of the museum's highlights, namely the extraordinary **agate bowl**, the natural pattern of whose stone is said to spell the name of Christ, and the so-called **horn of the unicorn**. The former was long revered as the Holy Grail, the bowl into which Christ's blood flowed at the Crucifixion. It probably dates to the 4C and is thought to have been plundered from Constantinople during the Fourth Crusade (1204), subsequently passing into Habsburg hands via the Burgundian inheritance. The fabled unicorn was viewed in the Middle Ages as symbolic of the incarnation of Christ and the Virgin birth. Miraculous powers were attributed to its horn and examples changed hands between Popes and potentates for fabulous sums. The 'horn' here (actually the tusk of a narwhal dating to the early 16C) was the gift of King Sigismund II of Poland to Ferdinand I in 1540. Room 8 adjoins the Sacred Treasury (see below).

The highlight of the section devoted to the **Holy Roman Empire** (**Rooms 9–12**) is the **Reich Insignia and Regalia**. Since the insignia were kept in Nuremberg, the Habsburgs had their own versions (see Room 2—the **Kaiserliche Hauskrone** (1602) of Rudolf II, made by the court jeweller, Jan Vermeyen. The orb and sceptre were made in Prague where Rudolf had his court). However, the original Reich insignia were subsequently brought to Vienna in the 19C, and the Nazis ostentatiously moved them back to Nuremberg.

The **Crown of the Holy Roman Emperor**, dating to 962 (**Room 11**), is particularly impressive. The octagonal form is everywhere encrusted with pearls and gems, and set with enamel plaques. A cross rises above the brow-plate, and behind it is an overarching jewelled rib. It is thought to be the work of a German goldsmith, who made it for the coronation (962) of the German king, Otto the Great. The Habsburgs obtained the Imperial Crown permanently in 1440 under Friedrich III, the last Holy Roman Emperor to be crowned in Rome. They held the title (with a brief intermission at the time of Maria Theresia) until compelled to renounce it by Napoleon in 1806. The orb and sceptre are of later date than the crown (12C and 14C respectively).

Other early treasures in this room are the 8C **Holy Lance**, once claimed to incorporate nails from the Cross, and the so-called **Sabre of Charlemagne** (probably of Avar origin); also the 11C **Imperial Cross** and the **Carolingian gospel** on which Charlemagne's successors swore their oaths.

Among the **Burgundian treasures** (**Rooms 13–16**) the **Chain of the Golden Fleece** (**Room 15**) is noteworthy. In an evocation of the heroic exploits of Jason, Philip the Good of Burgundy founded the Order of the Golden Fleece in 1429; under Karl VI it became a special mark of imperial favour for members of the higher nobility.

In this section too are a number of high quality portraits, the most striking being that of **Maximilian I** by Bernhard Strigel. It was Maximilian's marriage to Maria of Burgundy in 1477 that paved the way for the rapid expansion of Habsburg territory through inheritances (p 52).

The **Sacred Treasury** (**Rooms I to V**), reached from Room 8) contains 18C vestments and a silver gilt replica of the **Marian Column Am Hof** (**Room I**, p 101). **St Stephen of Hungary's Purse** is a rare example of 11C–12C Russian embroidery, probably a relique-holder. The tradition that it belonged to the great apostolic king of Hungary is an invention of the Capuchins who owned it in the 18C (**Room II**). In the same room, note the two exotic **scourges of Empress Anna**, the latter sharing with the Capuchins a taste for masochistic (but, of course, pious) 'self-correction'. There are also fine silver reliefs of the Coronation of the Virgin and the Adoration of the Shepherds, both made in Augsburg, as well as a crucifix after Giambologna (1590, **Room III**).

A speciality is the line in ornate reliquaries, the descriptions of whose contents vie with each other in implausibility. One beautiful jewelled artefact from Augsburg (17C) purports to contain a nail from the True Cross; a dramatic **monstrance** is said to enclose a fragment of wood from the same, thus joining the other claimed fragments in Europe, which have been calculated to make 40 crosses altogether (**Room IV**). Of the 18C and 19C reliquary holders, one is claimed to contain a tooth of St Peter (**Room V**). It was given to Franz Joseph by the Pope after the young emperor narrowly escaped assassination in 1853 (p 161).

A walk through the archway at the southwest corner of the Schweizerhof will bring you to the **Josefsplatz**, one of the finest squares in Vienna. Before you reach it, a detour to the right gives access to the Burggarten (p 136) and the Jugendstil **Schmetterlinghaus** (Butterfly House). Hundreds of species of butterflies from tropical parts of the world live in rainforest conditions created in this huge glasshouse.

The southwest of the Josefsplatz is taken up by the **Hofbibliothek**, the northwest by the **Redoutensaal**. To the southeast is Nikolaus Pacassi's extension of the J.B. Fischer von Erlach library, and the square is closed to the east by the Baroque Pálffy and Pallavicini palaces. (Movie buffs will recognise in these a key setting in *The Third Man*, Carol Reed's brilliant film of war-torn Vienna, with a screenplay by Graham Greene from his novel.)

The equestrian **statue of Joseph II** at the centre (Anton Zauner, 1807) again adopts the heroic Roman mode (the model was the monument to Marcus Aurelius on the Capitol in Rome). Joseph is shown blessing his people, while the reliefs on the plinth eulogise the enlightened emperor for his reform of commerce and recall his wide-ranging travels (many of which were fact-finding trips undertaken incognito).

The Hofbibliothek (Court Library)

The Hofbibliothek, entrance at Josefsplatz 1, is now part of the National Library. The building was commissioned from Johann Bernhard Fischer von Erlach by Karl VI, and after the architect's death was completed by his son, Joseph Emanuel, in 1735. Maria Theresia's court architect, Nikolaus Pacassi, extended the building to the southeast. The huge first-floor library includes the collection of Prince Eugene of Savoy (whose possessions passed into Habsburg hands after his niece squandered much of her inheritance and had to sell up the rest). There are also books from the monastic libraries which fell victim to Joseph II's policy of closing religious foundations not engaged in activities considered to be of practical value. Above the external central section is a sculpture (1725) of *Minerva and her chariot* by Lorenzo Mattielli and *Atlas figures* by Hans Gasser, the latter added in 1880.

The real glory of the building is the domed **Prunksaal** or Ceremonial Hall which is used for temporary exhibitions. In the dome is Daniel Gran's *Apotheosis of Karl VI*. The lateral spaces have allegorical ceiling frescoes representing the knowledge of heavenly and earthly things. The life-size marble statues of Karl VI and other Habsburgs in the cupola hall are by Paul and Peter Strudel.

Manuscripts and incunabula from the priceless collection (which goes back to the time of Albrecht III, 1365–95) are exhibited in display cases.

Among the library's most precious manuscripts are an illustrated Byzantine treatise on herbalism (AD 512), known as the *Vienna Dioskurides*, the illuminated prayer book of Duke Galeasso Sforza (Flemish work, about 1470) and a 15C Gutenberg Bible from Mainz.

Adjoining the Hofbibliothek is the **Old Reading Room**, previously the library of the adjacent Augustinian monastery, together with the **cartographical collection** (**Globenmuseum**). The latter includes a 4C Roman map for travellers and a map of the world (1551) made for Karl V, who ruled a great deal of it between 1519 and 1521. The interesting **collection of globes** has a Mercator globe, also made for Karl V in 1541, as well as four large globes by the Venetian Vincenzo Coronelli (17C). The Fleming, Gerhard Kremer, known as Mercator (1519–94), was the first to construct a flat projection of the earth's surface, using techniques that have been followed ever since.

The two other museums under the auspices of the Nationalbibliothek are worth visiting: the **Papyrusmuseum** contains a vast collection (180,000) of writing materials and papyri in various ancient Middle Eastern languages, mostly of Egyptian provenance. In a glass window on the first floor is the earliest surviving fragment of **St Paul's Letter to the Hebrews** found in the archive's cellar among materials acquired in 1883 by the Archduke Rainer, whose collection was given to the Emperor in 1899 and forms the basis of the present one. In the Batthyánystiege of the Hofburg (entrance from Michaelerplatz by the Michaelertor; see above) is the **Esperanto Museum** which documents the history of this artificially constructed language, the brainchild of a Polish oculist, Dr. Zamenhof, who first published his idea in 1887.

On the northwest side of the Josefsplatz is the **Redoutensaal**, converted from an opera house in 1748, probably by Jean Nicolas Jadot de Ville-Issey. Masked balls were held here in Maria Theresia's time. It has now become a conference centre

and was badly damaged by fire in 1992, but was subsequently restored in record time.

Adjoining to the north is the **Winterreitschule** (Winter Riding School) of the Spanish Riding School, home to some of the famous Lipizzaner horses. Performances by the Spanish Riding School are held here regularly and morning training sessions and starting times (p 78) are posted here. The riders wear traditional livery of black boots, white jodhpurs, brown frac and a gilded bicorne (which is doffed to the portrait of Karl VI at the end of the hall as the rider enters).

Lipizzaner, Spanische Hofreitschule

The Lipizzaners and the Spanish Riding School

In 1580 the Archduke Karl, brother of Maximilian II, founded a stud in the karst region at Lipizza near Trieste (now in Slovenia). This area had always produced a tough breed, having supplied the horses for the chariot races in Rome. These karst horses were cross-bred with Spanish thoroughbreds (hence the name for the school Spanish Riding School), themselves a cross of the Iberian breed with Arab and Berber stock. Under Leopold I (who needed horses for lavish Baroque spectacles such as the fabulous 'horse ballet' of 1667), the karst stud expanded and the Emperor himself was expert enough to issue a set of breeding rules in 1685, the application of which greatly improved the stock.

During the Napoleonic wars the horses had to be trekked twice to Hungary for safety (they are still bred there, as well as at Piber, near Graz in Styria). The French committed the unpardonable and pointless vandalism of destroying all the stud archives at Lipizza. The Lipizzaners had a second narrow escape at the end of World War II. During the war, they had been taken to Czechoslovakia, where they were being used as farm animals. The legendary General Patton, exceeding orders, mounted a bold rescue operation and snatched them from the clutches of the advancing Russians. (There is a memorial plaque to him in the school.)

Modern Lipizzaners, although no longer karst horses, have proved just as hardy as their ancestors. The foals are born dark, acquiring their snow-white coat slowly up to their seventh to tenth year. Their elaborate Baroque ballet is a stylised version of the manoeuvres of cavalry horses—for example, the *Capriole* (a leap in the air with a kick of the hind legs), *Levade* (standing on hind legs) and *Croupade* (mid-air leap with fore and hind legs folded under the belly) all have their origin in battle tactics. Nonetheless, all the movements of the *haute école*, whether on the ground or in the air, are based on nature, albeit carefully refined. The more advanced exercises in dressage come from the French tradition—the Versailles Master of the Horse, F.R. de la Guérinière, came to Vienna in 1789 when the Revolution broke out. However, Karl VI (1711–40) is credited with laying down the elaborate code of training and performance programmes.

Architecturally the **Winterreit-schule** is impressive, one of the most graceful works (1735) of Joseph Emanuel Fischer von Erlach. Its spacious interior is surrounded by a two-tier gallery, the lower one a columned arcade. It has seen a lot of history: Maria Theresia organised her famous 'ladies' carousel' here in 1743 to celebrate the reconquest of Prague from the Prussians. In 1848 the first 'Constitutional Assembly' met in the Winterreitschule during the Revolution. During the Congress of Vienna (29 November 1814) Beethoven conducted a monster concert of his works here with an all-star cast including Antonio Salieri (cannonades), Johann Nepomuk Hummel (drums) and Giacomo Meyerbeer (thunder machine).

Neue Hofburg

To reach the most modern part of the Hofburg from the Winterreitschule, the Neue Hofburg, walk back along the road from Josefsplatz to Michaelerplatz. On your right you will pass the lovely arcaded façade of the Renaissance **Stallburg**, originally built as quarters for the future Emperor Maximilian II. After he ascended the throne in 1564, he used it to house his art collection. Today the building provides stabling for the Lipizzaners. In the north corner, formerly occupied by the court pharmacy, is the relatively new **Lipizzaner Museum** (Reitschulgasse 1), which contains interesting documentation and videos concerning the Lipizzaners and, best of all, a chance to view them in their stalls through a picture-window. After your visit, bear left through the Michaelertor and walk through the Burg, continuing under the arches to the southwest and out into the **Heldenplatz** on the far side.

This substantial square and park was laid out at the end of the Napoleonic wars, at the same time as the Volksgarten to the northwest of it. In the late 19C, it acquired its name Heroes Square, when the sculptor Anton Fernkorn made its two splendid **equestrian statues**: to the west is that of the **Archduke Carl**, who led the Austrian army in one of its few victories over Napoleon at Aspern (22 May 1809). On this occasion, thousands of Viennese, dubbed '*Schlachtenbummler*', i.e. the army supporters' club, trooped out of the city to spectate and cheer on their side. The unveiling of the heroic monument (originally planned for the 50th anniversary of the battle) had to be postponed for a year because of Austrian defeats at Solferino and Magenta.

Facing the Archduke Carl in front of the Neue Hofburg is Fernkorn's similarly rhetorical representation of **Prince Eugene of Savoy**, the first monument to a non-Habsburg to be set up in the Hofburg. Unfortunately, the syphilitic Fernkorn was declining into mental instability when he got the commission and had great difficulty in fulfilling it. The Prince's horse is sculpted in the Levade posture, but could only be made stable by the device of resting the animal on its tail.

The concave sweep of the Neue Hofburg beyond the statue achieves some splendour from its very size, but a closer look reveals its overblown neo-Renaissance architecture as essentially empty bombast, the fag-end of Historicism. From 1881 four architects in succession worked on it, and the last blocks were set in place only in 1913. In 1938 Adolf Hitler stood on the central balcony and announced the *Anschluss* to a vast and hysterically enthusiastic crowd on the Heldenplatz.

On the left, the Neue Burg adjoins the 19C **Kongreßzentrum** (now used for international conferences and the November antiques fair). In the central part of the Neue Burg is the National Library (Reading Room on the ground floor, reader's card on application). The rest of the building is taken up with collections that are part of the Kunsthistorisches Museum (Weapons and Musical Instruments), and the **Ephesos Museum**. The latter exhibits the finds from the Austrian archaeological digs both at Ephesus and in Samothrace. Its star exhibit is a gigantic frieze commemorating the victory of Lucius Verus over the Parthians in AD 165. The fourth collection here is the Ethnology Museum (see below).

The **Hofjagd und Rüstkammer** is notable for its size and quality, and is unique in Europe. It is the legacy of assiduous Habsburg collecting of ceremonial arms, particularly by Ferdinand II (1619–37), who set out to acquire the arms and armour of all famous soldiers, both contemporaries and those of the past. In the 19C the hunting weapons and saddlery were added.

There are nine rooms and six galleries, which can be viewed in chronological progression from **Room I** (AD 500–1480) to the **Arcaded Gallery** (17C–19C).

Rooms I–III are devoted to hunting weapons. Highlights include the ceremonial armour worn by 16C Habsburgs (**Room VII**), a Medusa shield and morion given by Charles V to his brother Ferdinand, an exquisitely decorated half-armour made for the Grand Chancellor of Lithuania (c 1555), a blue-gold garniture made for Maximilian II (1557) and a Turkish embroidered saddle belonging to Kara Mustafa, the besieger of Vienna in 1683.

The **Sammlung Alter Musikinstrumente** is an amalgamation of a collection belonging to Archduke Ferdinand of Tyrol and that of the Union of Viennese Music Lovers. The selection of Renaissance instruments is considered the best in the world. Concerts using items on show are sometimes given in the museum's Marble Hall, (through the efforts of the conductor Nikolaus Harnoncourt, the Austrian public has become increasingly sensitised to music played on original instruments). The exhibits are arranged to show general developments in craftsmanship, with different rooms containing keyboard, stringed, plucked, woodwind and bass instruments. In the **Marble Hall** are a harpsichord and a table piano that belonged to Joseph Haydn, a grand piano presented to Beethoven and a Viennese piano which Schubert used for composing. A curiosity is a 16C claviorgan made in Southern Germany, which includes 'joke-stops' for special effects such as 'frog-dance' or 'birdsong'.

The **Museum für Völkerkunde** is an ethnological collection in the southern corner of the Neue Burg containing artefacts from all over the world. Its most famous—or notorious—possession is the so-called crown of Montezuma, a feathered headdress which Mexican patriots wish to have 'returned' to their homeland. It was originally acquired by Karl V, when Cortéz returned from the New World bringing with him several such headdresses as gifts for his sovereign. Captain Cook's *Oceania* collection is here.

2 • A circular tour ~ Michaelerplatz, Freyung, Am Hof, Kohlmarkt

The attractive Michaelerplatz is a few minutes' walk from the Herrengasse stop of the U3. In Roman times this was the 'rest and recreation' area (*canabae*) for the troops, just outside the camp's Porta Decumana at the Tuchlauben end of Graben. A few Roman remains (some of them said to be part of a brothel) are to be seen in the excavations laid bare at the centre, but mostly these remnants are Baroque, together with Renaissance relics of the Burg's *Paradeisgartl*, where vegetables were grown. To the northeast of the Herrengasse ran the east–west artery of Roman Pannonia (the Via Limes).

The southwest side of the square is closed by the Michaelertor of the Hofburg, in front of which stood the Burgtheater until the new theatre was built on the Ring (p 160). To the east is the historic Michaelerkirche, originally late Romanesque and Gothic, but much rebuilt and extended after fires in the 14C and 16C and an earthquake in 1579.

Michaelerkirche

Under Emperor Ferdinand II, the church came into the possession of the Barnabite Order and was subsequently barockised in the 18C. At this time (1724),

Antonio Beduzzi erected the elegant portal and Lorenzo Mattielli created the dramatic sandstone group above the pediment, which shows St Michael casting out the rebellious angels. This theme is picked up in the interior stucco, the plastic depiction of falling angels above the main altar (by Karl Georg Merville) being one of the most arresting examples of Rococo ornamentation in the city. This replaced an altarpiece on the same theme by Michael Angelo Unterberger in 1782, the change marking a transition from didactic Counter-Reformatory art to the more generalised treatment of the image favoured by the Enlightenment. The façade of the church was altered to neo-Classical style in 1792.

Some of the rich decoration of the chapels in the interior is hard to see in the prevailing gloom, but it is worth persevering. In the north side-chancel is a bronze Crucifixion made in Augsburg (1646). Against the triumphal arches are altarpieces by Tobias Pock (*Pentecost* and the *Fourteen Healing Saints*, 1643). The high altar (1781) by J.B. d'Avrange is inspired by neo-Classicism, but looks forward to the fashion for 're-Gothicising' that took hold a few years later. The icon on the altar was brought from Crete in 1667 and the surrounding figures (which include the plague protectors, Sts Sebastian and Rochus) are by Jakob Philipp Prokop. Johann Martin Fischer sculpted the four sitting Evangelists.

In the St Nicholas Chapel of the southern side-chancel are 14C Gothic remnants and further along near the side-entrance is a remarkable 15C **Man Of Sorrows** (circa 1420) carved in sandstone from the Leitha hills to the east of Vienna. Note also the Baroque organ by J.D. Sieber (1714).

From the north choir access is gained to the celebrated crypt, where many Habsburg loyalists and retainers were buried until 1783, when Joseph II put a stop to burials here. The constant temperature has to some extent preserved the remains; since many of the coffin lids have lifted, the occupants can still be seen in the tatters of their finery. On the north side too, a Romanesque door has recently been excavated. The church now has a permanent exhibition that includes church treasures and a tour of the refectory and crypt (May–Nov, Mon–Fri, tours at 11.00, 13.00, 14.00, 15.00 and 16.00). As you leave the building, walk round to the Michaeler Durchgang (Michaelerplatz 6) on the south side, where there is a polychrome limestone **relief** (circa 1480) by an unknown master, but restored and slightly altered by Hans Huber in 1494, showing *Christ on the Mount of Olives*. The foreground, with Christ praying while the disciples sleep, is realised with astonishing plasticity. In the background loom the Calvary and Crucifixion.

Between the Kohlmarkt and the Herrengasse is the **Loos-Haus**, which created a stir when it was built by Adolf Loos (see box, p 94) for the bespoke tailors, Goldman and Salatsch, in 1912. The unornamented façade was said to clash with the ambience of the Michaelertrakt of the Hofburg and the Michaelerkirche: Loos was obliged to add the ten window-boxes to appease the critics of his 'house without eyebrows'. The high entrance portal clad in green cipollino marble and its Tuscan columns were in fact intended by Loos as a harmonising reference to the portal of the church. The interior (restored in the 1980s) also makes use of costly materials such as mahogany and Evian marble. The house (now a bank) is accessible on weekdays between 08.00 and 15.00 (to 17.30 on Thursdays and when exhibitions are running in the upstairs rooms).

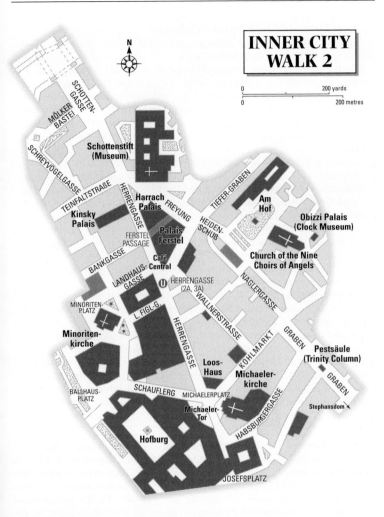

INNER CITY WALK 2

The Herrengasse

The name of the street recalls the fact that this was where the high nobility traditionally built their palaces, in order to be in close proximity to the court. The Herberstein Palace (1897) at nos 1–3 was built in 1897 on the site of the Baroque Dietrichstein Palace. On the ground floor was once the famous *Café Griensteidl*, a meeting place for literati. Karl Kraus devastatingly mocked its habitués in his essay *Literature Demolished* (1897), accusing the feuilletonists of following in the footsteps of Heine, who had introduced the feuilleton genre, and who had, according to Heine, 'so loosened the corset of the German language that today any salesman can handle her breasts'. A modern *Café Griensteidl* has arisen on the corner of Michaelerplatz.

Adolf Loos (1870–1933) and Ornament

The combative architect, aesthetician and cultural philosopher formed an alliance with the equally polemical writer, Karl Kraus, to attack what both regarded as the dishonest and overblown style of Historicism and the decorative excess of the Secession. In his famous diatribe, '*Ornament und Verbrechen*' ('Ornament and Crime'), Loos condemns ornament as libidinous and irrational, something that ignores the functional aspects of a building in favour of deceitful ostentation. Typically he writes that: 'The evolution of culture is synonymous with the removal of ornament from everyday objects.'

A vein of rabid puritanism runs through Loos's thought, which has been compared to certain attitudes of Sigmund Freud. His equation of ornament with eroticism chimes with Freud's tendency to see erotic symbols lurking in mundane artefacts, and the violence of Loos's language ('those who...smear walls with erotic symbols [i.e. ornament] are criminals and degenerates') suggests that his aesthetic has deep emotional and psychological roots. For example, he associates ornament with feminine appeal to (morbid) male sensuality, a phenomenon that can only be rectified when the complete economic independence of woman will render attraction through ornament no longer necessary.

It is interesting that the *Neue Freie Presse* referred to the 'obscene nakedness' of the Loos House, and that contemporary critics compared its lack of ornamentation to the naked body of a woman. Comparisons even went so far as to define the smooth façade as lacking the equivalent of secondary sexual characteristics (hairless, unrounded) and therefore suggesting the pre-pubescent female form. (Loos did, in fact, have a penchant for underage girls, a taste he shared with several turn of the century Viennese Bohemians, notably the writer Peter Altenberg.) Such far-fetched comments may now seem absurd as descriptions of architecture, but they do tell us much about the libidinous ambience of turn of the century Vienna.

Other palaces on the same side of the street include the Wilcek-Palais attributed to Anton Ospel at no. 5, the neo-Classical Modena-Palais at no. 7, which is today the Ministry of the Interior, the Mollard-Clary-Palais at no. 9, with a fine Renaissance well (1570) in the courtyard, the former Lower Austrian Statthaltereigebäude (no. 11), and at no. 13 Alois Pichl's monumental neo-Classical Lower Austrian Parliament (where the 1848 Revolution began). Lower Austrian institutions have been transferred to St Pölten, the new capital of the Province.

A left turn up the Landhaus Gasse brings you to the **Minoritenplatz**, flanked by Baroque palaces. Notable are the **Dietrichstein-Palais** at no. 3, whose present aspect dates from alterations by Franz Hillebrand (1755), and the **Liechtensteinisches Majoratshaus** at no. 4, still constitutionally-speaking part of Liechtenstein territory: so much building and alteration was involved with this pile (which had the first lifts in the city, operated by footmen) that it was known as the 'job-creation palace'. The first contract for interior design given to the *Thonet* firm was for the Liechtenstein Palace; they worked, with another enterprise (*Karl Leistler and Sons*) and the English architect, Peter Hubert

Devigny, to create a glittering ballroom and salons in the style of the Second Rococo (1836–47).

Minoritenkirche Maria Schnee

The square is dominated by the historic Minoritenkirche. The present mid-14C building succeeds a church and cloister erected by the Franciscans in 1250, where Ottokar Přemysl (II), Bohemian challenger to Rudolf of Habsburg (p 49) lay in state after his defeat at Dürnkrut (1278). The architect is thought to have been Duke Albrecht II's confessor, a certain Father James of Paris, to whom the fine Gothic decoration of the west portal is attributed. The steeple was decapitated in the Turkish siege of 1683 and has not been rebuilt. For many years (1569–1620) the Minoritenkirche was in the hands of Protestants who ripped out most of the decoration; barockisation took place on its return to Catholic ownership. The last major alteration was its 're-Gothicisation' by Ferdinand von Hohenberg (1784–89) which involved, *inter alia*, removal of the tomb of the Valois wife of Duke Rudolf III and in-filling of the crypt, as well as the removal of all Baroque fittings and the addition of a neo-Gothic pulpit, organ loft and high altar. The painting over the last-named is an 18C copy of the miracle-working image, *Salus Populi Romani*, in the Capella Paolina of Santa Maria Maggiore in Rome, the latter church having been built (according to legend) on the spot where snow fell in August. Hence the appellation of the Minoritenkirche.

The most prominent (and most tasteless) decoration of the interior is Giacomo Raffaelli's vast mosaic copy of Leonardo's **The Last Supper**. It was created for Napoleon as a substitute for the original, which he had hoped to remove from the wall of the refectory of the Monastery of Santa Maria delle Grazie in Milan and place in the Louvre. Franz I added Raffaelli's version to the imperial collection in 1816 and his successor, Ferdinand, bestowed it on the church. The Friars Minor (a Franciscan order) are again in possession of the Minoritenkirche, which has been the church for the Italian community in Vienna since 1784. However, the friars lost their cloister in the late 19C, when it was demolished to make way for the State Archives.

On the north side of Minoritenplatz is the Liechtenstein Majoratshaus (p 94) and the green painted **Starhemberg Palace**, the decoration of which has a touch of Mannerism. To the south is the new U-Bahn entrance and modern statuary; to the southwest the famous **Ballhausplatz**, the name being shorthand for the Foreign Ministry situated here, together with the offices of the Chancellor. To the north there is access to Bankgasse, in which is the attractive late Baroque Hungarian Embassy and the Batthyány-Palais (no. 2), with a façade after Fischer von Erlach. The street runs back down into Herrengasse, where you turn left, coming shortly to the *Café Central* on the other side of the street. The café is on the ground floor of the so-called Palais Ferstel.

Palais Ferstel

The 'palace', built on an awkwardly shaped site, only unofficially bears the name of the architect who created it. It was built between 1856 and 1860 with multiple use in mind (bank, stock exchange, shops and of course a café for the hard-working occupants). The *Café Central* has been restored to something of its former glory and was for a long time the venue for a rather fuddy-duddy and unctuous TV discussion on Sundays—it is a sign of the times that the contemporary equivalent of this show is confrontational and takes place in the yuppie-style café of Hollein's *Haas-Haus* (p 117). The original café was the haunt of turn-of-the-century literati, who migrated here after their main base, *Café Griensteidl*, was closed in 1897. One of them (Alfred Polgar) wrote a 'Theory of the Café Central', in which he asserted that it was 'not so much a café as a view of the world,' and that it lay 'on the Vienna latitude at the meridian of loneliness'. He continues, 'Its denizens are mostly people whose misanthropy is as great as their need for people, who want to be alone, but who need company to be alone in.' And further: 'It is a true asylum for people who have to kill time so as not to be killed by it'—which might stand as an epitaph for coffee-house habitués.

The façade on the café side is decorated with 12 figures representing the nations of the Austro-Hungarian monarchy. Above the café is the splendid former dealers' room of the Stock Exchange (until 1877) with its rich and colourful neo-Gothic ornament in the manner of the Munich Rundbogenstil. (Visits are possible during the November antiques fair). A glass-covered gallery ('Bazaar') runs through the middle of the complex, in the middle of which is a Danube Fountain with figures of mermaids, knights, burghers and peasants. Note also the ceremonial double-return stairway, a cunning solution on the irregular ground-plan.

Freyung

From the Ferstel Passage you emerge on the ancient Freyung, the town's rubbish heap in pre-medieval times. Its name refers to a right of asylum that existed here, derived from an ancient privilege granted to the monks of the cloister at the far side of the square, and confirmed by Albrecht I in 1287 (it lasted until 1782). The foundation of the convent dates to 1155, when the Babenberg (the future) Duke Heinrich II 'Jasomirgott', invited 12 Benedictines from Regensburg; they were sometimes described as 'Hyberner', more often as 'Schotten', after the medieval Latin name for Ireland (*Scotia maior*) and for Scotland (*Scotia minor*). However, it appears that most, if not all of them were Irish.

The originally Romanesque **Schottenkirche** was rebuilt in Gothic style after a fire in 1276, but very little of that remains. The present rather uninspiring aspect of the building is substantially the creation of Carlo Carlone in the 17C, while the interior was ruthlessly 'restored' by Heinrich Ferstel in the 1880s, but beautifully refurbished in the 1990s. Ferstel's most remarkable contribution is the monumental high altar, in early Renaissance style, that covers the whole of the east wall (1883). Also from the 19C are Julius Schmid's ceiling frescoes (*Nativity, Crucifixion, Resurrection, Assumption of Mary*, and depictions of the work of the Benedictines). Against a pillar on the right, half-way along the nave, is the noble funerary monument for Count Starhemberg, defender of Vienna from the Turks in 1683. (It was probably designed by Fischer von Erlach the Younger.) Of the various Baroque altar pictures, that by Tobias Pock of the *Assumption of Mary* (third chapel on the left) is of particularly high quality. Time should be taken to visit the mausoleum reached through a door to the north, where ornate gravestones are exhibited and from which steps descend to the impressive crypt containing the tomb of Heinrich II.

The Schottenhof and Museum im Schottenstift

Adjoining the church is the Schottenhof (Freyung 6), an elegant example of Josef Kornhäusel's neo-Classicism. Here the enticing monastery shop, that sells wine and other produce from Benedictine estates, also gives access to the recently created **Museum im Schottenstift** (entrance via the monastery shop; open Thur, Fri, Sat 10.00–17.00. Sun 11.00–17.00. Guided Tour on Saturdays at 15.00. ☎ 534 98-600 to confirm).

The museum of the Monastery of the Scots houses one of the most exciting new displays in Vienna (remodelled 1999–2000) in specially converted rooms of the Prelacy, built by Kornhäusel between 1826 and 1832. Much of the art collection dates to the abbotcy of Carl Fetzer (1705–50), but it also included furniture, tapestries, paraments and liturgical instruments (few of these are on show however) as well as paintings. As you leave the stairs at the entrance, note the large wooden panel (1708) showing the monastery's many parishes dotted around Lower Austria. **Room I** is devoted mainly to Dutch and Austrian still-lifes, but it is the second and further rooms that have some really superb paintings by Josse de Momper (Rudolf of Habsburg with the Priest) and other Netherlands masters, such as the Francken painter dynasty. The catalogue commentary stresses the move away from didactic religious painting to scenes where the religious motif is an excuse for description of nature. A typical example here is Joachim Beuckelaer's *Ecce Homo* (1564), where the biblical event takes place in the background, while the entire foreground consists of anecdotal depiction of daily life in the market. In the inner room are some delightful Biedermeier paintings by Thomas Ender, Johann Peter Krafft (in particular the characteristically sententious *Return of the Militiaman*) and others. In another room, the South German 18C townscapes made entirely from differently hued woods are notable.

In the innermost room is the museum's most precious possession, the **Winged Altarpiece** ('**Schottenaltar**') by the anonymous 'Viennese Master of the Scots', or probably with contributions by several different hands. Formerly in the monastery church, this masterpiece of Late Gothic painting is notable for its panel of *The Flight to Egypt*, the background of which is a view of Vienna, the earliest one recorded. Another scene (*The Visitation*) is set in the Spiegelgasse, with the towers of St Stephen visible in the background. Extensive documentation on its history and significance is supplied in commentaries posted on the wall, unfortunately only in German. There are 21 surviving panels out of the '*Wandelaltar*'s' original 24, painting of which began in 1469 (the date on the arch of the city gate for the panel showing *Christ's Entry into Jerusalem*) and was concluded in the late 1470s. During weekdays, the eight scenes of *The Passion* would have been displayed, while on Sundays, Feast Days and during Lent the 16 scenes of *Life of Mary* were shown.

It may be possible, on application, to see the huge Baroque altarpiece (1671) by Joachim von Sandrat featuring the **Heavenly Gloriole**. It is a typical hierarchical representation of all the Catholic saints in heaven, here with the Virgin Mary at the apex, although the composition was originally crowned with a Trinity. This immensely ambitious work was formerly in the Schottenkirche and is now located in the Prelacy Hall adjoining the museum. Access to the neighbouring Schottenstift library is also planned for the future.

From the Schottenhof it is worth the short detour along Schottengasse and left into the Mölker Bastei. At no. 8 is the **Pasqualatihaus** (1798), one of Beethoven's many residences in Vienna. (He is said to have moved 80 times in 36 years, often to the relief of landlords who were dismayed by all-hours piano playing and unemptied chamber pots.) On the fourth floor is a small collection of Beethoven memorabilia (open Tues–Sun 09.00–12.15 and 13.00–16.30), and in an adjacent room drawings and paintings by Adalbert Stifter (1805–68). The latter was the author of the quintessential Biedermeier novel of 'inner emigration' in the Metternich era, evoking in *Der Nachsommer* (Indian Summer) an idealised and becalmed world.

The Mölker Bastei connects with Schreyvogelgasse; the **Dreimädlerhaus** (1803) at no. 10 is probably unique, a perfectly preserved, harmoniously proportioned town house designed in the spirit of Josephin 'Zopf' style. There is no recorded connection between this house and Franz Schubert, but legend insists that some of his (mostly unsuccessful) courting took place here. The name Dreimädler seems to be of modern origin, an allusion to the sentimental 1920s operetta with this title which bastardised Schubert melodies.

Returning along Schottengasse to Freyung, note on your right as you regain the square the elegant, yellow and cream facade at no. 4, Lukas von Hildebrandt's **Kinsky Palais** (1716). The opportunity should not be missed to see the superb interior, newly opened to the public after renovation and housing showrooms for fine art auctions and a venue for other upmarket events such as wine-tastings. The glory of the palace is the noble stairway to the left, rising rectangularly through three stories and flanked by a carved balustrade thought to be by Georg Raphael Donner, of surpassing elegance, with statues and lanterns at the turns. The third storey is a rectangular gallery, overarched by a ceiling fresco of *The Triumph of the War Heroes* by Marcantonio Chiarini. At ground level, the surprisingly massive gateway incorporates a reception hall at *piano nobile* level with a mythological ceiling fresco by Carlo Carlone; it leads on to two further courtyards of great beauty (in the first one is a restaurant of distinction—*the Palais-Restaurant Daun-Kinsky*), at the end of the second being a modern bronze statue. It is easy to see why many contemporaries rated this palace the most aesthetically refined and impressive in Vienna. Next to it at Herrengasse 23 is the **Porcia-Palais**, a rare survival of a town house from the 16C. The great palace on the southeast side of the square, stretching between Herrengasse and the entrance to the Ferstel bazaar, was built by the Harrach family on whose estates, at Rohrau, Joseph Haydn was born. It used to contain their picture collection, but this has now been transferred to their country seat at Schloß Rohrau in Burgenland.

However, the newly renovated representation rooms of the **Harrach Palais** (Freyung 3; open Wed–Mon 10.00–12.00) are open to the public, a section of them being used for temporary exhibitions and smaller shows drawn from the depository of the Kunsthistorischen Museum. The palace was rebuilt in the 1690s to plans by Domenico Martinelli after its predecessor had burned down in the Turkish siege of 1683. The monumental concept of façade and interior (for instance, the superb **double stairway** in red marble that Count Harrach boasted was more elegant than that of the Tuileries) is the work of Martinelli, while Hildebrandt was involved with the scheme of works for the rooms. Most of the lovely stuccolustro and the fabulous gilded wall decoration of the ballroom are neo-

Baroque refurbishment of the 19C. The superb **oratorium** (1720), with wood panelling and elaborate decoration, is by Antonio Beduzzi, who was also responsible for the altar in the chapel and the allegorical ceiling fresco in the gallery.

If you walk into the courtyard from Herrengasse 16, you will see immediately on your left a display of Roman fragments unearthed when the underground car park was built here, together with a map of the Roman camp and description of the history of Freyung. Walk on through, emerging on Freyung, and you will see some of the square's original cobbles laid bare, with a plaque claiming that they date to the year 1200. Across the square from you, on the southern wall of the Schottenkirche, note the rather overblown 19C monument to Heinrich of Babenberg, erected in 1893.

To the right of the church (as you look at it) is the first block of apartments to be occupied by the Viennese bourgeoisie, the so-called **Schubladlkastenhaus** or 'Chest of Drawers House' (because critics claimed that it resembled one). Originally built (1774) on the cemetery of the Schottenstift, it included representation apartments for the abbot and rooms for the monastery scholars, but was later let out entirely as apartments, a necessity evidently forced on the abbey because of falling revenues from its country livings. Adolf Loos was supposedly inspired by the simplicity of the design, which attracted a storm of abuse in its day, remarkably similar to that provoked by Loos's house on the Michaelerplatz.

In front of the house is the **Austria fountain** by Ludwig Schwanthaler, erected at citizens' expense in 1846. The rather heavy-handed allegorical ensemble consists of Austria with lance and shield standing on a pedestal over figures representing the main rivers of the Empire at that time (Danube, Po, Elbe and Vistula). The four rivers, which flow into four different seas, also symbolise the main languages or language groups of the Empire (Germanic, Slav, Hungarian, Italian). The monument was cast in Munich and was thought to have contained the cigars that were smuggled over the border inside it, having been erected too quickly for the Viennese recipients to reclaim their booty. However no cigars were discovered when the monument was restored in the 1980s.

Am Hof

A short walk southeast brings you to a square, just off the **Heidenschuß,** called Am Hof.

The 'Heidenschuß' gets its name from the sculpted Turk wielding a scimitar as he gallops into battle (it may be seen at first-floor level on the corner of the Montenuovo Palais). According to legend, this figure recalls an incident in the siege of 1529 when a bakery stood on the site. Working late at night, the baker heard strange noises coming from the foundations and pulled up some floorboards to discover the Turkish invaders laying a mine shaft beneath his shop. He alerted the authorities and helped to pour water into the opening, which had the satisfactory result of drowning all inside the tunnel. Unfortunately, historians discount this picturesque tale, pointing out that 'Heiden-' (heathen) 'schuß' is a corruption of 'Haydenschuß', which in turn recalls an earlier house-sign with a Turkish archer placed on the residence here of the well-known Hayden family. You can in fact see the family name at the base of the ornament.

The ground rises from this hollow (once the bed of the Alserbach and Ottakringerbach, which merged just outside the walls of the old city before flowing into the Danube) as you approach the ancient core of Vienna where the Babenbergs first established their court (*hof*). Nothing remains to remind you of the days when Heinrich II laid on a fortnight of festivities for Friedrich Barbarossa here, except the name Am Hof.

Church of the Nine Choirs of Angels

The square's modern focal point is the Jesuit Church of the Nine Choirs of Angels on the east side.

History

It was from the balcony of this church that a herald announced the dissolution of the Holy Roman Empire in 1806. This ended 1006 years of a historical curiosity that had begun with the crowning of Charlemagne at Aachen on Christmas Day, AD 800, and which had remained a Habsburg prerogative with an interruption of only 23 years since Friedrich III was crowned in Rome in 1452. The fact that it was neither Holy, nor Roman, nor an Empire, as Voltaire rather unkindly remarked, scarcely lessened the significance of the adoption by Franz II of the title Franz I of Austria, effectively signalling the end of Habsburg pretensions to lead Christendom.

The church is built on the site of a Gothic Carmelite church that was largely destroyed in a fire of 1607. With its adjunctive cloister, it was the first toe-hold in Vienna for the Jesuits after Ferdinand I had invited them (1551) to lead the Counter-Reformation in his lands. The first rector was the indefatigable Petrus Canisius, who was asked by the Emperor to formulate the essentials of the Catholic faith in easily understandable and easily learned axioms; his answer (1555) was to produce the three famous catechisms for Christian pupils of different ages.

The gracious **façade** of the church is by Carlo Carlone (1662) and integrates living quarters with the church itself. Its sculpture alludes to the church's name, showing the Virgin Mary praised by the nine orders of angels (the highest are the ardent seraphim). It is difficult to visit the interior, which is generally in poor condition.

The narrow street to the left of the church leads to the **Obizzi-Palais** at Schulhof 2, which was long in the possession of the Starhemberg family, who were still the owners in 1683 during the Turkish siege. Count Ernst Rüdiger von Starhemberg was commanding the defence and the open fireplace of his palace was in constant use for the casting of lead cannon balls. The extremely interesting **Clock Museum** (open Tues–Sun 09.00–16.30) is now housed on the premises. The collection (over 3000 items) was made by Rudolf Kaftan (its first curator) and the novelist Marie von Ebner-Eschenbach. On the first floor are mechanisms from early tower clocks, and on higher floors astronomical and novelty clocks. Remarkable examples of clockmakers' ingenuity include a pictorial clock with a 'flowing' waterfall and an astronomical clock, one pointer of which requires 20,904 years for a complete revolution.

At Schulhof 4 is the **Doll and Toy Museum** (open Tues–Sun 10.00–18.00) containing mainly French and German dolls, as well as finely detailed dolls' houses from the turn of the century, and teddy bears.

Retracing your steps to Am Hof, note in the northwest corner of the square the former **Citizens' Armoury** (Bürgerliches Zeughaus), now part of the Fire Brigade Headquarters. The Viennese students helped themselves to the contents during the 1848 revolution, during which it was the command point of the National Guard. The building was designed (1732) during the reign of Karl VI by Anton Ospel. Under the broken pediment of the façade is the pompous sculpture of the Habsburg double eagle and crown. Lorenzo Mattielli supplied the attic statuary, crowned by the two allegorical figures of *Strength* and *Determination* (an echo of Karl VI's motto, '*constantia et fortitudine*'), which bear aloft a gilded globe. At either side are trophies, symbolising the heaped up weapons of defeated enemies.

In the middle of Am Hof is an **Immaculata Monument** (Mariensäule) erected by Ferdinand III, who ascribed the retreat of the Swedes threatening Vienna in 1645 to the intervention of the Virgin. The present column is an imitation of the original and was erected by Leopold I, who also commissioned the fabulous silver-gilt miniature of it from Philipp Küsel of Augsburg, which may be seen in the Sacred Treasury of the Hofburg (p 85). The original design was closely based on a column put up by Elector Maximilian of Bavaria in 1638 in Munich's Marienplatz, also in thanksgiving for deliverance from the Swedes. In the Viennese version, the Virgin Mary is shown standing on a dragon pierced by an arrow, the victrix over Satan and the enemies of the church. (These events were during the Thirty Years War.)

The southwest corner of Am Hof leads to the historic **Naglergasse**, which follows the course of the outer wall of the Roman camp and gains its name from the nail and needle-makers who plied their trade here in the Middle Ages. The Baroque façades of original Gothic houses have interesting detail and the street exhibits a lively mix of traditional crafts, antique dealers and atmospheric restaurants.

Kohlmarkt

At the end of Naglergasse, turn right (skirting the Graben) into Kohlmarkt, a fashionable shopping area, now pedestrianised, which leads back to Michaelerplatz and the Michaelertor of the Hofburg. The name of the street is derived from the charcoal market (Holzkohlen-Markt) that once existed here. No. 9 is

Michaelertor, Michaelerplatz

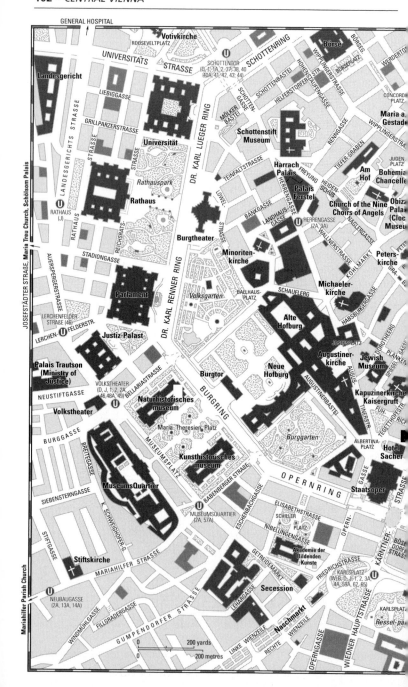

GENERAL HOSPITAL

Votivkirche

ROOSEVELTPLATZ

UNIVERSITÄTS STRASSE

SCHOTTENRING

Börse

BÖRSEG

SCHOTTENTOR
(1, 1A, 2; 37; 38, 40
(40A, 41, 42, 43; 44)

WIPPLINGERSTRASSE

BÖRSEPLATZ

WERKDERTO

Landesgericht

LIEBIGGASSE

GRILLPARZERSTRASSE

MÖLKER
BASTEI

SCHOTTENBASTEI

SCHOTTEN-
GASSE

HELFERSTORFERGASSE

HOHENSTAUFENGASSE

RENNGASSE

CONCORD
PLATZ

Maria a
Gestad

WIPPLINGERSTRA

Universität

Rathauspark

Rathaus

TEINFALTSTRASSE

Schottenstift
Museum

Harrach
Palais

Freyung

HERRENGASSE

HEIDEN-
SCHUSS

Am
Hof

JUGEN.
PLATZ

Bohemi
Chancelle

Palais
Ferstel

LÖWEL.

Church of the Nine
Choirs of Angels

Obizz
Palai
(Cloc
Museu

Burgtheater

LANDHAUS
GASSE

BANKGASSE

HERRENGASSE
(2A, 3A)

NAGLERGASSE

WALLNERSTRASSE

KOHLMARKT

Peters-
kirche

PETTE

GRA.

B

Minoriten-
kirche

Michaeler-
kirche

HABSBURGERGASSE

Parlament

Volksgarten

BALLHAUS-
PLATZ

SCHAUFLERG

Alte
Hofburg

Justiz-Palast

JOSEFSPLATZ

Augustiner-
kirche

AUGUS.

DOROTHEERG

Jewish
Museum

Palais Trautson
(Ministry of
Justice)

NEUSTIFTGASSE

VOLKSTHEATER
(D, J, 1, 2, 2A
46,48A, 49)

BELLARIASTRASSE

Burgtor

Neue
Hofburg

AUGUSTINERBASTEI

Kapuzinerkirche
Kaisergruft

Volkstheater

BURGGASSE

Naturhistorisches
museum

Maria-Theresien-Platz

BURGRING

Burggarten

ALBERTINA-
PLATZ

Hotel
Sacher

MuseumsQuartier

Kunsthistorisches
museum

BABENBERGER STRASSE

OPERNRING

Staatsoper

KÄRTNER

MUSEUMSQUARTIER
(2A, 57A)

ELISABETHSTRASSE

SCHILLER

OPERN-

NIBELUNGENGASSE

Stiftskirche

MARIAHILFER STRASSE

Akademie der
Bildenden
Kunste

FRIEDRICHSTRASSE

KÄRTNER-

NEUBAUGASSE
(2A, 13A, 14A)

Secession

KARLSPLATZ
(WB-D, J-1, 2, 3A
4A, -59A, 62, 65)

GUMPENDORFER STRASSE

Naschmarkt

KARLSPLAT

Ressel-pa

0   200 yards

0   200 metres

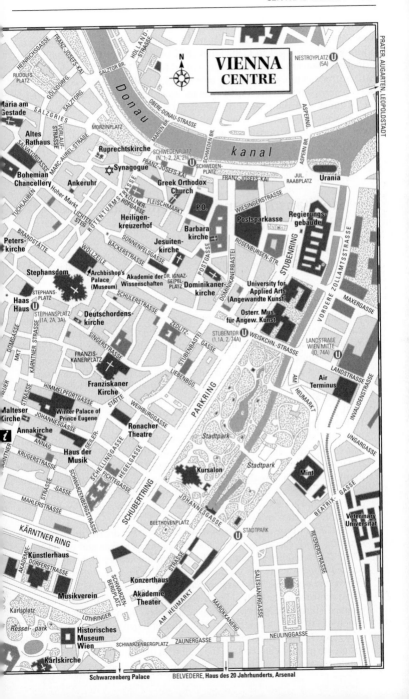

PRATER, AUGARTEN, LEOPOLDSTADT

NESTROYPLATZ (5A)

VIENNA CENTRE

N

Donau

HEINRICHSGASSE

FRANZ-JOSEFS-KAI

GÖLSDORFG.

HOLLAND.-STRASSE

SALZTOR BR.

OBERE-DONAU-STRASSE

RUDOLFS PLATZ

SALZGRIES

SALZGORG.

SALZDORFG.

ASPENG.

Maria am Gestade

VORLAUF-STRASSE

MARC-AUREL-STRASSE

MARIEN BR.

SCHWEDEN BR.

kanal

Altes Rathaus

SALVATORGASSE

MORZINPLATZ

Ruprechtskirche

SCHWEDENPLATZ (N. 1, 2, 2A, ZH)

FRANZ-JOSEFS-KAI

SCHWEDEN- PLATZ

FRANZ-JOSEFS-KAI

ASPERN BR.

JUL. RAABPLATZ

Urania

Bohemian Chancellery

Ankeruhr

Synagogue

Greek Orthodox Church

FLEISCHMARKT

Hoher Markt

KÖLLNER-HOFGASSE

P.O.

WIESINGERSTRASSE

Regierungs- gebäude

TUCHLAUBEN

Heiligen- kreuzerhof

Postsparkasse

LICHTEN- STEG

RIEMERGASSE

ROTENTURMSTRASSE

Peters- kirche

BRANDSTÄTTE

WOLLZEILE

SONNENFELSGASSE

Barbara- kirche

POSTGASSE

Jesuiten- kirche

ROSENBURSEN-STR.

STUBENRING

VORDERE ZOLLAMTSSTRASSE

Stephansdom

BÄCKERSTRASSE

Archbishop's Palace (Museum)

Akademie der Wissenschaften

DR. IGNAZ- SEIPEL- PLATZ

Dominikaner- kirche

DOMINIKANERBASTEI

University for Applied Arts (Angewandte Kunst)

MAXERGASSE

STEPHANS- PLATZ

Haas Haus

SCHULERSTRASSE

STEPHANSPLATZ (1A, 2A, 3A)

Deutschordens- kirche

ZEDLITZ-

Österr. Mus. für Angew. Kunst

DOMGASSE

MKT.

KÄRNTNER STRASSE

SINGERSTRASSE

FRANZIS- KANERPLATZ

STUBENBASTEI

STUBENTOR (1,1A, 2, 74A)

WEISKCHN.-STRASSE

LANDSTRASSE WIEN MITTE (O, 74A)

LANDSTRASSE

INVALIDENSTRASSE

NEUER

Franziskaner Kirche

HIMMELPFORTGASSE

LIEBENBGG

STÄTTE

PARKRING

AM HEUMARKT

Air Terminus

Malteser Kirche

JOHANNESGASSE

Winter Palace of Prince Eugene

WEIHBURGGASSE

UNGARGASSE

Annakirche

ANNAG.

Ronacher Theatre

KRUGERSTRASSE

SEILER-

Haus der Musik

SCHELLINGGASSE

RICHTEGASSE

HEGELGASSE

Stadtpark

KÄRNTNER

STRASSE

GASSE

MAHLERSTRASSE

SCHWARZENBERGSTRASSE

SCHUBERTRING

Kursalon

Stadtpark

Mint

BEATRIX

GASSE

KÄRNTNER RING

JOHANNESGASSE

STADTPARK

Veterinär Universität

REISNERSTRASSE

Künstlerhaus

AKADEMIE-

DORFERSTRASSE

SCHWARZEN BERGPLATZ

BEETHOVENPLATZ

STRASSE

Musikverein

Konzerthaus

AM HEUMARKT

SALESIANERGASSE

Karlsplatz

LOTHRINGER

Akademie Theater

MAROKKANERG.

Ressel- park

Historisches Museum Wien

SCHWARZENBERGPLATZ

ZAUNERGASSE

NEULINGGASSE

Karlskirche

Schwarzenberg Palace

BELVEDERE, Haus des 20 Jahrhunderts, Arsenal

the **Artaria House** (now the best map and guide shop in town), an example of Max Fabiani's Jugendstil (1901). At no. 14 is the famous **Demel Konditorei**, a business that dates back to 1786. From 1857 until 1956 the Demel family and its heirs ran it, having moved to the present address in 1888. The ornate interior, with mirrors, chinoiserie and blue or rose-tinted walls, is in fact a recreation of Rococo carried out in the 1930s. The most celebrated, or notorious, owner in recent times was the insurance swindler, Udo Proksch (recently deceased in prison), who entertained corrupt politicians in an upstairs room. Unfortunately, **Demel** has become a tourist trap, and even the undisputed quality of the food and the nostalgic pleasures of the ambience can hardly compensate for the crowds and often brusque service.

3 • Stephansdom and the Dom- und Diözesanmuseum

Stephansdom
Stephansdom, or St Stephen's Cathedral, (U1 or U3 to Stephansplatz) is Vienna's focal point.

History

According to sensational new discoveries made public in 2001, archaeologists have confirmed that an earlier church and cemetery built at least as early as the 9C and a burial area dating to Roman times occupied this site. In the 12C (following the important Treaty of Mautern of 1136, that allowed the Passau bishopric to erect a new parish church outside the city boundaries), the Romanesque church must have been largely replaced and from then on the building was enlarged, altered and embellished several times up to the Baroque age.

At the west end is the surviving **Romanesque** part, notably the **Heidentürme** (Heathen Towers), so-called because of their supposed resemblance to pagan architecture. It is also likely that the first church on the site was constructed above a pagan shrine (as was the church of St Vitus on the Prague Hradcany). The new church of the mid-12C was possibly intended for a suffragan bishop; like the Peterskirche, it was placed under the Passau episcopate, St Stephen being the patron saint of the Passau cathedral. Fire destroyed two early structures in 1193 and struck again in 1258 during the hegemony of Ottokar II of Bohemia.

The Heidentürme and the **Riesentor** (Giant's Door) are the result of reconstruction work carried out to St Stephen's under Ottokar and completed in 1263. (The reference to giants recalls the fact that mammoth bones were discovered when work began on the north tower (see below) and were hung to view by the west door. The Viennese took them to be the bones of an ur-race of giants drowned in the Biblical flood.) In the frieze above the door, Christ is represented sitting in judgement, resting on a rainbow with the left leg bared. This curious detail may refer to the initiation ritual of the stonemasons, whose powerful guild (*Bauhütte*) controlled the work on the cathedral. On either side of the portals are graphic depictions of the fight with the forces of evil. The male and female sex symbols on the shafts below the second-storey circular windows would seem to be a transmutation of pagan fertility motifs into a Christian allusion to Adam and Eve, quite a common motif on Romanesque façades.

Under the Habsburg Albrecht II (1330–1358) the beautiful Gothic (Albertine) **choir** begun in 1304 under Friedrich the Handsome, was completed (1340). However, the most striking feature of the cathedral, its great **southern tower**, known as the **Steffl**, was erected under Albrecht's successor, Rudolf IV, the Founder. Rudolf turned the first sod on 2 March 1359, and the foundation stone was laid on 7 April. It took 74 years to build, the 137m high tower being completed by Hans Prachatitz in 1433. Visitors can climb the stairs from the sexton's lodge just to the east of the tower as far as the Starhemberg seat (343 steps!), from where the defender of the city surveyed the manoeuvres of the Turks in 1683 (open daily 09.00–17.30).

Rudolf's idea was to build a complementary north tower—since the episcopal cathedrals of Germany possessed twin towers of great magnificence—although the Duke's ambition to have Vienna made a bishopric was frustrated by the Pope. In the event, the foundation stone for the north tower, the so-called **Adler** or Eagle Tower (access by lift from inside the cathedral, next to Pilgram's organ loft, 08.30–17.30) was not laid until 1450 under Friedrich III and was discontinued in 1511. (The copper Renaissance cupola was added in 1566.) It was long thought that the immediate cause for stopping work was the death of the tower's supposed architect, Hans Puchsbaum, who fell from the scaffolding. According to legend, he saw his fiancée on the ground below and called out her name, Maria. In so doing, he broke a secret pact he had made with the devil, who had promised him rapid progress with the work, provided no mention of any name sacred to Christians was made until the tower was finished. Unfortunately, like so many legends, this one too has been undermined by scientific research.

In 2001 a momentous discovery was made: after examination of remarkable Gothic draft plans found in the Academy of Fine Arts it was clear that the main architect and *Baumeister* for substantial parts of the cathedral (the vaulting in the main aisle, the west gallery, the Singertor and the unfinished north tower) was Laurenz Spenning, who worked on the church between 1455 and 1477.

Other features of the exterior worth noting are the decorated **tombstones** placed against the southwest façade. They were formerly in the cemetery that occupied the area in front of the cathedral up to the time of Joseph II. Moving anti-clockwise round the building we pass the **Singertor**, to the left of which is the much decayed tomb of the poet at the Babenberg court, Neidhart Fuchs. To the right is the Master of St Michael's deeply expressive *Man of Sorrows* (c 1370). In the portals of the Singertor (not always accessible) are sculptures of Rudolf IV and his consort (a recurring motif in the church's decoration) and a sopraportal relief of the *Conversion of St Paul*.

Skirting the south tower and the Sexton's Office, you pass more blackened Gothic reliefs around the apse before coming to a 15C stone **pulpit** against the northeast wall, built on the site where Giovanni Capistrano (1386–1456) preached in support of a crusade against the Turks in 1454–55. The Dominican monk was actually an inquisitor sent in 1451 to root out heresy, who realised that his rabble-rousing talents would be better employed against the Ottoman menace. The pulpit is thought to date to 1456 and is a memorial to János Hunyadi's victory

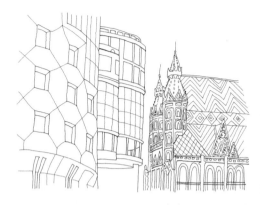

Stephansdom and the Haas-Haus (1990)

over the Turks at Belgrade in that year, a victory in which Capistrano played an important role, and on the anniversary of which all the bells of Christendom were to be rung annually in perpetuity by order of Pope Calixtus III. Hunyadi died of the plague immediately after his victory and Capistrano (who had accompanied him to Belgrade) died a little while later of exhaustion. The later Baroque sculpture (1738) above the pulpit depicts the Turks being trampled underfoot by the saint, who holds the crusader standard in his right hand.

Before entering, have a look at the striking tiled **roof** of the church, with its black and yellow chevrons framing (on the northern pitch of the choir roof) the crown-topped image of the Habsburg double-eagle, which the cities of Vienna and Krems were allowed to incorporate into their coats of arms by Friedrich III. A quarter of a million glazed tiles were required for restoration work after the cathedral mysteriously caught fire at the end of the last war. (The carved wooden roof of the nave and the Gothic choirstalls fell victim to this fire.) Money was received from every part of Austria for the repairs, and rebuilding of the nave was completed by 1948 (a plaque there recalls the contributions of individual provinces). It was not until 1952 that the choir was re-opened and the recast **Pummerin** (the great bell that had fallen from its moorings in 1945) hoisted into the north (Adler) tower. The original had been made from Turkish cannons abandoned by the besiegers in 1683, surviving fragments of which were used in the new casting.

Interior

The nave of St Stephen's (much of it the work of Spenning and Puchsbaum) is 107m long and 39m high, with beautiful reticulated vaulting. Hard on your left as you enter is the **Kreuzkapelle** containing the tomb of Prince Eugene of Savoy. Next to its wrought-iron gate is the fine Renaissance memorial to the family of Johannes Cuspinian (1473–1529), the latter having been Rector of the Vienna University and Maximilian I's personal doctor. The gravestone to another famous humanist scholar, Konrad Celtis (1459–1508), can be seen to the right of the organ loft on the north wall. These memorials to worldly fame are in stark contrast to the transcendental religiosity of the Gothic tombs.

In the main aisle you will see the Late Gothic **pulpit** (c 1500) set back in the lay area of the church, an unusual positioning before the Reformation that suggests its use by wandering preachers. On its sides are four beautifully carved panels showing the fathers of the church (Saints Ambrose, Jerome, Augustine and Gregory), depicted as personifications of the four humours (phlegm, blood, choler and black bile). Sculpted lizards and toads, the symbols of good and evil, crawl along the balustrade, a salutary reminder to the preacher of his responsibilities. Underneath the pulpit steps, a figure (believed to be Anton Pilgram, the pulpit's supposed sculptor) is portrayed leaning out of a window—staring from windows being an ancient Viennese pastime considered so normal that its practitioners are dignified with the term *Fenstergucker*. This motif—the autonomous artist admiring his handiwork, the servant of his commissioners but master of his craft—is repeated under the **organ loft** (1513) on the wall of the north aisle, despite the fact that self-representation was theoretically against the masons' code. The plunging stone ribs of the loft come together at this focal point, so that Pilgram appears to carry the structure on his back. For acoustical reasons, the organ itself was transferred to the (southern) Apostles Choir in 1991.

The entrance to the **catacombs** (guided tours as posted), containing the embalmed entrails of the Habsburgs, is in the north crossing. However, the tour is a half-baked affair with nothing much to be seen, although some may enjoy the frisson provided by the chamber containing the bones of thousands of plague victims, tipped into it from a hole in the ground above during the last epidemic of 1713. At the exit you will notice a plaque on the wall marking the place where obsequies were held for Wolfgang Amadeus Mozart on 6 December 1791, before the coffin was carted off to St Mark's cemetery.

Also in the crossing, on the wall of the chamber of the Adler Tower, is the so-called **Christ with Toothache**, a Gothic *Man of Sorrows* that once stood in St Stephen's cemetery and acquired its name from the (later regretted) mockery of drunken students. Making their way home after a night of carousing, they saw that the pious had bound their offerings of flowers to the head of the statue, so that it appeared to be swathed in head-bands. One of their number joked that Our Saviour must be suffering from toothache. In the morning each of them awoke with agonising toothache, the pain only being dispelled by a period of prolonged penance in front of the Christ figure.

At the end of the north ('Women's') nave (*Frauenchor*) is the remarkable **Wiener Neustadt Altar** (1447), an incredibly elaborate work brought to St Stephen's in 1883 from the Cistercians in Wiener Neustadt, and balancing the tomb of Friedrich III in the Apostles' Nave, since it is thought originally to have been a donation by him. On the exterior panels are painted images of 72 saints, which close on sculptured groups showing the *Life of Christ and the Virgin*. Among the saints featured is the legendary St Morandus, revered by the Habsburgs, who believed him to have been an ancestor. To the right nearby is the **tomb of Rudolf IV** (1339–65), on the lid of which are the sculpted forms (in sandstone, and originally gem-encrusted) of the Duke and his wife, Katharine of Bohemia. The latter had returned to Austria as a widow after her second marriage, following Rudolf's death on a visit to the Milanese court at the early age of 26. (The cause of death was described as a 'high fever' (malaria?), the effects of which were perhaps intensified by the muscular dystrophy from which he suffered.)

The Baroque **high altar** in the central apse shows the *Stoning of St Stephen* by Tobias Pock (1640), while the marble figures (1647) of Saints Sebastian, Leopold, Florian and Rochus are by his brother, Johann Jakob Pock. In the southern apse is the Late Gothic **sepulchral monument to Emperor Friedrich III** (1467), a superb work of red marble planned and partially executed by Niclaes Gerhaert van Leyden, who certainly did the sculpted figure of the Emperor in coronation robes on the lid of the tomb. The rest was completed by 1513 by Max Valmet and Michael Tichter. The sarcophagus, which unfortunately may only be viewed from a distance unless you are with a guided group, represents an immensely elaborate and subtle articulation of Habsburg dynastic and spiritual aspirations. What at first sight appears to be a balustrade enclosing it, is in fact a walkway (mounted from the rear), around which the Stephansdom canons progressed singing or praying in a ritualistic marking of the ruler's death and promised awakening to eternal life.

On the front pier of the south crossing is the Gothic statue known as the *Servant Girl Madonna* (c 1320), so-called from the legend that a servant-girl unjustly accused of theft successfully appealed to it to clear her name. Her harsh mistress was angered by the continual reminder of her injustice provided by the statue and donated it to the cathedral. Originally it stood in the former Mary's Altar in the women's nave, where early mass was attended by domestics. Not far off, on the fourth southern pillar of the nave, is another 14C Marian sculpture held in especial affection by the Viennese, namely the *Madonna with the Protective Cloak*, a popular medieval motif.

Returning towards the west door by way of the south aisle, you pass the **St Catherine Chapel** in the lower tower chamber of the south tower, containing an ornate baptismal font by Ulrich Auer (1481), with representations of the four evangelists at the base, and of Christ, John the Baptist and the Twelve Apostles on the basin itself. The impressive septagonal Gothic crown of the font features Christ's baptism with reliefs of the Seven Sacraments. Beyond the Catherine Chapel is a **Gothic baldachin** by Hans Puchsbaum over the Leopold altar. Towards the southwestern end is a late Gothic canopy (c 1510) over the **Maria Pötsch icon** brought from the southern Hungarian town of that name on the orders of Leopold I in 1697. The icon was supposed to have helped Prince Eugene of Savoy to victory over the Turks at the Battle of Zenta (14 September 1697).

There are many other Gothic features of the Stephansdom which repay study, as well as Renaissance tombstones and Baroque works of high quality. The Baroque altars against the great pillars of the naves replaced some 34 Gothic ones, but are nevertheless remarkably well integrated into the architectural ambience of the whole. Most of them are dedications by private individuals and are not therefore part of any general artistic or religiously didactic programme. Comprehensive tours of the interior are recommended for those who are interested in getting acquainted with detailed aspects of its decoration.

Erzbischöfliches Dom- und Diözesanmuseum

To the northeast of the cathedral is the **Archbishop's Palace** (1640) incorporating the Dom- und Diözesanmuseum or Cathedral Museum (Stephansplatz 6, Stiege 1/1. Open Tues–Sat 10.00–17.00), entered from the passageway running between Stephansplatz and Wollzeile.

Room 1, at the top of the stairs from the lobby, contains Baroque paintings by Austrian masters such as Anton Kraus, Kremser Schmidt, Franz Anton Maulbertsch (a *Crucifixion*) and Michael Angelo Unterberger (*The Fall of the Angels*). In **Room 2** is the powerful *portrait of Cardinal Khlesl* (1552–1630) attributed by some to Annibale Carracci. Khlesl was the son of a Protestant baker who became a fanatical and ruthless proponent of the Counter-Reformation. The historian, Stephan Vajda, describes him as 'a forerunner of Metternich' who 'played the political game with cold passion'. His type is not extinct in the Austrian Catholic hierarchy. In the same room, note the marquetry-like panels of the *Deposition* and *Lamentation of Christ* which are, however, made of straw.

Highlights of **Room 3** are the **Nürnberg treasure chest** (1678) and the picture of *Nicholas of Tolentino* by one of the greatest of the Czech Baroque artists, Karel Skréta. Also two fine pictures by J.M. Rottmayr, The *Apotheosis of Carlo Borromeo* and a *Trinity* (both dating to 1728). **Rooms 4, 5,** and **6** contain wooden religious statuary from the 14C–18C, while in **Room 7** there are 16C and 17C altarpieces. The ecclesiastical treasures in **Room 8** include some fine monstrances, notably one in the form of the **Tree of Jesse** (17C). The adjacent room, which lights up automatically as you enter, has a famous **Reliquary of St Leopold** with a fragment of his scapula and another reliquary with part of St Stephen's cranium. The further chamber displays the celebrated *Portrait of Duke Rudolf IV* by a Bohemian master, painted between 1360 and 1365, the earliest royal portrait in the German-speaking world. In the corridor are Lenten and Christmas cribs, and another especially vivid one featuring the *Crucifixion* in **Room 9**. This last room also contains Beethoven's quill pen.

If you descend to the U-Bahn by the entrance on Stephansplatz in front of the cathedral, you will pass on your left the picture-window looking onto the **Virgilkapelle**, access to which is by the adjacent stairs. The sanctuary dates to the 14C and was probably the crypt for a burial chapel which stood in the cemetery formerly occupying the area above. It now lies 12m below the surface of the street. There are periodic exhibitions here, usually of archaeological finds.

4 • Hoher Markt, Maria am Gestade, Judenplatz, Graben

This walk begins at Stephansplatz (U1, U3 or the Inner City hopper bus 1A). A short walk to the northeast of the square along Rotenturmstraße brings you to a left-hand turning (Lichtensteg) into the Hoher Markt, reputedly the oldest square in the city. Leading off from it to the north is the narrow Rotgasse, to the south the Kramergasse, which follow the line of the earliest city wall, itself built over the perimeter of the Roman camp.

Hoher Markt

On the northwestern edge of the Hoher Markt stood the residence of the Roman commander of Vindobona (the lodging of Marcus Aurelius during his visit, but not, as was long thought, the place where he died). In this same 'Berghof' (claimed to be the oldest house in Vienna), resided the various overlords of the town in the Dark Ages, as an inscription on the wall of a neighbouring (post-war) building relates. On the other side of the square at **no. 5**, you can visit the remains of **quarters for Roman officers**, comfortable dwellings with sanitation and hypocaust heating (open Tues–Sun 09.00–12.15; 13.00–16.30).

In the Middle Ages the square was the focal point of the economic life of the city, flanked by merchant and guild houses and hosting a fish market, the latter making use of a fountain with water piped from distant Hernals for keeping the fish alive. Public executions (a popular spectacle) were carried out here.

On entering the square from the east, you are confronted by the would-be imposing

Ankeruhr (detail) designed by Franz Matsch

but in fact uninspiring **Wedding Fountain** to a design by Fischer von Erlach the Younger. Leopold I had promised in 1702 to erect a monument to St Joseph if his son (Josef I) was victorious in the siege of Landau during the War of the Spanish Succession. Fischer von Erlach the Elder's original wooden monument was replaced by the present marble one under Karl VI. The wedding group beneath a canopy supported by Corinthian columns is by Antonio Corradini, while the basin of the fountain is the work of Lorenzo Mattielli. Reliefs on the base show the *Adoration of the Magi*, the *Presentation in the Temple* and the *Adoration of the Shepherds*.

The major attraction of the Hoher Markt is the great **Ankeruhr** (Anker Clock) to the northeast, built onto the elevated corridor that joins two buildings at the corner of the square, one of them the *Anker Insurance Company*. The late Jugendstil clock (1913) is the work of Franz Matsch, formerly the third member of the Painters' Company with the brothers Klimt. Each hour a different figure from Viennese history appears on the clock-face, and at noon all twelve figures traverse it in sequence. The selection of personalities is somewhat idiosyncratic: it begins with Marcus Aurelius, continues with Charlemagne, then Leopold the Glorious of Babenberg with his consort, followed by the *Minnesinger*, Walther von der Vogelweide. Next comes Duke Rudolf IV of Habsburg (the Founder), and after him one of the most important architects of the Stephansdom, Hans Puchsbaum. These are followed by Emperor Maximilian I (1459–1519, initiator of the great expansion of Habsburg hegemony through 'marriage-bed diplomacy'), Andreas Liebenberg (mayor during the 1683 Turkish siege of Vienna), Count Starhemberg (the garrison commander during the siege) and Prince Eugene of Savoy. The 18C is represented by Maria Theresia and her husband, Franz Stephan of Lorraine, and the last figure is Joseph Haydn. The inauguration of the clock was planned as part of the celebrations for the confidently expected victory of Austria-Hungary in World War I.

Crossing the mouth of Marc-Aurel-Straße, you enter Salvatorgasse, soon passing the rear of the Alten Rathaus (see below) and the lovely Renaissance doorway to the **Salvatorkapelle** (open Mon, Wed, Sat 09.00–11.00; Sun 10.00–12.00). In the tympanum of the sopraportal arch are half-figures of Christ and Mary and the archivolt bears an inscription to the 14C founder of the chapel, Otto Haimo (see below). The adjacent statues of knights are copies of originals from the same period as the door (1520), and are now in the city museum. The chapel belongs to the so-called 'Old Catholic' community, whose adherents refused to accept the arbitary doctrine of papal infallibility promulgated by Pius IX in 1870.

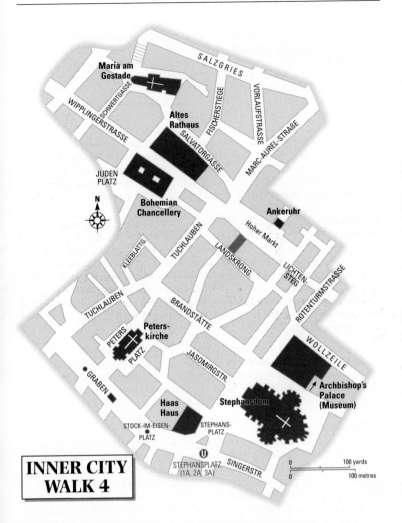

INNER CITY WALK 4

Maria am Gestade

Salvatorgasse leads to one of the most beautiful of the city's Gothic churches, Maria am Gestade—at the time it was built, the Danube lapped against the city wall at this point). Its **tower** with a fine open-work lantern is a Viennese landmark and can be seen in the earliest view of Vienna by the 15C Master of the Scots (p 97).

History

The nave was built by Michael Knab between 1394 and 1414, extending an earlier choir. The tower had to be reconstructed after damage in the first Turkish siege (1529).

In 1786 the now decayed building was threatened with demolition, from which it was saved only because the municipal authorities baulked at the cost of removing the rubble. Instead it was used as an arsenal, suffering a further indignity in 1809, when occupying French forces stabled their horses in it. Franz I gave Maria am Gestade to the Redemptorist Order, whose charismatic local leader was the Moravian preacher, Clemens Maria Hofbauer (1751–1820).

Hofbauer made the church the centre of a mission to the increasing number of Czechs living in 19C Vienna. He was a protagonist of the religious revival in the Romantic period, and was therefore viewed with distrust by the enlightened Josephin establishment, which had him watched by the secret police. He was a major influence on both German and Austrian writers and philosophers of the day, including the Schlegels, Joseph von Eichendorff and Clemens Brentano. After his canonisation in 1909, he was made patron saint of the City of Vienna (and is similarly honoured by Warsaw).

The **interior** (closed off with an iron gate at the choir, but accessible with permission, ☎ 533 2282) is of interest. The irregular site has necessitated a noticeable misalignment between choir and nave. Hans Gasser's tomb (1862) for Hofbauer has pride of place in the choir, while the southern apse contains part of a Gothic wing altar showing the *Coronation of Mary*, together with Leopold Kupelwieser's painting (1836) of the *Apotheosis of the Founder of the Redemptorist Order*. Medieval stained glass has been reinstated above the main altar and the piers of the nave were embellished in the 19C with mostly neo-Gothic canopies and statuary.

If you glance down the steps from the fine western façade of the church, you will see the **Hannaken Fountain**, a modern (1937) sculpture narrating the medieval legend of a quack who lived nearby. His method of generating business was to have his servants abduct and beat up passers-by, the unfortunate victims then being little disposed to refuse his offer to dress their wounds for a substantial fee.

Judenplatz

From the church walk down Schwertgasse, passing the splendid portal of the Baroque House of the Seven Swords at no. 3, where the writer, Adalbert Stifter, lived in 1831–1832. At the southern end bear left into Wipplingerstraße. Shortly on your right a turning opens onto **Judenplatz**, once part of the ghetto that nestled against the walls of the Babenberg court. The great synagogue here was pulled down in the appalling pogrom of 1421 and its stones used in the building of a university for the gentiles. One of the earliest post-pogrom buildings on the square is **Great Jordan's House** (no. 2), so called after its original owner, one Jörg Jordan. Around 1500 a punning relief was placed on the wall showing the *Baptism of Christ in the River Jordan*. Its Latin inscription is curiously described in some of the local histories as 'commemorating' or 'marking' the burning of the Jews on the Goose-Meadow of the Erdberg during the 1421 pogrom. The exact nature of this 'commemoration' is perhaps best conveyed by a full translation:

The River Jordan washes the body clean from disease and evil. Even secret sins take flight. The flame rushing furiously through the city in 1421 purged the horrible crimes of the Hebrew dogs. The world was once cleansed by the Deucalion flood; but this time punishment came by means of raging fire.

Perhaps as a counter-weight to this grim text, Siegfried Charoux's statue to the enlightened German dramatist, Gotthold Ephraim Lessing (1729–81), author of *Nathan the Wise*, was placed in the middle of the square in the 1930s. The Nazis had it removed, but it was re-erected in the 1960s. A **holocaust monument** by the British sculptress, Rachel Whiteread, was unveiled on the square in 2000 and consists of a monolithic concrete block whose sides represent the book shelves of a library. Around the bottom of the monument are engraved the names of the places where Austrian Jews were put to death by the Nazi regime. In the northwest corner of the square is the Misrachi House, now a multi-media **Museum of Medieval Jewish Life** (Judenplatz 8, Open Sun–Thur, 10.00–18.00, Fri 10.00–14.00). There is an excellently written and informative catalogue (available also in English) with sections on Jewish customs and the life of Jews in medieval Vienna, together with a dispassionate but sobering account of the '*Wiener Gesera*' (pogrom) of 1420–21. The lower floor shows remains of the medieval synagogue. This all represents the fulfiment of a long-nurtured desire by Simon Wiesenthal of the Jewish Documentation Centre to create a fitting memorial to Austrian Jewry, which was liquidated or forced into exile by the Nazis.

Backing onto the Judenplatz is Johann Bernhard Fischer von Erlach's fine **Bohemian Chancellery** (1714), extended to the east and west by Matthias Gerl between 1751 and 1754. (However, Bohemian affairs were transferred to the competence of the Privy Council following Maria Theresia's administrative reform of 1749.) Walking round the building, you will see massive Atlases supporting the portals, together with allegorical figures by Lorenzo Mattielli on the façade of the *piano nobile*. Note also the splendid coats of arms of Bohemia, Moravia and Silesia, crowned by eagles with sunbursts and horns of plenty (the latter being flattering allusions to Karl VI). The Chancellery is now occupied by the Constitutional Court.

Opposite the Bohemian Chancellery at Wipplingerstraße 8 is the **Altes Rathaus** (former town hall), a building that belonged to a powerful burgher family named Haimo in the 14C. Unfortunately, Otto Haimo was involved in a conspiracy with the City Magistrate against Friedrich the Handsome of Habsburg, and paid for his temerity with confiscation of his property. In 1316 Friedrich gave Haimo's house (inclusive of the chapel—see above) to the city, which had asked for it to extend its adjacent Town Hall. More extensions were subsequently made. The Council Chamber's ceiling was given a rich stucco moulding in 1712–13 by Alberto Camesina, and J.M. Rottmayr covered the existing frescoes with oil paintings which are now in the New City Hall (Rathaus). In the courtyard is Georg Raphael Donner's graceful **fountain** (1741) showing Perseus and Andromeda under a baldachin supported by putti.

The last session of the City Council in the Old Town Hall was on 20 June 1885. The building is now occupied by the **District Museum of the First District of Vienna** (Wipplingerstraße 6-8, open Wed and Fri 15.00–17.00), the Archive and **Museum of the Austrian Resistance in World War II** (open Mon–Thur 09.00–17.00), Council Offices and City Archives. Over the two sides of the portal are allegorical sculptures (1781) by Johann Martin Fischer, *Justice and Mercy* complementing *Piety and Confessional Faith*.

Instead of walking back to the Hoher Markt, take the first right after the Rathaus into Tuchlauben, in medieval times the street of the cloth merchants. At no. 19, frescoes dating to 1400 (the oldest profane ones extant in the city) were discovered in 1979 in the Baroque interior. The scenes of a rustic idyll illustrate poems by the *Minnesinger*, Neidhart von Reuenthal (c 1180–1237), one of the glittering stars of the Babenberg court (visiting hours: Tues–Sun 09.00–12.00). Of the several historic houses in this ancient thoroughfare, the visitor is most likely to penetrate the attractive Hochholzerhof (Tuchlauben 5), whose convex façade with fine Baroque ornamentation dates to 1719. In the 1980s, the interior was gutted and modernised for a bank (BAWAG), which has instituted a gallery in the arched interior of the ground floor and a small café. (The excellent occasional exhibitions are gratis and usually offer a detailed look at one of the masters of Modernism since 1900.)

The Graben

At the southwestern end of Tuchlauben is the junction with Kohlmarkt and (to your left) Graben.

History

Originally the Graben was the protective southern ditch of the Roman camp. The work of levelling this moat was undertaken in the reign of Leopold of Babenberg and paid for with the ransom obtained for the release of Richard Coeur de Lion in 1194 (a sum of 150,000 marks shared between the German Emperor and Leopold). Various markets were held on the Graben and by the 18C it was the most elegant shopping street in the city. Its reputation took a knock, however, as the numbers of '*Grabennymphen*' plying their trade here dramatically increased in the 19C, prompting a police official to complain to the Prime Minister, Count Taaffe, that one could no longer distinguish between the virtuous ladies and the prostitutes. 'Maybe you and your officers can't,' replied Taaffe drily, 'but the rest of us manage perfectly well.'

The Graben is a showcase of Historicism and Jugendstil. At the corner with Kohlmarkt, a house formerly dealing in firearms is topped by a hussar on horseback. This is an architectural folly and not (as a few romanticists have claimed) a reference to Jan Sobieski, the King of Poland who led the armies that rescued Vienna in 1683. Hard on the left (Graben 21) is Alois Pichl's graceful neo-Classical bank (**Erste Österrreichische Spar-Casse**) built in 1836. The gilded bee on the gable is a symbol of middle-class thrift and diligence. At nos 14–15 is the imposing **Grabenhof** (1876), recently cleaned and restored to its original splendour, even down to the gilding of the balcony railings. Otto Wagner, in his pre-Secessionist phase, built this to a design by Otto Thienemann. At no. 10 the **Ankerhaus** (1893) is a realisation of Wagner's own design, notable for its impressive glassed-in roof. The latter was for a while Wagner's own studio and more recently, the atelier of the late painter Friedensreich Hundertwasser. The fashionable clothing shop at no. 13 (*Knize*) boasts an interior designed by Adolf Loos. Jugendstil houses can be seen at no. 16 (again with a partially preserved Loos interior), and at no. 30 (the confectioners, *Altmann & Kühne*), designed by Josef Hoffmann and Oswald Haerdtl. The two below-ground public conveniences are also picturesque examples of Jugendstil.

Noteworthy modern façades are those for the jeweller *Schullin* (no. 26), at the time (1974) a daring departure from Inner City shop façades by Hans Hollein, who designed a similarly arresting pseudo-archaic façade for the same firm at nearby Kohlmarkt 7 in 1982. The bookshop *Frick* (nos 27–28) has an eye-catching entrance consisting of an ornamental bridge from which the lower ground floor can be seen (Michael Schluder and Hans Kastner, 1988). The only surviving Baroque building is the former Bartolotti-Partenfeld palace at no. 11, possibly designed by Hildebrandt (1720; the top floor is a later addition). The **Trattnerhof** (nos 29–29A) is named after the 18C court printer, Thomas von Trattner, who pirated Goethe and introduced Shakespeare to the Viennese with such success that he could afford to build a Baroque pile here in 1773. (The present building on the site dates to 1912.)

At the far end of Graben on Stock-im-Eisen-Platz (nos 3–4) is a large Neo-Renaissance palace (the so-called **Equitable Palais**, named after its original owner, the *Equitable Life Insurance Company* of New York); it is worth walking in to view the fine ornate courtyard, hall and stairway decorated with Hungarian Zsolnay ceramics. The panels on the door tell the story of the locksmith's apprentice who made a pact with the devil, a legend connected with the Stock-im-Eisen (p 117) after which the square is named.

The three monuments on the Graben repay study. The two fountains were erected on the orders of Franz I to honour his predecessors Leopold II and Joseph II. To the west is the **Joseph Fountain** (J.M. Fischer, 1804) with figures of the father of Christ accompanied by a boy holding a scroll of the 'line of David'. The socle reliefs show the *Flight into Egypt* and the *Annunciation*. The figures on the **Leopold Fountain** (also by Fischer), to the east are St Leopold (III of Babenberg, 1075–1136) and a boy exhibiting on a parchment roll the façade of the Klosterneuburg church. The reliefs illustrate the legend of the founding of the monastery on the spot where the veil of Leopold's consort, St Agnes, came to rest after the wind had blown it away, and also the laying of the foundation stone of the church.

Between these fountains and dominating the Graben is the famous **Pestsäule** (Plague or more precisely Trinity Column), one of the loveliest and most elaborate in Austria. Its origin lies in the vow made by Leopold I, 1640–1705) to set up a monument in thanksgiving for the city's deliverance from the horrific plague of 1679. However, the present work (replacing an earlier wooden column) dates to 1692 and was primarily conceived by the court architect, Ludovico Burnacini and Johann Bernhard Fischer von Erlach. The pyramidal arrangement of clouds was Burnacini's idea, while Fischer von Erlach was reponsible for the reliefs, figures and emblems. The symbolic realisation of the Trinity was worked out by Franciscus Menegatti, Leopold's confessor, and adroitly combines the three symbolic and actual pillars of Habsburg '*Hausmacht*' (Bohemia, Hungary and the Crown Lands) with the doctrinal religious motif (God the Father, God the Son and God the Holy Ghost). Much of the final work on the column was done by Paul Strudel, who executed the spiral of clouds and angels and the crowning Trinity group. In particular, Strudel is responsible for the vivid reliefs of *Faith Driving Out the Plague* and (on the south side) the pathos-filled representation of *Leopold I at Prayer*.

Peterskirche

Just off the Graben to the north is the Peterskirche.

History

Begun in 1702 to plans by Gabriele Montani it was largely completed by Johann Lukas von Hildebrandt, with further work on the choir and towers by Franz Jänggl (1730–33). It stands on the probable site of the earliest Viennese church which was thought to have existed in Roman times (late 4C—the legend perpetuated by Rudolf Weyr's 1906 relief on the southeast external wall that Charlemagne founded a church here is unhistorical). The successor to that early church was transferred to the Diocese of Passau in the significant Treaty of Mautern (1137), in which Vienna was for the first time dignified with the title '*civitas*'. This second church, however, was destroyed by fire in 1276. A subsequent three-aisled Gothic church was restored by the scholar and antiquary, Wolfgang Lazius, in the mid-16C using his own money (his tomb is in the interior). Nonetheless, the building had so greatly decayed by the beginning of the 18C that the Emperor determined that a new church should be built. Leopold I himself was present at the laying of the foundation stone in 1702, when a trench collapsed, injuring members of the imperial retinue.

From the outside, the church seems wonderfully compact and perfectly adjusted to the narrow confines within which it must achieve its spatial effects. The two towers seem to hug the two-storeyed façade, above which rises a mighty oval cupola. The gable of the portico by Andrea Altomonte shows allegories of Faith, Hope and Charity, and an inscription over the middle door reads: 'What I vowed for man's salvation, that will I fulfil.'

Peterskirche by Gabriele Montani and Lukas von Hildebrandt

The **interior** likewise achieves an effect of compression and harmonious unity through its total subordination to the dome of 56m diameter. The latter is frescoed with the *Assumption of Mary* by Johann Michael Rottmayr (1714). The trompe l'oeil architectural effects in the choir and around the altar are by Antonio Galli-Bibiena, the last of an Italian craftsman dynasty renowned for its skills in illusionistic architecture to work in Vienna. Above Galli-Bibiena's **high altar**, realised by Santino Bussi, is an altarpiece by Martino Altomonte (*The Healing of the Lame by Peter and John*). The pristine unity of the faith is alluded to in the choice of figures flanking the high altar—Constantine and Charlemagne. Jesuitical influence is apparent in the highlighting of a local Central European saint, John of Nepomuk: Lorenzo Mattielli's **gilded wood and stucco scene** (1729) to the right of the choir shows John being thrown into the Moldau from the Charles Bridge in Prague on the orders of Wenceslas IV, whose Vicar-General he was. According to legend, he had refused to reveal the secrets of the Queen's confession to Wenceslas. This is the most striking of Mattielli's works in Vienna, but was for a while attributed to Matthias Steindl, whose carved pulpit (1716) to the left of the choir is also a noteworthy example of Baroque plasticity.

Leaving the Peterskirche, turn left along the Graben. You soon reach **Stock-im-Eisen-Platz** again abutting Stephansplatz. This area takes its name from a stock on the wall of the Equitable Palais (see above) hammered with nails by apprentice locksmiths in the Middle Ages; it was probably the upturned stump of a tree from the ur-forest that once covered the area. Superstition required that journeymen coming to Vienna had to hammer a nail into the stump in order to ensure a safe return home, the last such nail being hammered in 1832.

Facing Stephansdom on the northeast end of Graben at Stock-im-Eisen-Platz 6 is Hans Hollein's controversial **Haas-Haus** (completed 1990). This replaced an ugly 1950s building, which in turn filled in the gap left by the 1945 bombing of Siccardsburg and Van der Null's Historicist retail store (1867), the first such in Vienna. Critics of Hollein's building (and they are many) complain inter alia that it is wholly inappropriate opposite the Stephansdom, that its layered internal terraces of up-market shops are too much the expression of today's lustfully materialistic society, and that it interferes with a favourite snapshot view of the cathedral from the Graben corner. On the other hand, like the Hundertwasser house, it has become a tourist attraction in its own right. Its elegant rounded glass façade darkly reflects the cathedral, and there are marvellous views of the latter from the roof-level bar. At night, the lights set in the surrounding paving and the foliage of fairy lights draped on the façade around Christmas produce some striking visual effects.

5 • From Oper to Stephansplatz via Albertina, Neuer Markt and Kärntner Straße

The walk begins at the Opera House (Oper) (walk 7, p 130), reached by U1, U2 and U4 and trams 1 and 2 on the Ringstraße. Immediately behind the Opera House is the famous *Hotel Sacher* (Philharmonikerstraße 4), built for Eduard Sacher in 1876 on the site of the old Kärntnertortheater. The hotelier (1843–92) was the son of Metternich's cook, who had opened the first delicatessen in Vienna and is credited with creating the recipe for Sacher Torte in 1840. (A long-running dispute with neighbouring *Demel* over the rights to market the cake was settled in 1965—only Sacher can call its product 'original', but few could tell the difference between that and the other versions on offer.)

The *Sacher* offered *chambres séparées* on the Parisian model and was a convenient watering hole for the upper classes to keep their assignations with ballet dancers from the opera and other ladies of ill-defined repute. Eduard's widow, Anna, a cigar-smoking matriarch who turned away potentially disagreeable guests, but also fed the poor from the kitchens at the rear, ran the hotel from 1892 until shortly before her death in 1930. In the First World War, the *Sacher* was known as 'Hotel World History', so popular was it with officers and

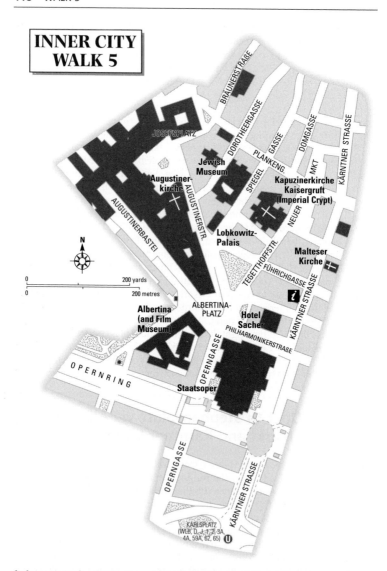

INNER CITY WALK 5

diplomats. In the 1980s it was a favourite haunt of Austria's greatest and most controversial modern playwright, Thomas Bernhard (1931–89); the then owner raised his profile by marrying the American ambassadress to Austria.

Philharmonikerstraße debouches westwards into **Albertinaplatz**, across which you will see the Albertina itself, rising above an ornamental wall enclosing the remains of the Augustinian bastion. At the salient angle is Johann Meixner's **Danube Fountain** (1869), representing (in the centre) the Danube and Vindobona flanked by emblems of the rivers Save and Tisza. The lateral sculptures representing the Raab, the Enns, the Traun, the Drave (on the right) and the Inn, the Mur, the Salzach and the March (on the left) were restored to their niches in 1989.

Above the Danube Fountain is an equestrian monument to Archduke Albrecht (Caspar von Zumbusch, 1899), the victorious Habsburg general against the Italians at the battle of Custozza in 1866, when the young Italian state was in alliance with Prussia. (The victory, overshadowed only a month later by the catastrophic defeat of the Austrians by the Prussians at Sadowa, was largely in vain.)

The Albertina

Vienna's Albertina (Augustinerstraße 1), the largest of the Habsburg residential palais, is one of the most important museums in the world. It houses the famous graphic collection of Duke Albert of Sachsen-Teschen (hence its name) who was a son-in-law of the Empress Maria Theresia, and an architectural collection. The museum, currently undergoing a massive restoration programme, reopens in March 2003 with an exhibition on Edvard Munch, followed by one on Dürer in September 2003 and will offer the unique experience of a modern museum within a historic palais.

The world famous collection of 60,000 drawings and one million graphics will be joined by a new photographic collection with works by Helmut Newton and Lisette Model (among others). Exhibitions will be presented in the newly erected exhibition halls, one of which is embedded in the Bastei (bastion), the former city wall of Vienna. The palace staterooms will also be open to the public for the first time, among them the *Musensaal* (Hall of the Muses) and *Goldkabinett* (Gold Cabinet).

There are exhibitions of facsimiles in the Albertina meanwhile, and select items of the originals are displayed periodically in small exhibitions in the National Library. The excellent **Austrian Film Museum**, showing retrospectives of major directors, still operates in the gallery's entrance lobby at Augustinerstraße 1 (☎ 533 70 54-0).

Originally guest apartments for the Hofburg, the palace was altered and enlarged by Louis von Montoyer (1801–04), although rebuilding after damage in the war has left little of his imprint. A new entrance was made from the Augustinerstraße, next to the old bastion ramp, at the base of which is Fritz Wotruba's statue of a *Reclining Boy* (1933).

Highlights of the collection include Dürer's *Hare* and *Clasped Hands*, two of the most frequently reproduced works in the world (the originals have been owned by the Albertina for centuries) and works by Rubens, Schiele, Cézanne, Klimt, Kokoschka, Picasso and Rauschenberg.

Augustinerkirche

At Augustinerstraße 3 (but entered from the Josefsplatz round the corner) is the Gothic Augustinerkirche, founded by Friedrich the Handsome in 1327 and made the parish church of the court in 1634. After many vicissitudes it was returned to the possession of its original Augustinian owners in 1950. Augustinian monks who were members of the *Totenbrüderschaft* (Brotherhood of the Dead), which had been founded in 1638 and was modelled on a similar body in Rome to which Michelangelo once belonged, attended executions in the 17C with their faces shrouded in black cowls, and removed the corpses to the common burial ground.

The **exterior** of the church is fairly unremarkable, except perhaps for the clock in the tower: it was a gift from an 18C Hungarian aristocrat and general

(Count Nádasdy) who lived opposite the Augustinerkirche, and thought it would be convenient to see the time from his window. The **interior** was completely 're-Gothicized' by Ferdinand von Hohenberg in 1783, at which time many Baroque works of art were swept away. Near the entrance is the remarkable **tomb of Marie Christine of Habsburg** (see above), a masterwork (1805) of neo-Classical sculpture by Antonio Canova. Allegorical figures (*Virtus* and *Caritas*) process through the entrance into a pyramidal burial chamber, watched from the right by a genius resting on a lion. Above the entrance is a medallion of the Archduchess with the simple inscription *uxori optimae* (the best of wives), a testament to her famously happy marriage to Albert of Sachsen-Teschen. (The latter had every reason to be happy, as it was Habsburg money that enabled him to build up his great collection of drawings.)

Off the right-hand aisle is the **Loreto Chapel** (moved from the centre of the church in 1784), which contains silver urns with the hearts of Habsburgs, beginning with that of Emperor Ferdinand II (d. 1637) and ending with the father of Franz Joseph (d. 1878). Among them is the heart of the Duc de Reichstadt, Napoleon's son by the daughter of Franz I. Following the somewhat gruesome prescriptions of Habsburg necrolatry, the embalmed entrails (together with brains and eyes) are in the catacombs of St Stephen's, while the bodies are in the Imperial Crypt (Kaisergruft) below the Kapuzinerkirche (Capuchin Church) on the Neuen Markt (see below). The idea behind the ritual (which represented the influence of Spanish imperial customs) was to create separate focal points for Habsburg devotion in the city. However, opinions are divided as to the psychological significance of the death cult for its practitioners—did it represent the celebration of the transience of individual life in the eternity of a shrine, or simple morbidity, in Hilde Spiel's acid phrase, 'the saturnalia of death'?

To the right of the choir, a door leads to **St George's Chapel**, an assembly point for the crusading order founded in 1337 to convert the heathen Prussians and Lithuanians. Maria Theresia's personal physician and enlightened counsellor, Gerhard van Swieten, is buried here and there is also an (empty) tomb for Leopold II by Franz Anton Zauner, originally intended for the Capuchin crypt.

A number of treasures have been brought to the church since Hohenberg's restoration, notably J.M. Rottmayr's **Vision of Mary Magdalene** (originally in the chapel at Schönbrunn), figures of St Augustine and St Ambrose from the Schwarzspanierkirche, the **Twelve-Year-Old Jesus in the Temple** by Michel Angelo Unterberger from the Stiftskirche, and other works. A modern pulpit near the choir stands on the spot where the most celebrated of the Augustinian friars delivered his vivid fulminations in the plague years of the 17C. Ulrich Megerle (1644–1709; known to the Viennese by his adopted name of Abraham a Sancta Clara) has been characterised by Stephen Vajda as 'a fairground barker for intolerance ... but remembered above all as a great stylist and original literary talent.' His legendary fire and brimstone outbursts castigated the people of Vienna, warning them to mend their ways in the face of the dangers posed by the armies of the Turkish infidels, the Protestant heretics and, of course, the hated Jews. The plague was convenient to his rhetoric, being the punishment of God for the sin that the preacher saw all around him; his most famous sermon (*Merck's, Wienn!*; 1680) and an exhortatory polemic (*Auf, auf, ihr Christen!*; 1683) were later exploited by Schiller for the coruscating Capuchin sermon in *Wallenstein* (1796–9).

The horrific consequences of racism in our own age are marked by Alfred Hrdlicka's controversial memorial at the centre of Albertinaplatz. His **Monument against War and Fascism** was erected on the 50th anniversary (1988) of the *Anschluss*. Two monolithic marble blocks represent the Gate of Violence and behind them stands a bronze image of the Jew washing the streets (as Jews were forced to do in 1938, to erase the campaign slogans of the Fatherland Front for the plebiscite forestalled by Hitler's invasion). Separated from this group are representations of Orpheus entering Hades and the Stone of the Republic, engraved with the Austrian Declaration of Independence circulated on 27 April 1945. Controversy arose because the site for the monument is above the cellar of a house destroyed by allied bombing, with much loss of life.

At the northwest end of the square is the **Lobkowitz-Palais** (Lobkowitz-Platz 2), the façade (1710) of which is by Johann Bernhard Fischer von Erlach. The original palace was built on what had been the pig market by Giovanni Tencala for Count Dietrichstein in 1687. In 1753 Prince Wenzel von Lobkowitz acquired it, his descendant Franz Josef Max being the patron of Beethoven, who conducted the first performance of his Third Symphony in 1804 before an invited audience in the palace. There were splendid balls here during the Congress of Vienna. It now houses the **Theatre Museum** (open Tue–Sun 10.00–17.00, Wed to 21.00). The collection includes one hundred Secessionist stage designs by Alfred Roller, who worked closely with Gustav Mahler, then musical director at the imperial opera house. (Another branch of the museum— the Memorial Rooms—is nearby at Hanuschgasse 3, open Tue–Fri 10.00–12.00 and 13.00–16.00, Sat, Sun 13.00–16.00.)

A few paces back along the Augustinerstraße brings you on the right to the **Dorotheergasse**, a street that bears witness to Joseph II's Edict of Tolerance, promulgated in 1781. There are two Protestant churches close together: the **Lutheran** at no. 18 and the **Reformed** (Presbyterian) **Church** at no. 16. They were built on the site of an abandoned Clarissan cloister and their exteriors long remained indistinguishable from ordinary house façades (Joseph's Edict prohibited any indication—including a belfry—of religious activity which might seem provocative to pious Catholics). The tower of the Reformed Church was added in 1887, together with its neo-Baroque façade. At no. 17 is the State Auction House, known as the **Dorotheum** (or 'Aunt Dorothy' to the Viennese), and founded under Josef I in 1707 as a cheaper alternative to rapacious pawnbrokers. Its name recalls the cloister of Dorothean nuns, who had previously occupied a building here, replaced by the present neo-Baroque edifice of Emil Förster in 1901. It is well worth wandering around the huge galleries, and it can be advantageous to buy at auction, although commission, taxes and other expenses add some 30 per cent to the successful bid price.

At Dorotheergasse 11, situated in the former Eskeles-Palais, is the recently (1993) opened **Jewish Museum of the City of Vienna** (open Sun to Fri, 10.00–18.00, Thur 10.00–20.00) (Jüdisches Museum der Stadt Wien), which owes its existence substantially to the commitment of the (non-Jewish) former mayor of Vienna, Helmut Zilk. The 18C Baroque palace transferred from noble ownership to the Jewish bankers, Arnstein and Eskeles, in 1823. Around the turn of the century the famous Gallery Miethke operated here, dealing in the works of the Secessionists and the Wiener Werkstätte. The museum, which has a bookshop and café, stages regular exhibitions with a Jewish theme.

Neuer Markt

A turn off Dorotheergasse into Plankengasse brings you to the Neuen Markt (in the Middle Ages the Mehlmarkt—Flour Market). In the centre is a copy of Georg Raphael Donner's lovely **Providentia Fountain**, the original of which dates to 1739. The putti and some of the allegorical figures were considered indecent by Maria Theresia's notorious and absurd Chastity Commission and had to be removed in 1773 (since 1921 they have been in the Baroque Museum in the Lower Belvedere). The figure of Providentia presides over the surrounding personifications of Austrian rivers—the Styrian Enns (a bearded ferryman with an oar), the Lower Austrian March (a river goddess), the Upper Austrian Traun (a fisherman with trident) and the Lower Austrian Ybbs (a river nymph with a flower vase).

Also on the Neuen Markt below the **Kapuzinerkirche** (Capuchin Church) at the western corner of the square, is the **Imperial Crypt** or Kapuzinergruft (Tegetthoffstraße 2, open daily 09.30–16.00) of the Habsburgs.

History

The first Capuchins (a branch of the Franciscan order) came to Vienna in 1599. Eighteen years later, the wife of the Emperor Matthias invited them to found a cloister and a burial chapel, the latter to be occupied by herself and her husband (as it happened, the crypt proved to be on the site of a Roman burial ground, discovered in 1824). However, it was not until 1632 that construction was completed (under Ferdinand II) and a year later the founder and her husband were the first of 143 Habsburgs and one commoner to be buried here. (The commoner is Maria Theresia's governess, Countess Fuchs, who thus obtained an honour refused even to Field Marshal Radetzky.) There are some absentees: the last Emperor, Karl I, was buried in exile in Madeira; Marie Antoinette (a daughter of Maria Theresia) was buried on the spot where she was executed in Paris; and the remains of the Duc de Reichstadt (Napoleon's son by Marie Louise) were transferred to Les Invalides in 1940 by the Germans as a diplomatic ploy.

Many of the coffins are those of prematurely deceased little archdukes and archduchesses, but the larger Baroque tombs are amongst the finest funerary monuments of Europe. The most beautiful is Balthasar Moll's double tomb (1753) for Maria Theresia (d. 1780) and her husband, Franz Stephan of Lorraine (d. 1765). On the lid of the sarcophagus, the Emperor and his consort are portrayed as if awakening to eternal life; they gaze fixedly into each other's eyes, while above them a genius, holding the trumpet with which he had roused them, bears aloft a crown of stars. At the foot of the tomb are mourning female figures carrying the four Habsburg crowns (of the Holy Roman Empire, of Hungary, of Bohemia and of Jerusalem). Reliefs on one side depict Franz Stephan's arrival in Tuscany as Grand Duke (1739) and the imperial coronation procession at Frankfurt (1745); on the other side are Maria Theresia's coronation as Queen of Bohemia in St Vitus's Cathedral (1743) and her ride to the coronation mound in Pozsony (Pressburg) as newly crowned Queen of Hungary (1741). Balthasar Moll also designed the tombs for Maria Theresia's father, Karl VI, and his wife, Elisabeth Christine, on which may be seen J.N. Moll's moving representation of a mourning

Austria. In striking contrast to the ornate Rococo of Balthasar Moll's double tomb, is the simple copper coffin of the rationalist emperor, Joseph II, son and successor to Maria Theresia, which lies at the foot of his mother's sarcophagus. (Joseph actually had the crypt closed in 1787, but his successor, Leopold II, re-opened it.)

The **Kapuzinerkirche** was altered and renovated in 1935–36. It is uninspiring from the outside, and the façade, with its huge cross, is not improved by the tasteless fresco showing *St Francis with Angels* (Hans Fischer, 1936). In a wall niche to the right is the bronze figure of Marco d'Aviano, a favourite preacher of Leopold I, who joined the imperial armies (as Papal Legate) in their battle with the besieging Turks in 1683. Inside the church, note the Kaiserkapelle with statues of the Emperors Matthias, Ferdinands II and III and King Ferdinand IV. In the chapel of the Holy Cross is an altar by Lukas von Hildebrandt and a fine *pietà* with weeping women and angels by Peter Strudel and Matthias Steinl. Originally (1717) this was made for the crypt, but moved to the church when the latter was closed by Joseph II.

Kärntner Straße

To the east of the Neuen Markt is the fashionable pedestrian precinct of the Kärntner Straße, Vienna's Bond Street where there are many shops of interest to lovers of Viennese applied arts. *Joh. Backhausen & Söhne* at no. 33 sells the textile designs of the Wiener Werkstätte; at *Lobmeyr* (no. 26), glassware made to 19C Historicist designs is on sale (there is a small museum of their products above the shop) and *Prachner* at no. 30 has the best selection of books on architecture in Vienna.

Kärntner Straße has little to detain us from the architectural point of view. However, towards the southern end is the charming **Malteser Kirche** (no. 37) belonging to the Knights of St John, who were rewarded for their defence of Christendom with the Island of Malta in 1530 by Emperor Karl V. The last Babenberg Duke (Leopold VI) had called the Knights to Vienna in the 13C, when they built a chapel and hospital for the pilgrims arriving from Carinthia and points south. The present church dates to the 14C, with a neo-Classical façade added between 1806 and 1808. Inside is an epitaph and monument to the Grand Master (Jean Parisot de la Vallette) who defended Malta from the Turks (1557–58). The neo-Classical relief (1806) shows the fortress of Valletta under siege and is flanked by the figures of two manacled Turks. Beyond the church at no. 41 is the diminutive **Esterházy-Palais** (mid-17C with later additions), whose aspect is perhaps more bourgeois than aristocratic. It now houses a casino.

Architectural buffs should also make their way to the Kärntner Durchgang, off the northern end of the street to the left, where they will find the curious **American Bar** (1909) by Adolf Loos (p 94). Loos was an enthusiast for American civilisation, which he admired for its practicality, modernity and optimism; this work is a kind of homage to American lifestyle. The tiny bar (originally for men only, on Loos's instructions) is made to seem larger by the use of wall-mirrors. The interior (restored 1990) uses costly materials such as mahogany, Skyros marble, brass and glass for the portals and window decoration of polished onyx. From here, the U-Bahn (Stephansplatz—U1, U3) is two minutes' walk away.

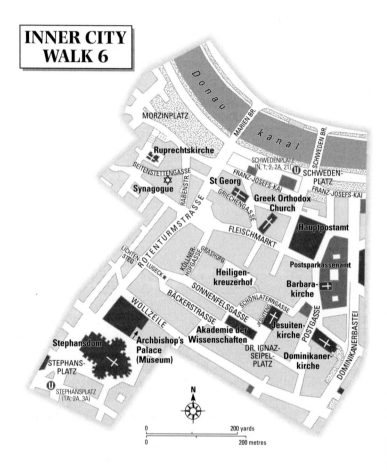

| INNER CITY |
| WALK 6 |

6 • Stephansplatz to Dr.-Ignaz-Seipel-Platz, Heiligenkreuzerhof, and Ruprechtsplatz

From Stephansplatz walk northwards on Rotenturmstraße (the name recalls the medieval tower that once stood on the fortifications at the street's northern end). After a short distance turn right into the Wollzeile, another ancient street once occupied by wool merchants and weavers, later notorious for its 'baths' (a euphemism for brothels). A *Durchgang* (alley) reached shortly on the left leads to the famous *Wiener Schnitzel* restaurant of *Figlmüller*, opposite which is the same firm's wine-bar (*Vis-à-Vis*), offering a large selection of open wines by the glass. Towards the end of the Wollzeile, a left turn brings you into Postgasse, at no. 4 of which is the **Dominikanerkirche** or Basilica ad S. Maria Rotundam.

The Dominicans

The Dominicans were called to Vienna under Leopold VI of Babenberg in 1226; two churches, Romanesque and Gothic (the second entirely financed by the sale of indulgences) preceded the present Baroque one (1634) on this site. Two of its architects were Italian, Cipriano Biasino and Antonio Canevale and their work shows a strong influence of Rome's ecclesiastical Baroque style. Originally a dome was planned but the foundations proved too weak to sustain it—or so the builders successfully maintained before a commission set up by the sceptical sponsors to investigate why one had not been built as ordered.

The Dominicans ('*Domini canes*' or 'Hounds of the Lord') were scholars and persuasive advocates of the faith (in Vienna they were simply known as 'The Preachers').

On the **façade** of the church are statues of their two greatest luminaries, Albertus Magnus (c 1200–80) and Thomas Aquinas (c 1225–74), whose works were crucial in the reconciliation of learning from the ancient world with the spirit and teachings of Christianity. Over the entrance portal is a representation of the *Rosary Madonna*, a reference to the fact that the prayer cycle of the rosary is said to have begun with Saint Dominic in the 13C. The rosary theme is taken up inside the church with Leopold Kupelwieser's altarpiece (1839) of *The Institution of the Festival of the Rosary*, celebrating Pope Gregory XIII's foundation of this popular ceremony. To the left of the high altar is a statue of St Dominic, represented as a wandering preacher, staff in hand, his dog beside him.

The striking architectural unity of the basilical **interior** is aesthetically enhanced by the adroit use of stucco and frescoes by Matthias Rauchmiller, Nikolaus van Hoye and Carpoforo Tencala, while the *trompe l'oeil* cupola is a late (1836), neo-Baroque addition by Franz Geyling. Of the many fine Baroque works, that of Johann Spillenberger next to the pulpit (the *Adoration of the Shepherds*) commands attention, as does the Dominican altarpiece in the second chapel of the left transept, a work by Tobias Pock (the *Ecstasy of St Dominic*). Underneath this altar lies the second wife of Leopold I, Claudia Felicitas of Tyrol (her decorative gravestone is by Balthasar Herold). The most sumptuous of the other chapels is that of St Vincent Ferrer (c 1350–1419), which boasts a Rococo wrought-iron gate and lavish decoration in red marble by François Roettier. (Ferrer, born of an English father and a Spanish mother, was one of the most celebrated Dominican preachers, and a remarkably successful missionary amongst the Jews and Moslems.)

The Barbarakirche

Just beyond the Dominican Church at Postgasse 10 is the small Barbarakirche or **Church of St Barbara**, belonging to the Uniat (or Uniate) Community, a halfway house between Orthodoxy and Catholicism set up under Maria Theresia to accommodate Christians in the eastern regions of the Empire.

The Uniates are in communion with Rome, but retain their respective languages, rites and canon law. However the term 'Uniat' was originally used by the opponents of the Union of Brest-Litovsk (1596) that imposed this politically driven religious compromise, and is disowned by those to whom it is nevertheless applied by others. There are probably some 15 million Uniats or Eastern Rite Catholics, including Copts, Maronites, Ukrainians and others. Their Viennese church (which had originally belonged to the Jesuits) dates to 1654 and contains an iconostasis and a picture of St Barbara by Moses Subolic, a Serbian painter of the Kiev school. It was given to them by Maria Theresia in 1775, originally with the intention of preparing Uniat priests. Today the congregation is in the majority Ukrainian, but includes many Slavs and an increasing number of Arab Melkites settled in the city.

The adjacent former Jesuit cloister was altered by Franz Hillebrand in the 18C and used as a customs building, then enlarged by Paul Sprenger in 1852 and occupied by the Ministry of Commerce. More recently it became the **Main Post Office**, and has recently undergone massive refurbishment. The old, forbidding halls flanked by officious and not always genial counter-clerks have been transformed into a communications super-mall, complete with coffee-house and cybernetic boutiques (entrance at Fleischmarkt 19).

Dr.-Ignaz-Seipel-Platz

Retracing your steps along Postgasse, turn right under an arch into Dr-Ignaz-Seipel-Platz. The square is remarkable for retaining historic buildings on all sides, and made an ideal open-air theatre for 17C Jesuit propaganda spectacles (performances are still sometimes given here). It is named, appropriately, after the controversial Catholic priest and university professor, Ignaz Seipel who was twice Chancellor of the First Republic in the troubled 1920s, and whose greatest achievement was the stabilisation of the Austrian currency after a period of hyper-inflation. He was seriously wounded in an assassination attempt in 1924 but returned as Chancellor for three years and died in 1932.

The building ahead of you, to the northwest, is the **Academy of Sciences** (Akademie der Wissenschaften), built to a design by Nicolas Jadot de Ville-Issey between 1753 and 1755. (A fine view of it, painted by Bernardo Bellotto around 1760, hangs in the Kunsthistorischen Museum—at that time the Academy housed university faculties and still had its astronomical observatory.) On the pleasing late Baroque façade are two ornamental fountains by Franz Lenzbauer.

It is difficult to get inside, except for functions, but well worth the attempt in order to see the **Ceremonial Hall** on the first floor. Its ceiling has a careful reconstruction of Gregorio Guglielmo's frescoes, allegories of the university faculties based on a programme by Pietro Metastasio (the original was destroyed by fire in 1961). In the neighbouring **Theological Hall** are thematically appropriate frescoes (1756) by Franz Anton Maulbertsch. It was in the Academy that Haydn made his last public appearance, aged 75, to hear the first performance of his *Creation*. Legend has it that Beethoven pushed forward to kiss the composer's hand; as he rested his palm on Beethoven's unkempt locks, the old man murmured: 'You shall finish what I have begun.'

The **Old University** (Alte Universität) faces the Academy and dates to the Jesuit take-over of higher education in the early 17C, the single most significant of Ferdinand II's counter-reformatory measures. A plaque on the wall recalls that Schubert was a pupil-chorister here in the days when the building was occupied by the *Hofsängerknaben* (later the Vienna Boys' Choir).

Adjacent, to the north, there was originally a student dormitory, inappropriately known as the *Bursa agni* (the house sign showed a lamb). The word *bursa* referred to the *bursarii*, that is, scholars supported with bursaries, from which the words *Bursche* and *Burschenschaft* (fraternity) are derived. Since the 19C, these words have become somewhat tainted by nationalism. In the Middle Ages, however, licentiousness was evidently the main problem with students: in a letter of 1438, Aeneas Silvius Piccolomini (later Pope Pius II) complained that they spent their time 'marauding through the city', harassing law-abiding citizens, eating, drinking and womanising. (However, he himself had illegitimate children.)

Probably the citizens were relieved when the Jesuits demolished the Bursa and built their **University Church** (now **Jesuitenkirche**) on the site (1627–31). Alterations between 1703 and 1705 enriched the façade and remodelled the interior. The figures in the upper niches (late 17C) represent Sts Catherine, Joseph, Leopold and Barbara. Below them (early 18C) are Sts Ignatius Loyola (founder of the Jesuits) and Francis Xavier (Loyola's co-founder and contemporary). The spectacular interior with *trompe l'oeil* effects is the work of Andrea Pozzo, who created the high altar with its painting of the **Assumption of the Virgin Mary**, the latter cunningly illuminated by an angled oriel. The illusionistic ceiling frescoes illustrate the **Life of Mary**, the **Fall of the Angels** and **The Trinity**, while the altarpieces in the chapels (by Pozzo's workshop) represent **Theology**, **Philosophy**, the **Sacraments of Life and Death**, and leading Jesuit fathers. The marvellous barley-sugar curlicue columns are a deliberate imitation of Bernini's solomonic originals for St Peter's in Rome.

Two parallel streets, Bäckerstraße and Sonnenfelsgasse run northwest from Dr.-Ignaz-Seipel-Platz. Originally there was a single, wide street here, which declined in importance, since (unlike the Wollzeile) it did not lead to a city gate with access to the Vorstadt. The pressure on accommodation from a rising population resulted in an extra row of houses being erected along the middle in the 16C. Earlier architectural features of the houses are now mostly hidden behind later façades, but at no. 12 Bäckerstraße (which retains a Renaissance oriel) an interesting **house sign** came to light during restoration, showing a bespectacled cow playing backgammon with a wolf (of which only the snout is visible). This visual fable is said to be an ironic comment on the struggle between the Catholics (the cow) and the Protestants (the wolf) in 17C Vienna. No. 7 has a particularly fine Renaissance courtyard, something of a rarity in the city; since so much money that might have been spent on building in the Renaissance period was ploughed into vastly expensive *tracé italien* fortifications, Viennese architecture often gives the appearance of evolving straight from medieval to Baroque.

Bäckerstraße debouches into Lugeck, once the site of a large inn (the Regensburger Hof) accommodating Bavarian merchants. The towering eclectic building (1897) now on the site recalls the German Renaissance in its façade, but is nevertheless an obtrusive and largely graceless building. In the centre of Lugeck is Max Fabiani's sculpture of Johannes Gutenberg, erected in 1900 to mark 500 years of printing in Vienna.

The walk back towards Dr.-Ignaz-Seipel-Platz takes you along Sonnenfelsgasse, named after one of Maria Theresa's wisest counsellors, Joseph von Sonnenfels (1732–1817). He persuaded her to abolish torture of criminal suspects and also introduced street lighting to Vienna. At no. 3 is the *Zwölf*

Apostel-Keller, a *Stadtheurige* (city tavern) with two subterranean levels of cellars (Baroque and medieval). The fine Baroque façade (1721) is in the style of Lukas von Hildebrandt. No. 15 has a beautiful Renaissance portal with a horseshoe arch whose keystone is in the form of a mask, above which is a finely carved pine-cone motif. No. 19 once housed the university administration and archives.

A left turn down the narrow Jesuitengasse brings you to Schönlaterngasse, where another left brings you to the inconspicuous east gate of the Heiligenkreuzer Hof.

Heiligenkreuzer Hof

The Cistercian Abbey of Heiligenkreuz (p 200) had a convent here from the 13C, its rooms later being let out as flats. The courtyard is an oasis of tranquillity in the heart of the city and is surrounded by Baroque buildings, mostly dating to the abbacy of Clemens Schäffer in the 17C. On the south side is the entrance to St Bernard's Chapel. Apply to the *Hauswart* (janitor) if you wish to see inside. The chapel's portal, with sculptured angels flanking a bust of the most celebrated Cistercian, St Bernard of Clairvaux, is the work of Giovanni Giuliani (1729). The interior (1730) has an altarpiece (St Bernard and the Virgin Mary) by Martino Altomonte, on either side of which are Giuliani's wood sculptures of Saints Leopold and Florian. Giuliani also created the side altars.

The prelacy next to the chapel is set back behind a wall and is now an extension exhibition hall for the University of Applied Arts (Universität für Angewandte Kunst). A number of artists and writers have had rooms in the Heiligenkreuzer Hof, most recently the satirist Helmut Qualtinger (1928–86). He created a quintessential Viennese character, the time-serving Kleinbürger ('Der Herr Karl'), who deployed an equal degree of cynicism and sycophancy to survive the changing political dispensations of the pre-war and war years. The deadly accuracy of Qualtinger's portrait aroused furious indignation when first shown on TV.

Lieber Augustin

In the plague year of 1679, the legendary bagpiper Marx Augustin (1643–1705) (who featured in the preaching of Abraham a Sancta Clara) regularly frequented the inn. One evening, while returning home the worse for wear, he fell into an open pit of infected corpses. After snoozing all night on a heap of rotting flesh, he arose happily in the morning to continue his riotous living, much to the astonishment of the burial gang who had arrived to pour lime on the bodies. Augustin never caught the plague and died in his cups, a symbol of the Viennese *Lebenskünstler*, the ultimate survivor. However, the famous song, *O du lieber Augustin*, which is associated with him, only appeared in Vienna around 1800 and is thought to be an adaptation of a scurrilous contemporary *Gassenhauer* (popular ballad) written in 1704 to cash in on the overthrow of the Elector of Saxony and would-be successor to Jan Sobieski as King of Poland, Frederick-Augustus II:

Oh my dear Augustin, everything's gone!
Saxony's gone, Poland is gone,
Augustin lies in the shit.
Oh my dear Augustin, it's all up with you!

Leaving the Heiligenkreuzer Hof at the northwest end (Grashofgasse) you soon meet the Köllnerhofgasse. At its northern end is the Fleischmarkt, across which you will see the *Griechenbeisl* restaurant.

If you go down the narrow Griechengasse beside the Beisl, you come to St George's Chapel, a diminutive church (no. 5) which, like the Barbarakirche, largely owed its existence to the support of Maria Theresia. In 1776, she gave the Viennese Ottoman Greek community (i.e. those Greeks still subject to the Sultan, later to the Greek monarchy) unrestricted possession of this chapel, thus laying to rest a long dispute with the aggressive Orthodox Serbs. The church was rebuilt in 1803 by Franz Wipplinger, but its iconostasis dates to 1780.

Back on the Fleischmarkt at no. 13 is the marvellous **Greek Orthodox Trinity Church**. It was built in the 1860s (together with a presbytery and school) for Greek subjects of the Habsburgs by Theophil Hansen and financed by the magnate and Maecenas, Baron Sina, who was of Greek (Aromunian) origin. The colourful brick façade with its oriental glow is as striking as the lush interior decorated in Byzantine style, with gilded columns, a ceiling ornamented with Greek-style painting and a fine iconostasis.

The Fleischmarkt leads eastwards to the main post office (p 126), but head west now across the Rotenturmstraße and up a flight of steps to the **Seitenstettengasse** and the **Kornhäusel-Turm** at no. 2, which bears the name of the distinguished neo-Classical architect who built it. His atelier was situated in the prominent and rather grim-looking tower rising above the dwelling, a refuge, according to cynics, from his fierce wife. The façade on the Seitenstettengasse side is attractively ornamented with reliefs and plant motifs. The house is now the centre of the Jewish religious community (Israelitische Kultusgemeinde, Seitenstettengasse 4), which explains the armed police usually hovering in the neighbourhood. Kornhäusel also built the fine neo-Classical **Synagogue** (Wiener Stadttempel, 1826; Seitenstettengasse 4), whose oval interior has a star-studded cupola, below which an Ionic colonnade supports a running gallery. Partly because of its inconspicuousness (itself dictated by the conditions attached to Joseph II's Edict of Tolerance), but more perhaps because of the danger to the adjoining houses if it was burned, the synagogue escaped major damage in the horrifying Reichskristallnacht of 9 November 1938 and was restored in the 1970s. The contents of the **Jewish Museum** have been transferred to the new premises at Dorotheergasse 11 (p 121). Worship is at 09.00 on Fridays, 21.00 on Saturdays and prospective visitors must bring a passport.

Ruprechtsplatz

Just to the west of Seitenstettengasse is the Ruprechtsplatz. On its northern edge is the ancient **Ruprechtskirche**, the oldest surviving church in Vienna, part of it supposedly built over a Roman chapel. In the so-called Dark Ages it was patronised by the shipmen bringing salt from the Salzkammergut (hence the name of the nearby 'Salzgries' and hence also the church's subordination before 803 to the Salzburg diocese. St Rupert, a Salzburg bishop, was by tradition the founder of the salt industry and patron saint of salt miners).

While a revised and extended 17C edition of Wolfgang Lazius's famous history of Vienna claimed a foundation date as early as 740, there is certain documentation for the church's existence in 1137, when the representative of the Passau bishopric

Ruprechtskirche

was based here. The building has preserved Romanesque elements; its tower also dates to the 11C, with a Gothic window and pitched roof added in the 15C.

Although much restored, the interior is atmospheric. A 13C stained glass window of the *Crucifixion* and the *Virgin Mary Enthroned* has survived. An impressive modern work in stained glass is Lydia Roppolt's cycle (1953) on the theme 'God be praised, our saviour in time of deepest trouble'. This includes representations of *Daniel*, *Jonah* and the *Burning Fiery Furnace*. On the wall of the choir is a painting of St Ruprecht by J.M. Rottmayr. In the early 19C, St Ruprecht's saw the foundation of the Marian Society, an organisation that revived the (still popular) annual pilgrimages to the shrine of Mariazell in Styria (see *Blue Guide Austria*).

There are some good restaurants in the vicinity, notably the *Salzamt* at Ruprechtsplatz 1 (an establishment so assured of its clientele that it needs no name-sign). In Sterngasse, leading out of the square, academic books in English (including a good selection of Austriaca) may be purchased at *Shakespeare and Company*.

Steps lead down to Morzinplatz, on which once stood the Hotel Metropole, destroyed by bombing in 1945. During the war it had been the headquarters of the Gestapo and many suspects were interrogated and tortured here. A **Monument against War and Fascism** (1985) now stands on the site. Leopold Grausam's sculpture shows a bronze figure striding forward with clenched fist. Between symbols of victimised homosexuals and Jews are the words 'Never forget!', while on the front is the following inscription dating to the 1950s:

> Here stood the house of the Gestapo. For patriotic Austrians, it was a hell. For many others, the forecourt to death. It is in ruins, like the 1000 year Reich. But Austria is resurrected and with Austria, her dead, the immortal victims.

From this chilling memorial it is a short walk east along the Franz-Josefs-Kai to the transport connections at Schwedenplatz.

7 • Oper to Stephansplatz

Annagasse

Starting from the junction at the Oper (U1, U2, U4, Trams 1 and 2) walk northeast along Kärntner Straße and turn right into Annagasse, a rather narrow street lined with Baroque façades. Almost immediately on your left is the diminutive **Annakirche**, whose richly decorated Baroque interior is arresting. The highlights are the ceiling fresco of the *Immaculate Conception* by Daniel Gran,

INNER CITY WALK 7

and the same artist's altarpiece representing the *Holy Family*. Above the first altar to the left is a copy of what had been the church's greatest treasure, a **wood-carving** of St Anne with the Virgin Mary and the infant Jesus (1505) attributed to Veit Stoß of Nürnberg (the original is now in the Dom- und Diözesanmuseum; p 108).

Adjacent to the church, its former convent (originally Clarissan, later a school for Jesuit novitiates) was the home of the Imperial Academy of Fine Arts between 1786 and 1876; it was here that the first art exhibition (1813) was held in Vienna. In the three-storeyed cellars under the convent, a famous dance-hall (Neues Elysium) existed in Biedermeier times, offering such exotic peripheral attractions as Baroque grottoes and an imitation Turkish seraglio.

Johannesgasse

Shortly beyond the Annakirche, a left turn brings you into the Seilerstätte, originally so-called from its workshops which made ropes for shipping on the Danube and the Save. At Seilerstätte 30 is an exciting new project, the **Haus der Musik** (open daily 10.00–22.00), an interactive display devoted to the experience of all types of music housed in the modernised and air-conditioned former palace of the Archduke Karl. Apart from practising your skills as a conductor, you can enjoy a journey back in time through the Viennese music tradition and visit a room devoted to the Wiener Philharmoniker. There is a good gift shop with CDs and café-restaurant Cantino. However, at ten Euros, the combi-ticket is quite expensive.

The first left out of Seilerstätte is the **Johannesgasse**, on the corner of which is the former convent and church of the Ursuline Order, now the High School for Music and the Performing Arts. On the second floor at no. 6 (Annagasse 5) is the **Hofkammerarchiv**, which preserves the office of the playwright Franz Grillparzer (1791–1872) exactly as he had it. (Open Mon–Fri, 08.30–14.30. To visit, apply to the porter or ring ☎ 512 54 34 for information.) In the archive itself you can see the original fascicles of imperial documents filed with Germanic precision. Between 1832 and 1856 Grillparzer held the post of chief archivist, a job that was apparently not so taxing as to interfere with his writing and journeys round Europe. The chief benefit of such a sinecure was that it allowed him the 'inner emigration' in which many intellectuals took refuge during the Metternich era. Some of Grillparzer's plays had been badly received and he had sporadic troubles with the censor.

Himmelpfortgasse

If you retrace your steps and leave Johannesgasse by turning right onto **Kärntner Straße**, and then turn right again into Himmelpfortgasse, you come (at no. 8) to the **Winter Palace of Prince Eugene of Savoy**. The first phase of the palace was commissioned from Johann Bernhard Fischer von Erlach in 1696, and work was continued by Johann Lukas von Hildebrandt between 1708 and 1709. (However, Fischer von Erlach was at pains to claim credit for the overall design in his *Treatise on Historic Architecture* which appeared in 1721.) The magnificent reliefs flanking the portals show *Hercules* and *Antäeus*, and *Aeneas* and *Anchises* in the middle, Achilles with the body of *Hector* and *Perseus with the Head of the Gorgon* (to the east), *War and Peace* (to the west). All are the work of Lorenzo Mattielli, who also supplied the decorative sculpture elsewhere on the façade. The exceptionally high rusticated socle is a device to ensure that the piano nobile gets enough light in a narrow street. The building is now the Finance Ministry, but is visitable from time to time for exhibitions, when you can enjoy the **Ceremonial Hall** with its allegorical painted panels depicting the deeds of *Apollo* and *Hercules*, an allusion to Prince Eugene's double role as cultivated patron of the arts and soldier. Even if the interior is closed to visitors, you should be allowed to look into the vestibule, from which rises a magnificent staircase with Giovanni Giuliani's Atlas figures supporting the balustrade. You may also be able to see the courtyard with a dolphin fountain and rich stucco by Santino Bussi.

Continuing down Himmelpfortgasse you rejoin Seilerstätte at a point opposite the Ronacher Établissement, a musical theatre built by the firm of *Fellner and Helmer* (which obtained contracts for theatre design all over the Habsburg Dual Monarchy). In its time Ronacher has been a variety theatre (where Josephine Baker once performed), a hotel, a broadcasting studio and an alternative stage for the Burgtheater. The sumptuous eclectic interior has recently been restored and the Ronacher now puts on hit musicals.

Franziskanerplatz

If you walk northeast along Seilerstätte, the next street to the left is the top half of the Weihburggasse; after a few yards, you come to Franziskanerplatz and the **Franziskanerkirche**.

The Franciscans had been called to Vienna under the Babenbergs, but the Habsburgs were also their strong supporters, several belonging to the Third Franciscan Order, following a tradition that reached back to the dynasty's founder, Rudolf of Habsburg. Their earlier convent having been destroyed, in 1589 the Franciscans obtained possession of the former house for the city's fallen women, which had a small chapel attached. The much altered building with curious roundels in the wall adjoins the church. (This convent or asylum for *Büsserinnen* was dedicated to St Jerome and had been founded in the 14C, when the city councillors decided to help Vienna's exploited prostitutes to go straight. Viennese burghers were encouraged to take the inmates as wives, the only stipulation being that they should not have known them in their professional capacity.)

The present church dates to 1611, its idiosyncratic architecture being doubtfully attributed to a Father Daum. The façade is a somewhat arbitrary mixture of Gothic and German Renaissance. The Baroque portal (1750) is crowned by the figure of St Jerome with cardinal's hat and lion, flanked by two angels. The Baroque interior is notable for the **high altar** in the form of a triumphal arch framing a *trompe l'oeil* painting by Andrea Pozzo (1707). Illusionistic architecture is also evident on the north wall's stucco: an enormous green curtain, patterned with fleurs-de-lys, seems to fall away from a high window in a series of ample drapes.

As you leave the Franziskanerplatz, note the attractive **Moses Fountain** (1798) by J.M. Fischer in the centre of the square. On the socle is an animal mask that acts as water spout; on the other side, a relief of the children of Israel thirsting in the desert, and Moses striking the rocks to make the water flow.

Deutschordenskirche und Schatzkammer

The northeastern corner of the square leads to the Singerstraße, at the western end of which (no. 7) is the **Church and Treasury of the Teutonic Knights** (Deutschordenskirche und Schatzkammer). The interior of the church contains a Flemish winged altarpiece of the *Passion* (1520) and a number of sumptuous red marble tombstones for members of the order.

The order was founded in the 12C and subsequently launched a crusade to convert the Prussians and Lithuanians. After the Hohenzollern leader of the Teutonic Knights turned Protestant in 1525, their extensive lands were secularised and later incorporated into Prussia. By the Treaty of Pressburg (1805), the office of Grand Master passed to the Habsburgs, who later (1840) reconstituted the order as a spiritual and charitable body under the leadership of a Grand Duke. Apart from their centre in the Singerstraße, the knights possessed a huge 19C palace on the Ringstraße built by Theophil Hansen (Deutschmeisterpalais, Parkring 8, formerly owned by OPEC and scene of an Arab terrorist attack led by the infamous 'Carlos' in 1975).

The **Treasury** is approached through the adjacent courtyard (Singerstraße 7) and has somewhat complicated opening times (Nov–Apr, Mon, Thur and Sat 10.00–12.00, Wed, Fri and Sat 15.00–17.00; May–Oct, Mon and Thur–Sun, 10.00–12.00, Wed, Fri, Sat, 15.00–17.00. If in doubt ☎ 512 10 65 to see whether it will be open when you plan to visit). The collections of the Grand Masters include medals, coins, ecclesiastical silver, ceremonial objects, paintings and carvings, mostly of very fine quality.

Turn north along Grünangergasse, passing the Fürstenberg-Palais (no. 4) with a façade after Hildebrandt and two naturalistically carved greyhounds above the portal. At the far end of the street is the Neuberger Hof (no. 1), one of the most ancient houses in the city, although much altered from its 14C shell. As it was spacious and conveniently situated, the French set up their headquarters here during the occupation of 1805. Its two inner courtyards have good examples of the windowed galleries known in Vienna as *pawlatschen*. In rooms on the second floor, Monsignor Otto Mauer founded his celebrated *Galerie nächst St Stephan* in 1954. Here he exhibited avant-garde art and worked tirelessly (ignoring the sniping from reactionary clerics), for a greater understanding in the church of modern art and of the inspiration of its practitioners. Unfortunately, much of the work of reconciliation of Mauer and of his contemporary, the former Cardinal-Archbishop of Vienna, Franz König, has recently been undermined by the Pope's strategy of packing the Austrian hierarchy with ultra-conservative elements.

Domgasse
The narrow Domgasse runs west off Grünangergasse towards the cathedral. At no. 5 is the Figarohaus, where Mozart wrote *The Marriage of Figaro* during his years here as lodger (1784–87). On the Schulerstraße side, the house is joined to the **König von Ungarn hotel** (Schulerstraße 10), a 16C building subsequently altered, which boasts the most delightful glassed-over Hof in Vienna. Renowned for its Viennese cooking, the hotel was popular in the 18C and 19C with aristocrats visiting Vienna on business from their country estates. From the hotel it is only a few minutes' walk westwards to Stephansplatz and the U-Bahn connections.

Two Walks on the Ringstraße

The Ringstraße

History

In an epoch-making decree issued on Christmas Day 1857, the Emperor Franz Joseph ordered the demolition of the city's cincture of bastions, which had stood since the 16C. This, the only initiative in urban planning ever undertaken by the Habsburgs in Vienna, opened the way for a building boom just as dramatic as that which had followed the defeat of the Turks in 1683. The extensive area of 'glacis' (military parade and exercise grounds in front of the bastions) was to be turned into a boulevard flanked by the representative buildings of an emergent entrepreneurial class of merchants, bankers, developers and industrialists. The styles chosen for these buildings symbolised the values of democratic Liberalism, and by the same token opposed the dynastic absolutism which had formerly made social or financial advance dependent on the patronage of the court.

Ringstraßen architecture represents the apotheosis of Historicism: its creators (Theophil Hansen, Heinrich Ferstel, Friedrich Schmidt, Karl von Hasenauer, Gottfried Semper, Eduard van der Null and August von Siccardsburg) looked to the architectural models of the past in order to express the bourgeois aspirations of the present and future. The neo-Classical Parlament harks back to the Athenian cradle of democracy; the neo-Renaissance University embodies the notion of the humanistic scholarship of the Italian Renaissance; the neo-Gothic Rathaus (City Hall) recalls the civic freedom and burgher wealth of medieval Flemish towns.

The grandiose nature of Ringstraßen public buildings and noble *Mietspaläste* (luxury apartment blocks) attracted cynical comment from the Viennese of the day. A reaction set in against over-ornamented façades and portentous symbolism, most acerbically articulated by the architect and apostle of functionalism, Adolf Loos. In a famous article entitled *The Potemkin City* (1898) he attacked the empty presumption and sterile ostentation of Historicism, which he likened to the fake villages erected by Count Potemkin to impress Catherine the Great when she visited the Ukraine. 'Whatever the Italian Renaissance produced in the way of lordly palaces' (wrote Loos) 'has been plundered, in order to conjure up before the eyes of His Majesty the Plebs a new Vienna, in which live only people in a position to own an entire palace from socle to cornice.' Loos was not alone in disliking Historicism—the Secession also reacted against Ringstraßen architecture by developing its local version of *art nouveau*, a sensual, liberating style drawing inspiration from natural forms.

In the first half of the 20C it was fashionable to take Loos's strictures at face value and few writers let slip the opportunity for a word or two of abuse about the excesses of Historicism. More recently, art historians and public alike have begun to appreciate the not unworthy ideals of the best architects of the Ringstraßen era, above all their commitment to fine craftsmanship and eloquent symbolism—the '*saxa loquuntur*', that Friedrich Schmidt conjured up when presenting his design for the Rathaus. These great public buildings combined the personal vision of the architects who designed them with a public statement about the society they represented and the assumptions of the age in which they were built.

8 • Burgtor to Schwedenplatz

The **Burgtor** and the two museums opposite it across the Ringstraße (**Naturhistorisches** and **Kunsthistorisches museums**) are reached by Trams 1 or 2 on the Ringstraße; nearest U-Bahn: Oper (U1, U2, U4) or Babenberger-straße (U2).

Burgtor

The original outer gate leading through the city fortifications to the Hofburg had been built under Leopold I (1660), but was destroyed by the Napoleonic army in 1809. Emperor Franz I was therefore underlining the reconquest of Austrian sovereignty when he ordered (1821) a new triumphal arch to be erected in memory of the victory over Napoleon at Leipzig ('the Battle of the Nations', 1813). Designed by Luigi Cagnola and Peter Nobile, the monument was built by soldiers, 'in the Roman way', as a contemporary put it. There is a Latin inscription on the inner side: 'Justice is the Foundation of Governance'; on the outer side, the Emperor's name is blazoned next to the date of construction (1824). Only the imperial family was permitted to use the middle arch, normal traffic being confined to the side passages. In modern times the Burgtor has become a monument to the Austrian dead in World War I (cf. the further Latin inscription meaning 'Glory to the soldiers, who are deserving of glory' and the references to the Austro-Hungarian army added in 1933/34, together with the coats of arms of the Habsburg Crown Lands). On 1 November, All Saints (or *Allerheiligen*, when the dead are commemorated in Austria) the urns on the Ringstraßen side of the arch are lit, the flame burning for 24 hours.

To the east of the Burgtor is the **Burggarten**, one of the more delightful green oases in Vienna. This was also laid out in the wake of the French occupation, during which the bastions here had been demolished. Louis von Remy's intimate garden plan with meandering paths and an ornamental pond was realised in 1818. The earliest iron and glass construction of Vienna was built in the garden (1826), but replaced (1907) by the present massive glasshouse of Friedrich Ohmann, which is a version of Jugendstil. There are several important **monuments** in the garden: that of the **Emperor Franz Stephan** (Maria Theresia's husband) is an equestrian statue (1780) by Balthasar Moll, transferred here from the old '*Paradeisgartl*' of the Hofburg that had also been destroyed by the French. The **statue of Franz Joseph** (Johann Benk, 1904), represented as an old man in military uniform, is easily overlooked in a byway of the garden. On the other hand, you can hardly miss the **Mozart Monument** near the Ring (Viktor Tilgner, 1896). Mozart appears in abandoned pose, the incarnation of sublime genius as the 19C liked to imagine him. The relief on the front of the plinth shows two scenes from *Don Giovanni* (the rash dinner invitation to the entombed Commendatore, and the arrival of the statue to send his victim to hell).

Opposite the Burgtor and west of the Burgring is the park dominated by a **monument to Maria Theresia** (Caspar von Zumbusch, 1888) and flanked by two huge museums. The great, reforming Habsburg ruler (1740–80) is shown enthroned and surrounded by her ministers, her generals and contemporary composers (Gluck, Haydn and Mozart). Her left hand rests on the famous Pragmatic Sanction (1713), a legal document by means of which her father, Karl VI, had tried to ensure the succession in the female line. It was, however, never accepted by the states hoping to carve up the Habsburg Empire, and the early part of her reign was devoted to fighting off opportunistic attacks by the Bavarians and the Prussians.

Maria-Theresien-Platz

History

The Maria-Theresien-Platz and its monumental museums represent the surviving elements of a hugely ambitious plan for a *Kaiserforum* drawn up in the 1870s by the German architect, Gottfried Semper. The latter was a romantic figure, a friend of Richard Wagner who had to flee Germany for England after the revolution of 1848; in London he had been the co-founder of the South Kensington Museum (later the Victoria and Albert Museum). His idea had been to extend the Hofburg southwards in two crescent-shaped wings and link them across the Ringstraße with a vast museum complex (the Outer Burgplatz). In the event, only the southeastern crescent of the Hofburg (the Neue Hofburg) was built, reaching as far as the Ring but no further.

Franz Alt's drawings of this planned apotheosis of metropolitan image-making have survived. From these and from the architects' plans we know that it was to have been a magnificent exercise in architectural symbolism, 'binding old and new: the court and the popular centres of high culture, the residence of ancient royalty and the institutes of bourgeois science and art ...' (Carl Schorske).

Semper had originally been called in (in 1869) to give his opinion of Karl von Hasenauer's plan for the museum quarter, and his own design was to some extent a reworking of Hasenauer's. The two architects began working together on the project, but then quarrelled acrimoniously; in the end Semper withdrew, leaving the completion of the museums in Hasenauer's hands. The Naturhistorisches Museum opened in 1889, the Kunsthistorisches Museum in 1891.

Naturhistorisches Museum

The façade of the Naturhistorischen Museum (Natural History Museum, Burgring 7; open Thur–Mon 09.00–18.30, Wed 09.00–21.00) mirrors that of its twin across the square, but its interior is less richly decorated. Its most interesting feature is the ceiling fresco by Hans Canon above the stairway, representing the *Circle of Life*.

The collection is arranged on two floors, the zoological exhibits and temporary exhibition being on the first floor. The star exhibit of the mineralogical collections (ground floor, to the left) is the famous **Venus of Willendorf**, which is thought to be 25,000 years old, while the **Galgenberg Fanny**, at 32,000 years, is the earliest surviving artefact in Austria. The 11cm high limestone fertility symbol of the **Venus**, with its grotesquely enlarged dugs, was found in the Wachau area upstream from Vienna. Other pre-history exhibits of interest are the casts of dinosaur skeletons, a vast collection of skulls illustrating the evolution of man, and an instructive section on extinct birds and mammals. The collection was based on that of Franz Stephan who was a keen amateur scientist, but also incorporates items acquired by Rudolf II and Prince Eugene of Savoy. It was for long the poor relation of Viennese museums (the upper floor only got electric lighting in 1988), but now has a lively programme of events and a better, more effectively didactic display.

Kunsthistorisches Museum

On entering the Museum of Art History (open Tues–Sun 10.00–18.00; Thur 10.00–21.00) you will immediately be struck by the luxurious and noble architectural scheme, which brilliantly exploits the effects of multi-coloured granites, variegated marbles and stucco lustro. Not only was the interior designed to be worthy of the fabulous art treasures amassed by the Habsburgs since the time of Friedrich III (1440–93), but Hasenauer also tried to integrate the designs of showrooms with their contents. (For example, in the Egyptian collection, Luxor columns presented by the Khedive to Franz Joseph are built into the structure.)

RINGSTRAßE
WALK 8

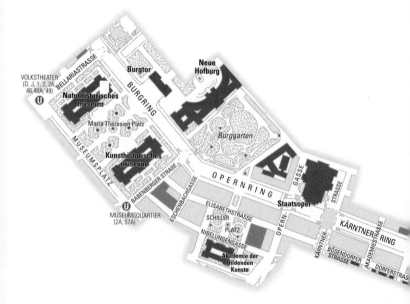

Our tour begins at the picture gallery. To reach this, climb the stairs from the lobby to the first floor. On the landing is Antonio Canova's ***Theseus Fighting the Centaur***, which had originally been commissioned by Napoleon and was for a while in the Theseus Temple in the Volksgarten. The ceiling fresco of the stairwell is by the Hungarian, Mihály von Munkácsy, and represents ***The Apotheosis of the Renaissance***. Other distinguished artists to work on the decoration included

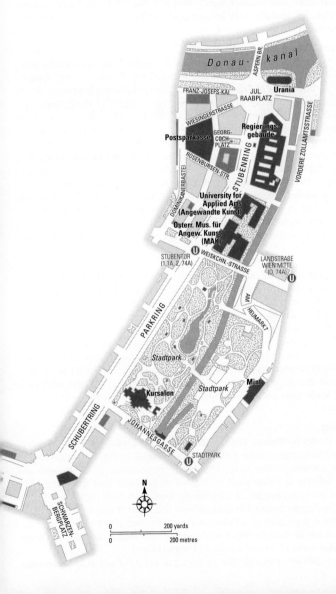

the painter-idol of the Ringstraßen generation, Hans Makart, and the Artists' Company (Gustav and Ernst Klimt and Franz Matsch). Makart painted 12 of the stairway lunettes showing great artists of the past and allegories of artistic genius. The Artists' Company painted the spandrels of the arches, symbolic representations of artistic golden ages. At the top of the stairs, you reach the cupola Hall of Fame, the decoration of which honours the great collectors of the Habsburg dynasty: Maximilian I, Karl V, Rudolf II, Karl VI, Franz Joseph and others are depicted in medallions by Johann Benk, while Rudolf Weyr did the reliefs of artists who served them.

The picture collection

The collection reflects the Habsburg taste for decorative religious painting and a princely interest in portraiture. The items featured are also indicative of dynastic influence in those parts of Europe that were under Habsburg hegemony at one time or another. In practice this means that the strengths of the Italian (especially North Italian) collection and that of the Low Countries are offset by under-representation of some other areas. French and English painting in particular are hardly featured. The actual founder of the collection was Archduke Leopold Wilhelm (1614–62), brother of Ferdinand III and Governor of the Low Countries, whose pictures were transferred to Vienna in 1656. Parts of the once vast Prague collection of Rudolf II were also added and under Joseph II many Flemish and Italian religious paintings were collected from dissolved churches and monasteries. In 1776 the pictures were transferred to the Belvedere Palace, the gallery there opened to the public and the first scientific catalogue made. By the time the Kunsthistorische Museum was opened in 1891, 1734 entries were recorded.

The rooms open off either side of the central stairwell; in the **West Wing** (Rooms I–VIII) are primarily Italian and some Spanish works; in the **East Wing** (Rooms IX–XV) are the German, Flemish and Dutch collections. This description begins in the West Wing, moving clockwise through the larger rooms; on the periphery of these rooms is a continuous corridor, divided into cabinets for smaller works.

Note that I have numbered the cabinets in order of access from the first one, *not* according to the museum's somewhat opaque scheme, and grouped them according to their proximity to each *room*. Unfortunately, the vanity of curators requires that many pictures may be rehung (intelligently or not) with each change of leadership, but the principal contents of the large rooms is not likely to be affected.

West Wing

Room I Works by **Titian**. The Habsburg arms on a soldier's shield in a dramatic *Ecce Homo* executed for a Flemish businessman in Venice remind us that Titian was a court painter to the Habsburgs. In the same room, *Nymph and Shepherd* belongs to Titian's last period, an erotic 'fable' that the aging artist painted for his own pleasure. A glimmering work with hazy background landscape, it is in distinct contrast to the sparkling definition of line and colour in the early *Violante*, a portrait of a Venetian courtesan, but also an idealised representation of female beauty. Other works include the *Danae*, *Diana and Calisto* and a sinister scene of a hired assassin at work (*Bravo*).

Cabinet 1 contains a marble-like rendering of *Saint Sebastian* by **Mantegna**, together with his *David and Goliath* and *Abraham and Isaac*.

In Cabinet 2, Antonello da Messina's *Madonna with Saints* (1476) is one of the first Italian paintings to abandon the traditional tempera for the Franco-Flemish technique of oil painting. This altarpiece for the church of San Cassiano in Venice had a lasting influence on Venetian painting.

In Cabinet 3 is a rare secular work by Giovanni **Bellini** (*Young Woman at her Toilette*), which anticipates the work of **Giorgione** (Cabinet 4). The latter's *Laura* served as a prototype for later courtesan portraits in Venetian art. The most striking Giorgione here is the enigmatic *Three Philosophers*, where the delicately hued landscape assumes the same importance in the picture as the human figures, possibly representing the three ages of man.

Room II is chiefly devoted to **Veronese** and Dosso **Dossi**. Of the former, the Manneristic *Judith with the Head of Holofernes* and *Jesus at the Samarian Well* serve to contrast the painter's earlier stage-like scenes with his later focus on a central character enhanced by stylish chiaroscuro. Dossi's *Jupiter and Mercury* has great charm—the normally terrifying Jupiter sits on a cloud painting butterflies while Mercury, with his finger to his lips, prevents the great man from being disturbed by Virtue. The painting has been interpreted as an allegory of art.

Room III contains works by **Tintoretto**, Paris **Bordone** and Francesco **Bassano**. Tintoretto's *Susanna and the Elders* is one of the major works of Venetian Mannerism, skilfully deploying both exaggeration and distortion, and the play of light and dark, to bring home the sinister tension between virtuous beauty and malign ugliness.

Room IV contains a number of **Peruginos**, an impassioned *Pietà* by **Andrea del Sarto** and **Raphael**'s *Madonna in the Meadow*, the last-named a classic pyramidal composition of figures strongly influenced by Leonardo da Vinci. The smiling Virgin, with the infants Christ and St John, is set against an enchanted green landscape, shading to blue in the distance. Benvenuto **Cellini**'s famous **salt cellar**, made for the king of France around 1540, is currently displayed in this room.

Cabinet 5 is devoted to works of **Palma Vecchio**, while Cabinet 6 contains two interesting paintings by Lorenzo **Lotto**. His *Sacra Conversazione* (*Mary with Child and Saints Catherine and James*) is a lyric rendering of this well-worn theme, in which, however, Mary is not exalted but blended into the warm intimacy of the group. Also unusual is his *Portrait of a Goldsmith in Three Views*, partly a device to substantiate the claims of painting against the three-dimensionality of sculpture.

In Cabinet 7 are two magnificent works by **Correggio**, dealing with subjects from Ovid's *Metamorphoses*. The lushly erotic *Jupiter and Io* depicts the nymph in the cloudy embrace of Jupiter, whose face is just visible emerging from the swirling mists. (Almost certainly this supplied the inspiration for Gustav Klimt's tenderly erotic *Love* (1895), a first version of the celebrated *Kiss*.) The second picture is the *Abduction of Ganymede* and was intended for the same setting (the ducal palace in Mantua).

Cabinet 8 is dominated by **Parmigianino**'s dramatic version of the *Conversion of St Paul*, of which the rearing white horse is the main focus; St Paul lies in the foreground with one arm raised for self-protection as the voice of the Lord rebukes him from the fulminant clouds.

Cabinet 9 contains a powerful *Noli me tangere* by Garofalo. In Cabinet 10 are works by Bernardo Luini and a *Salome* by Cesare del Sesto, while the most striking painting in Cabinet 11 is Giovanni Battista Moroni's 'career portrait' of Alessandro Vittoria, the most distinguished Venetian sculptor in the 16C.

Room V contains Orazio **Gentileschi**'s superb *Rest on the Flight to Egypt*, painted for the Duke of Buckingham in the 1620s (Gentileschi was painter to the English court from 1626). The strongly naturalistic depiction of the nursing mother, settled beside an exhausted Joseph asleep on the travelling pack, reflects the influence of Caravaggio, whose works are also represented in this room. Caravaggio's *David with the Head of Goliath* presents a curiously muted hero, distanced and stylised in a way that drains the brutality from the scene. On the other hand, the psychological cruelty of *Christ Crowned with Thorns* is heightened by the preoccupied look of the tormentors, picked out in a shaft of bright light that illuminates the shoulders and head of Christ.

Cabinet 12 contains the *Holy Family* by **Bronzino**, a masterpiece combining the tactile values of sculpture with compositional sophistication and intimacy. Cabinet 13 is notable for Alessandro Allori's vivid portrait of *Maria de' Medici* and in Cabinet 14 is Jacopo Bassano's strongly Manneristic *Adoration of the Magi*.

Cabinet 15 contains works of the Tintoretto school and Cabinet 16 offers **Spanish paintings** as a prelude to the celebrated **Velázquez Room**. The Infanta Margarita Theresa was promised in marriage to her uncle, the future Emperor Leopold I of the Austrian Habsburg line. Three portraits of her at different ages were sent to the prospective bridegroom; Velázquez painted her first in a pink dress when she was about three years old. At about five years she is depicted in white and at eight years she appears in a huge blue dress expanded with hoops. Equally charming is Velázquez's portrait of the *Infante Philip Prosper*, Margarita Theresa's two-year-old brother, who was to die only two years later, and who is shown in a white smock covered with bells and amulets.

Cabinet 17 contains works by **Guercino** and **Carracci**, while in Cabinet 18 is Salvator Rosa's *Return of Astraea*, a glorious evocation of the Golden Age as imagined in the Georgics of Virgil. In the same cabinet is Pietro da Cortona's *Return of Hagar*, a stylish Baroque work showing Abraham mediating between his wife Sarah and Hagar, who is pregnant with his child. Cabinet 20 contains works by Bernardo Strozzi and others, while in Cabinet 21 may be seen Johann Heinrich Schönfeld's Poussin-like *Gideon Reviewing his Troops*.

Of the works by Francesco **Guardi** in Cabinet 22, the *Miracle of a Dominican Saint* is a powerful and unexpected masterpiece from a painter usually associated with views of Venice (it was painted for the Chapel of St Dominic in a Murano church). Cabinet 23 contains works by Giovanni Pellegrini and Francesco Solimena.

Room VI features important canvases by Guido **Reni**, including a *Baptism of Christ*, where a darkly masculine St John contrasts strongly with a humble, almost effeminate Christ; also a *St Jerome* suffused with glowing colour. Nearby is Francesco **Solimena**'s pathos-filled *Descent from the Cross*.

Room VII, the last room in this wing, is notable for Bernardo **Bellotto**'s exact views of 18C Vienna (*View from the Belvedere, Schönbrunn, Freyung, The Dominican Church*). Note also Pompeo **Battoni**'s double portrait of two enlightened Habsburgs, Emperor Joseph II and his brother, Leopold of Tuscany. A portrait by Battoni was an obligatory part of the programme for 18C aristocrats on the Grand Tour. The importance of the Enlightenment as inspiration for both emperors (Leopold succeeded his brother) is underlined by Montesquieu's *L'Esprit des Lois* unrolled on the table. Nearby is a fine portrait of the composer Gluck by Josèphe-Sifrède Duplessis.

East Wing

The east wing of the picture gallery contains German, Dutch, Flemish and a few English paintings.

Rooms IX and X In Room IX are five of Lucas van Valckenborch's lyric versions of *The Seasons*, rather more idealised representations than the treatment of the same theme by Pieter **Brueghel the Elder** in the following room. Here is perhaps the best collection of Brueghels in Europe, featuring three of the six *Seasons* he painted in 1565: the *Gloomy Day*, the *Return of the Herd*, and *Hunters in the Snow*. These works are the culmination of the calendar landscape tradition that reaches back to antiquity; the cycle starts with March (originally the beginning of the year) and progresses in a continuous frieze through the dominant images of the changing year in the Flemish medieval countryside. A more enigmatic picture is *The Peasant and the Nest Robber*, which may illustrate a forgotten proverb. Brueghel's uncompromising realism is seen in the *Peasant Wedding*, the *Peasant Dance* and the brutal *Massacre of the Innocents*, an oblique reference to the Spanish occupation of the Netherlands. A moralistic early work, *The Tower of Babel*, is inspired by the Coliseum in Rome, seen by Christians as a symbol of pagan hubris and the site of Christian persecution. The impossibility of the tower's construction only becomes apparent on close inspection, the rational details taken from Roman models proving illusory and pointless when applied to an architectonic concept that stems from inflated human pride.

Room XI Jordaens' exuberant burlesque, the *Feast of the Bean King*, owes much to Rubens. It depicts a custom associated with Twelfth Night, when the guest who finds a single bean hidden in the cake is appointed king of the feast and can appoint his courtiers from the company, as well as having his pick of female companions.

Cabinet 1 on this side contains works by Geertgen tot Sint Jans, the *Lamentation of Christ* and the *Legend of the Relics of John the Baptist* (the latter painted to mark the return of St John's bones to the Order of the Knights of St John by the Sultan in 1484). Cabinet 2 has portraits by **Jan van Eyck**, a fine Gothic triptych of the *Crucifixion* by Rogier van der Weyden and portraits of *Philip the Handsome* and *Johanna the Mad* by Juan de Flandes. Cabinet 3 features Joos van Cleve's *Madonna with Child*, a masterly fusion of Netherlands tradition with the sfumato and other technical innovations of the Italian Renaissance; also a portrait of *Catherine of Aragon* by Michiel Sittow.

The most notable painting of Cabinet 4 is a *Baptism of Christ* by Joachim Patenier, where the painter is clearly as much interested in the dramatic depiction of landscape as in the foreground subject. In Cabinet 5 is Jan Gossaert's charming *Saint Luke Painting the Virgin*, where the Madonna is represented as a vision, which the evangelist paints assisted by an angel. In Cabinet 6 is Pieter Coecke van Aelst's *Rest on the Flight to Egypt*, where again the Netherlandish love for landscape almost overwhelms the *sujet*.

Passing the Flemish portraits in Cabinet 7 and Joos de Momper's marvellously atmospheric *Storm at Sea* in Cabinet 8, you reach the remarkable *Adoration of the Trinity* by **Dürer** in Cabinet 9, a representation inspired by St Augustine's conception of the City of God after the Last Judgement. The superb frame is a modern copy of the Renaissance original in Nuremberg.

Adjacent is the **German Renaissance Room**, containing Dürer's famous portrait of *Emperor Maximilian I*. Also here are examples of the Danube School, in particular Albrecht **Altdorfer**'s dramatic renderings of the *Resurrection* and the *Nativity*, which show the influence of medieval mystical and devotional literature. Here also are **Cranach**'s depressing scenes of mass animal slaughter, the excuse for which was a 'stag hunt' organised for the Elector of Saxony. Nearby is the same painter's *Judith with the Head of Holofernes*, where Judith appears, somewhat surprisingly, as an elegant lady of the Saxon court.

In Cabinet 10 may be seen **Holbein**'s ungallant portrait of the very plain *Jane Seymour*, third wife of Henry VIII. Equally striking is Holbein's rendering of Henry's grim-faced physician, *Dr John Chambers*.

Room XII This room is devoted to **Van Dyck** and includes a powerful *Samson and Delilah*, a tender and psychologically profound depiction of the *Vision of the Blessed Hermann Joseph* and several fine portraits (among them *Prince Rupert of the Palatinate* and *Nicholas Lanier*, Master of the King's Music under Charles I of England).

Cabinet 11 features Habsburg portraits, while Cabinet 12 contains works by Rudolf II's court painter, Bartholomäus Spranger, whose interest in obscure allegory and eroticism appealed to the epicurean taste of the Habsburg recluse. Rudolph's penchant for the exotic is here epitomised by the surrealist allegories of Giuseppe **Arcimboldo**, who represents seasons and the elements as busts of humans, the individual features being composed of natural objects such as fruits, or man-made objects such as pistols, candles and flints. Cabinet 13 contains fine Flemish landscapes.

Room XIII and Room XIV These rooms are given over to the museum's important collection of **Rubens**, and demonstrate every phase of the artist's development. Of the earlier works, the *Annunciation*, painted for the Jesuits after Rubens returned home following his eight-year sojourn in Italy, presents an intriguing contrast between the sensuousness of the angel Gabriel and the severe, almost affronted, posture of Mary. The *Lamentation of Christ* is a noteworthy fusion of religious didacticism and strongly felt human emotion, while the *Ildefonso Altar* is a major work of the late period, commissioned by the Habsburg Regent in memory of her late husband. Other masterpieces include a marvellously rich and colourful evocation of nature in destructive mode (*Stormy Landscape with Philemon and Baucis*) and *The Worship of Venus*, whose large acreage of dimpled flesh, signifying unbridled sensuality, is a showcase for Rubens' painterly skills, if also a powerful depressant to male desire. In contrast, the semi-nude portrait of his wife (*The Fur*) is a touching study in feminine vulnerability.

Room XV is devoted to **Rembrandt** and contains a couple of self-portraits, as well as a striking picture of the artist's mother, represented as the Prophetess Hannah. Perhaps the most delightful work here is the portrait of Rembrandt's son, *Titus*, the only one of his children to survive into adulthood. The approximately 15-year-old boy is depicted absorbed in his reading, his delicately expressive features beautifully captured in a moment of unselfconscious intimacy.

Cabinet 14 contains flower pictures and animal studies by Brueghel, while in Cabinet 15 are smaller works by Rubens.

The Corner Room features painting by **Teniers**, in particular his famous showpiece of the *Archduke Leopold Wilhelm in his Gallery at Brussels*. The Archduke (1614–62) was the most important of the Habsburg collectors and acquired many paintings during his governorship of the Spanish Netherlands (1647–56). The fall of the British monarchy enabled him to acquire further works from England. The 51 paintings that appear in Teniers' meticulously accurate picture are all in the Kunsthistorischen Museum.

Cabinet 16 contains 17C Dutch genre pictures, while Cabinet 17 is mostly devoted to works by Franz Hals and Jan van Goyen. In Cabinet 18 are smaller Rembrandts and some attractive landscapes by Jakob van Ruisdael. The evocative *Fishing by Moonlight* (Aert van de Neer) is a refined study of light effects that looks forward to Romanticism.

In Cabinet 19 are works by Wouwerman, while in Cabinet 20 there is an interesting view of the Vienna *Amalienburg*, painted in 1652 by Samuel von Hoogstraten. In Cabinet 21 is an attractive van Ostade (*Stopping by the Inn*), that ingeniously integrates landscape with genre painting; the latter is represented here by Jan Steen's *Beware of Luxury*, a humorous depiction of a feckless and dissolute family reminiscent of Hogarth.

In Cabinet 22 is **Vermeer**'s lovely depiction of the *Artist's Studio*, an allegory of the painter's craft that captures and fixes the iconographical timelessness of an image, while investing it with the warmth and immediacy of human feeling. In the same cabinet, Pieter de Hooch's *Woman and Child with Serving Maid* is compelling in a different way, a paean of praise for bourgeois domesticity and tranquillity in Holland's Golden Age.

The last Cabinet (23) displays the few **English pictures** in the collection—a portrait by Raeburn, an appealing landscape by Gainsborough, portraits by Reynolds and Joseph Wright of Derby.

The **top floor** of the museum (not always open) contains the **Graphik-Kabinett** with some fine works, notably the capriccios by Goya.

Egyptian and Near Eastern Antiquities collection

On the ground floor in the West Wing is the Egyptian and Near Eastern Collection (Rooms I to VIII) and the Collection of Greek and Roman Antiquities (Rooms IX to XVIII).

Room I This description proceeds anti-clockwise, starting with Room I, entered from the lobby. Prominent in the centre of the hall are the bundled papyrus stalk columns dating to c 1410 BC, intriguing examples of prototype building materials subsequently imitated in stone. The columns have been incorporated into the museum structure. Here also are highly decorated mummy-shaped coffins with representations of, and invocations to, Osiris.

Room II to IV Room II contains **pottery** from ancient Nubia and the Yemen area. There are a number of exquisitely sculpted smaller objects in Room III, in particular, a gracefully streamlined mongoose (*Ichneumon*). This useful killer of mice and snakes was associated with the God of Creation. Nearby is the **standing**

falcon, possibly a container for a mummified sacred bird to be buried with its owner. Note also the fine working of a votive offering in the shape of a ram's head, dating from 1150 BC. In Room IV are examples of **Books of the Dead** on papyrus, the scenes and inscriptions of which contain information about the life hereafter.

Room V A striking exhibit here is the great **relief of a snarling lion**, made from glazed brick and originally part of the gate of Babylon (6C BC). Also a gracefully erotic statue of a goddess with elongated legs (possibly a queen in goddess-like pose).

Room VI contains a vivid portrayal of a woman grinding corn, a limestone statuette, possibly for a tomb, the sculpted servant being there to supply the deceased with food in the after-life. In the same room is a model of a **Nile boat** (c 1900 BC), with a married couple sitting under the canopy surrounded by their servants. This too was an object to be placed in a tomb. Most of **Room VIA** is taken up with a richly frescoed tomb chamber, the frescoes showing aspects of the life of the occupant.

Room VII contains the large-scale representation of **Horus and King Horemheb** (end of the 4C BC). A remarkably realistic statuette here shows **King Amenophis III**, ruler of the Egyptian Empire between 1403 BC and 1365 BC. Perhaps the most delightful item in the collection is also to be found in Room VII, namely the diminutive blue-glazed **hippopotamus**, dating from 2000 BC. Also notable is the head of a **sphinx** as Sesostris III (1850 BC), an awe-inducing portrait of a powerful ruler.

Room VIII contains numerous standing or sitting figures that were made as funerary statues. An interesting example is the alabaster figure of a high official (Ba'ef-Ba), who is wearing a sort of kilt. Two husband and wife groups show familial devotion in ritualised form. A tomb relief from Giza features scenes of a funerary repast, bull slaughter and dancing.

Greek and Roman collection

Note Reorganisation of this section of the museum may still be in progress, so the new arrangement may not appear in the order in which it is described here.

Rooms IX and X The collection starts in Room IX with artefacts from Cyprus. A large votive statue of a priest is typical of archaic sculpture of the 6C BC, with almond eyes and thick ringlets of beard. In Room X is the dramatic **Amazonian Sarcophagus** (4C BC), also from Cyprus. A series of vivid scenes depicts the battle between Greek heroes and the mythological female warriors.

Room XI The later **Mithraic relief** (2C AD) here shows a great advance in plasticity; the main scene is of Mithras (God of Light) killing a bull, while his helpers stand on either side, with raised and lowered torches. Another relief in the same room shows a lion hunt, probably one of the standard scenes for sarcophagi that were made in advance of their purchasers' deaths. In the middle of the room is a marble and limestone floor mosaic of *Theseus and the Minotaur*, discovered in a Roman villa near Salzburg. The four pictorial cameos show scenes from the Theseus legend.

Rooms XII and XIII Room XII displays an exotic **mirror stand**, a youth standing on a turtle, with hands supporting horses' necks (now missing); above, a female figure that held the reins. In Room XIII are several more mirrors and an interesting **Etruscan brazier** in the form of a cart with lions at each corner. Also Etruscan is the Minerva figure (missing lance and shield) and the cinerary urn from the 2C BC with a relief of the dragon demon of Death. The Etruscan-style **Harigast helmet** is an intriguing item of bronze headgear in the shape of an Alpine hat. The Germanic name of this one is derived from a dedicatory inscription on the brim, which is one of the earliest (1C BC) surviving references in a Germanic language, although the alphabet used is Etruscan.

Rooms XIV and XV Room XIV contains vases and cups, while in Room XV are a number of busts of Roman emperors. The star item in this room, however, is the famous **Gemma Augustea** (1C AD). In this onyx cameo, Augustus is represented as Jupiter, together with Roma, patroness of the city, to his right. Allegorical figures represent the inhabited earth, rivers of the world and Italia. Also featured are Germanicus and Tiberius. The lower scene shows the erection of a victory monument after the defeat of the Dalmatians. This is one of several rare cameos in the collection. Another is the **Eagle Cameo**, part of the Imperial Treasury that was stolen and taken to Byzantium in the 5C and returned to the West after the sacking of Constantinople by crusaders in 1204. The **Gemma Claudia**, also here, dates from the 1C and shows Emperor Claudius with his fourth wife, Agrippina, together with Germanicus and Agrippina the Elder.

Room XVI and XVII Room XVI is part of a Byzantine ivory **diptych**, showing the Empress (possibly Ariadne, d. 515 AD) receiving homage. In Room XVII is a remarkable monogrammatic bronze cross from the 5C. The Latin form has been transformed into a christogramm by the addition of the Greek 'R' (P) at the top and A (for Alpha) and W (for Omega) on either side, symbolising the Christ of the Revelation.

Finally, in **Room XVIII** are items from the fabulous **Nagyszentmiklós treasure**, probably proto-Bulgarian from the late 9C, and showing a mixture of cultural and symbolic influences from Asia, Byzantium, Greece and Rome. In the same room is the handsome Byzantine silver bucket with reliefs of Mars and Venus, a survival of pagan motifs in an already Christian 7C context.

Sculpture and Decorative Arts (Rooms XIX to XXXVII)
This section is now refurbished and open again.

Room XIX follows the last hall of the Greek and Roman antiquities. In the centre is the **rock crystal pyramid** by Dionysio Miseroni, made in Prague around 1653, a unique example of craftsmanship that was long the *mirabilium* of the court treasury. The same craftsman created the citrine vase in this room, featuring artificial flowers made from precious stones. Of several table decorations, the **rock crystal dragon** (Milan, 1650) is ingenious, a table fountain on wheels, into the tail of which the drink was poured. Round the walls are marble **busts of Habsburgs** living at the turn of the 17C–18C made by the court sculptor, Paul Strudel. The one of Leopold I (who kept the busts in Vienna, although they had been commissioned by his German brother-in-law,) succeeds in making this ugliest member of the dynasty look imposingly regal.

Room XX contains a fine **bust of Marie Antoinette**, portrayed in the year of her marriage, at the age of 15, by Louis XIV's court sculptor, Jean Baptiste Lemoyne. In the same room are a gold Viennese coffee set and a washing set, both made for Maria Theresia and her husband by Anton Matthias Domanek. There are several cases of **figurines**, notable being an ivory *Fury* from the early 17C and (by the same master) a *Hesperide deceiving the Dragon*. Matthias Steinl's ivory equestrian statues of Emperor Leopold and the young Joseph I were probably made for the coronation of the latter as Holy Roman Emperor in 1690. Nearby are some exquisite reliefs done in cedar wood (*Battle of the Amazons*), ivory (*Phaeton Scorching the Earth*) and coloured wax (*Dragon Fight*). A masterpiece of ivory carving is the tankard decorated with hunting and fishing scenes (Vienna? 17C).

Room XXII As you enter the room, you pass Camillo Rusconi's naturalistic bust (c 1719) of the aunt of Pope Clement XI, commissioned by the latter for her tomb. The finest piece in this room is Alessandro **Algardi**'s group for private meditation showing the *Scourging of Christ* (1635–40). It inspired numerous copies and over thirty replicas were made. Of the figurines, Johann Casper **Schenk**'s *Martyrdom of St Sebastian* (1655) and Leonard **Kern**'s *King David* (c 1620–25) are exceptional. The stone relief of **John the Baptist Preaching** by George Schweigger is inspired by Dürer; and there is a striking variant of Bernini's *Ecstasy of St Teresa* by Tommaso Amantini (c 1600–70). The room also contains lockets and medallions, as well as delicate ivory work from Germany.

Room XXIV and XXV contains treasures made for and collected by Emperor Rudolf II (1576–1608), who ruled from Prague. It includes a **narwhal tankard** made by Jan Vermeyen and inset with precious stones; and the same master's curious **bezoar goblet**, made from the hard material that forms into a stone in the stomach of the Asian goat. It was thought to have miraculous properties such as protecting one against poisoning, for example. Vermeyen, who was court jeweller, also made the exquisite **prase bowl**, its lid decorated with a net-like pattern of gold and garnets. Towards the centre of the room is the **portrait bust of Rudolf II** by Adrian de Vries, and *Allegories of the Seasons* by Gregor van der Schardt, the latter originally having been made as supports for a silver fountain, now lost. Notable is the cabinet of pietra dura (or 'Florentine mosaic'), featuring beautiful landscapes by Giovanni Castrucci, which have been made only from variegated stone, utilising its natural colours.

Room XXV contains work either commissioned or collected by Ferdinand II of Tyrol taken from part of his huge *Kunst- und Wunderkammer* (cabinet of art and curiosities) at Schloss Ambras near Innsbruck (see *Blue Guide Austria*). In the middle of the room is an **ebony coin chest** with gilded ivory figures and crystal ornament. Also of interest are the vessels in the form of humorous figures made by Christoph Gandtner between 1580 and 1590, particularly the **Jolly Bottle with Tantalus**, in the form of a glutton punished by having food and drink put just beyond his reach. Note in addition the elaborate **Venetian wax figures** by Francesco Segain, including a portrait of Ferdinand that is the oldest existing portrait in wax. Also of interest is the fine **cabinet** with its twenty-six drawers, in which were kept small curios.

Rooms XXVI and XXVII Room XXVI has a superb set of 16C **Limoges enamelware**; also a striking example of Parisian goldsmiths' work in the form of an ornate ewer of 1570 given to Ferdinand by the French king. Equally fine is the **St Michael Goblet**, so called because it was probably made for the order of that name, a work of gold and precious stones topped by the figure of St Michael slaying a dragon. Room XXVII contains the celebrated **saliera** by Benvenuto **Cellini**. Completed in 1543 it was commissioned by François I of France and is worked in pure gold with partial enamelling. The sea united with the earth is represented by two opposed sitting figures (*Neptune* and the *Earth Goddess*). The composition is completed with animal figures and (on the base) allegories of the *Four Winds, Morning, Noon* and *Midnight*. Nearby is the dignified **bronze of Queen Mary of Hungary** (1555), the highly intelligent younger sister of Emperor Karl V and longtime Governor of the Netherlands, by Leone Leoni. In the same room is a magnificent *Mercury*, made in the late 16C by **Giambologna**, and Leoni's bust of Karl V. Leoni's son, Pompeo, made the astonishingly life-like **portrait bust of Philip II of Spain** (1556), achieving brilliant effects with painted copper and enamel. The combination of scientific curiosity with aesthetic considerations, that was characteristic of the age, may be seen in the terracotta *écorché* by Paludanus, a flayed figure showing the muscular structure with anatomical precision.

Rooms XXVIII and XXIX Room XXVIII contains the huge **Wandelaltar** made around 1540 for the abbey church of Mont Gélliard, and having 156 panels featuring biblical instances and citations in German. Wendel Jamnitzer's **Escritorio** (c 1560), with its drawers showing gilded allegories, is notable and a curiosity is the board for a game similar to *tric trac*, but known as *Der lange Puff*, made by Hans Kels around 1537 and having delicately carved relief pieces, together with reliefs of the Habsburgs on the lids. The realistic beechwood figures by Conrad Meit (*Adam and Eve, Lucretia* etc., 1520) are after Dürer. Room XXIX again features bezoars made into cups and bowls by Gasparo Miseroni. The highlight here, however, is a beautifully delicate **house altar** by Christoforo Gaffuri. It shows *Jesus and the Samaritan Woman at the Well*, the figures and objects being made with precious stones and the whole set against a pietra dura background. It is surely one of the most exquisite things of its kind ever made, and it comes as no suprise to learn that it took ten years of highly skilled craftsmanship to complete it.

Rooms XXX to XXXIII Room XXX has a remarkable gold plaque of the *Scourging of Christ* (1510) by Moderno, which however takes its iconology principally from antiquity. Also of note are the **bust of Bacchus** (1520–25) by Antico, and Tullio Lombardo's reliefs of *Bacchus and Ariadne*, probably made in honour of a Venetian wedding couple. Room XXXI contains huge cabinets crammed with small figurines and statuettes, displayed as Renaissance princes would have displayed them, but somewhat indigestible in this form for the modern viewer. As well as the bronze and ivory cabinets, there is also one of ornate glass crystal. Room XXXII has a fine polychrome terracotta relief designed by Verrocchio and glazed by Andrea della Robbia, which features *Alexander the Great*; another della Robbia relief (but by Luca) shows *Mary with the Infant Jesus*. The same subject is treated by Donatello in a tondo of 1444, and there is also a tabernacle after Donatello, dated to 1460. Perhaps the most lovely item in this room is the marble of a *Laughing Child* (1464) by Desiderio da Settignano. Notable also are the idealised portrait of Petrarch's *Laura* (1488) by Francesco Laurana and the relief portrait of Duke Federigo da Montefeltro. A further arresting work is Antonio Rossellino's large marble relief of the *Madonna and Child*, made in 15C Florence. In Room XXXIII, to the side, are astronomical, geometrical and other instruments of measurement, including an elaborate counting machine made for Karl VI.

Rooms XXXIV and XXXV Room XXXIV has a notable section of a larger ensemble for a winged altar, featuring a *Madonna and Child on a Crescent Moon* by Niklaus Weckmann the Elder, and (on the outer wall) a gilded sculpture of *Christ Sitting in Judgement on the World* (Dutch, 1470). The highlights are the superb **reliquary bust of Saint Cassian** (?) from the late 14C, the **Krumau Madonna** (Prague 1390–1400), a fine example of the late Gothic soft style, and the celebrated portrait of *Emperor Sigismund* made by a Prague master around 1420. There are two highly naturalistic works by Jörg Muskat, a bust of **Emperor Maximilian I**, and another of the **Empress Eleonora**. Room XXXV, to the side, contains table decorations and automatons in the forms of ships etc., some of which could move across the table surface. Perhaps the most ingenious is **Diana and the Centaur** (Augsburg,1605), a combined clock and 'drinking game' automaton, on which the figures moved, the dog barked silently and finally the centaur loosed an arrow from his bow.

Rooms XXXVI and XXXVII Room XXXVI (nearest the entrance lobby) contains Byzantine and Venetian work. Seven portrait busts of prophets line one wall, while sarchophagus lids from the 13C line the other, all Venetian work, the sarcophagi somewhat harshly carved. Byzantine are the **cameos**, to which a case is dedicated, and which were brought to Venice after the plundering of Constantinople by the crusaders in 1204. They feature the Holy Family and assorted saints. The other important object here is the **Wilten Chalice**, a masterpiece of Romanesque goldsmith's work made in Lower Saxony around 1160. Room XXXVII (to the side) is filled with clocks, all of interest, but perhaps especially Jobst Bürgl's **Planetenuhr** (1605), an astronomical clock, and the same craftsman's delicate and brilliantly worked **Crystal Clock** (1622).

Schillerplatz

A short walk along the southern side of the Ringstraße brings you to Schillerplatz, whose focal point is the statue of the poet and dramatist Friedrich Schiller. (Almost opposite, across the Ring, identification with German culture is replicated with a monument by Edmund Hellmer to **Johann Wolfgang von Goethe**.)

Akademie der Bildenden Künste

Beyond the Schiller statue is the Academy of Fine Arts, (Schillerplatz 3). A fine neo-Renaissance building by Theophil Hansen (1876), it was erected on a site originally reserved for the Parliament.

- Open Tues–Sun and holidays 10.00–16.00, except 1 Jan, 1 May, Corpus Christi and the Friday after it, 1–2 Nov, 31 Dec (last entry 15.45). The gallery is on the second floor but a lift in the left wing of the building allows wheelchair access (ask the porter for assistance). U-bahn U1, U2 to Karlsplatz/Oper, Trams 1 and 2 on the Ringstraße.

History

The professors at the Academy have entered history for turning down the 18-year-old Adolf Hitler, who applied to study here in 1907. They complained that his drawing of the human head was incompetent. Thereafter Otto Wagner refused him for the Architectural School because he lacked a high school diploma, although in fact Hitler had some skill in architectural drawing. Another subsequently famous figure then studying at the Academy was the young Egon Schiele; unlike Hitler, he could not wait to escape from the place, which he regarded as stifling and reactionary, and left (or was asked to leave) in 1909.

The strict Historicism of the exterior, reproducing the decorative elements of an Italian palazzo, is continued in the ornate interior. On the ceiling of the basilical hall are frescoes by Anselm Feuerbach (painted between 1875 and 1880) representing the *Fall of the Titans*, *Venus*, *Prometheus Chained to the Rock*, *Gaia* and *Uranus*. Other artists completed Feuerbach's scheme after his death, adding *Eros*, *Oceanus*, *Demeter* and *Prometheus as Founder of Hearth and Home*. The gallery is on the second floor. The star item of the picture collection is the triptych of the *Last Judgement* by Hieronymus Bosch (see below).

The picture collection

This delightful gallery (whose collection has recently been rehung against a green background) covers European art from the 14C to the 20C, although the few modern paintings (mostly gifts from the Academy's professors) are hung in the lateral corridor and seem rather marginalised. (These corridor exhibits are rotated.) Nor is the main collection in any sense comprehensive, but more of a lucky dip, offering several unusual paintings of the second rank and a number of Baroque sketches for more ambitious works. One reason for this is that the original items were acquired to serve as models for the students of the Academy and not selected to reflect a collector's taste. However, this changed in the 19C, when several private bequests considerably fleshed out the collection.

Room 1 Indisputably the most important work in the gallery (and much better lit and displayed than previously) is Bosch's *Last Judgement* (in Room 1, entered to the right of the reception desk). The three wings of the triptych show scenes from the *Garden of Eden* on the left, *Christ Sitting in Judgement over the World* in the centre and *Hell* on the right. The immensely detailed representations of horrors that have overtaken the earth and punishments meted out in hell have their source in medieval visionary writings. The unrelenting emphasis on sin and torment (later an important inspiration for works of existential angst by Expressionist painters and other Modernists) appealed to the gloomy mentality of the Spanish Habsburgs and their coteries of mumbling confessors. Philip II acquired several works by Bosch, and Philip the Fair is thought to have commissioned this particular triptych in 1504. A Habsburg commission is suggested by the saints chosen for the outer panels: St James (supposedly buried at Compostela and the patron saint of Spain) and St Bavo, patron saint of the Netherlands.

Other works in Room 1 include a fragment of a 12C Byzantine fresco of the *Empress Helena* and early wall paintings from a church in South Tyrol (now Italy). Notable are the *Landscape with Christ Carrying the Cross* by Herri met de Bles, with its visionary setting of rugged terrain and wild mountains, and the 16C *Sibyl of Tibur* (the sibyl points out a vision of the Madonna to the Emperor). A thought-provoking work by Lucas Cranach is the subtly erotic representation of *Lucretia contemplating suicide*.

Room 2 On your left, as you enter, is a cabinet containing mostly 15C religious works, including Giovanni di Paolo's *Miracle of St Nicholas*, a sophisticated exploitation of perspective that draws the viewer into the composition. Nearby is an eye-catching *Portrait of a Young Venetian* by Marco Basaiti. Of the larger works in Room 2, the tondo of *Madonna and Child with Angels* from Botticelli's workshop reveals the influence of the master in its lineal clarity, harmonious composition and idealised grace.

The late Titian (*Tarquin and Lucrece*) is striking, the murderous moment here recorded being given menace and urgency by the steeply falling contours of the composition, all following the threatening poise of the dagger. There are two powerful Spanish paintings: the realistic *Boys Playing Dice* by Murillo and the depiction (by Juan Carreno de Miranda) of the *Founding of the Trinitarian Order*, a sketch for an altar painting.

Room 3 is a long gallery containing the bulk of the pictures dating from the 17C–19C. The oil sketches (*modelli*) by **Rubens** (made for his patrons so that they could grasp the plan for the final picture) are encountered first. These include the pathos-ridden *Circumcision of Christ*, mythological subjects and a superb *Apotheosis of James VI and I* intended for the ceiling of the banqueting hall in Whitehall. In this sketch, War is seen being driven off by Minerva, two well-endowed ladies (Concord and Plenty) embrace each other and Mercury looks on approvingly. We move on to a powerful Jordaens (*Paul and Barnabas at Lystra*), a precocious self-portrait by Van Dyck at the age of 14, and Gaspar de Crayer's fine *Portrait of a Lady*.

In contrast to the lush Baroque painting of Catholic Flanders, the next section illustrates the down-to-earth middle-class world of the Protestant Netherlands, together with its taste for genre scenes and landscapes. Notable are Pieter de Hooch's solid-looking *Dutch Family* and the attractive landscapes by Ruisdael, Jan van Goyen (an unexpected seascape) and van Ostade. Protestant Holland was hostile to depiction of sacred themes, so that such religious works as were painted may be ascribed to private patronage by Catholic families. One such is Benjamin Cuyp's arresting *Conversion of St Paul*, which achieves its brilliant effects with adept use of chiaroscuro. Note also the allegorical *Self-Portrait* by Barent Fabritius (brother of the celebrated Carel), where any feeling of absurdity provoked by his shepherd's costume is stilled by the subject's darkly penetrating gaze. In Room 3 also are the works of Dutch painters whose art was influenced by travels in Italy, notably Jan Asselijn's *The Ford* and *Coastal Landscape with Resting Riders*. Some of these painters were inspired by Claude Lorraine, represented here by an untypical early work (*Herd of Sheep in the Campagna*).

In a section devoted to Baroque painters of the 18C is Tiepolo's *Allegory of the Day Dawning*, a sketch for frescoes in a Milan palace. The gallery's notable collection of Guardis consists of eight superb scenes of Venice, of which four were painted over religious pictures that he had difficulty in selling after the taste of the Enlightenment had superseded the traditional demand for devotional images. An important Austrian work from the same period is Martin van Meytens' portrait of *Maria Theresia*, a formal representation of imperial power painted by the contemporary director of the Academy, and one that was much copied. Of Austrian Baroque painters, and painters active in Austria, there are sophisticated *modelli* by Daniel Gran, 'Kremser' Schmidt and Franz Anton Maulbertsch. The last-named submitted the *Allegory of the Destiny of Art* as evidence of his credentials when applying to teach at the Academy.

Room 4 starts with the late 18C and moves on to the 19C, notably Biedermeier works by Ferdinand Georg Waldmüller (the sentimental *Refused Ride*) and Friedrich Amerling (*Self-Portrait*).

In the **corridor** (entered from Room 3) is Carl Moll's delightful Secessionist picture *My Studio*, a *Still-life* by Albert Paris Gütersloh and several superb Romantic landscapes by M. Wutky (*The Sulphur Pit on the Gulf of Baiae*, *Vesuvius Erupting*, *Moonlit Landscape*).

Staatsoper

Leaving the Academy, continue along the Ringstraße anti-clockwise, coming shortly to the **Staatsoper** (**Opera House**). Rebuilt after wartime bombing (although the interior lacks many of the original details), it is still a shrine to operatic genius, attracting musical directors and performers of world rank.

History

The Opera House was built between 1861 and 1869 by Eduard van der Nüll and August von Siccardsburg, their efforts meeting with (now incomprehensible) abuse ('the Königgrätz of architecture', 'looks like an elephant lying down to digest its dinner', etc.). Unfortunately, the Emperor himself (who had personally financed the building) made a very mild criticism of the fact that it looked a little sunken, due to the Ringstraße having been raised by a metre during the construction. His remarks are said to have contributed to the deaths of the ultra-loyal architects (Van der Nüll hanged himself, Siccardsburg died of a heart attack), events which so shocked the Emperor that he thereafter confined his official comments to the formula: 'It was very nice. I liked it very much.' What is not very nice is the recent idea of glassing in the arcade on the façade in winter with a Post-Modern rib-structure totally out of sympathy with the building.

The best known musical director was **Gustav Mahler**, who imposed ruthless discipline on musicians and audience alike during his tenure (1897–1907). These ten years, in which stage design was also revolutionised by the Secession artist, Alfred Roller, constituted a golden age with many historic productions, particularly of **Wagner** and **Mozart**. The Viennese were less enthusiastic about Mahler's own works, with the exception of his songs, and during his lifetime not one of his symphonies was premiered in Vienna, nor did he ever conduct any of them in the city. Moreover, his autocratic ways (banning latecomers and the claque, sacking incompetent musicians) provoked enormous enmity amongst the empowered nonentities of the music establishment, who managed to force him out after years of vitriolic intrigue.

Beyond the Staatsoper are the **Ringstraßen Galerien**, a huge new shopping mall with some good restaurants, and further down on the other side of the Ring, the *Imperial Hotel*. Once the Ringstraßen palais of Prince Württemberg, this has long been the *Staatshotel* for visiting dignitaries, having been converted for hotel use to exploit the World Exhibition of 1873. Richard Wagner ran up debts here; in its lobby Adolf Hitler received the Cardinal Archbishop of Vienna (Theodor Innitzer), who responded with a Nazi salute; and the Russian military administration occupied it between 1945 and 1955.

Joseph Lanner (1801–1843) and the Strauss Dynasty

The origins of the **Wiener Walzer** lie in a folk dance in triple time, possibly of German origin, but known in Upper Austria as a *Ländler*, apparently from the village with which it was associated. As with the inspiration from folk art that informed the work of some Cubists and Expressionists, the waltz (like jazz and folk song later) is a notable example of grass roots music emerging as a major influence on 'high culture' and high society. It gradually (1780–1790) supplanted the courtly minuet, and by the time of the Vienna Congress in 1814, waltzing was already a craze embraced with equal enthusiasm by the royal and aristocratic delegates to the Congress and the burghers of the city. Acceptance of the waltz as a form also suitable for the classical repertoire dates from Carl Maria Weber's very popular *Invitation to the Dance* (1819).

In the same year of 1819, a virtuoso violinist named **Johann Baptist Strauss** joined **Joseph Lanner**'s musical ensemble and a profitable partnership ensued. Both men conducted their own compositions, which enormously refined and expanded the waltz repertoire. Lanner's waltzes (or '*Wiener Ländler*', as he called them) with their gentle Schubertian lyricism, were an ideal complement to the more fiery and energetic style of Strauss.

The ensemble was too small an arena to accommodate the musical egos of two such gifted artists. After their separation, Vienna was divided into Lanner and Strauss factions, but it was Strauss who demonstrated modern managerial talent, building a pool of 200 musicians who could be called upon to play a venue at short notice. Despite Strauss Senior's efforts to steer his son to a less precarious profession, Johann Strauss Junior displayed just as much managerial skill and even greater compositional gifts than his father. His breakthrough came with with an evening performance in October 1844 at the elegant Dommayer Établissement in the upper-class district of Hietzing. The journals and newspapers carried rave reviews and Strauss never looked back, although for many years there was an undignified jockeying for position between the father (who still monopolised the most important music venues) and the increasingly frustrated son. In the Revolution of 1848 father and son were on opposite sides, Strauss Senior supporting the dynasty, the son a bourgeois radical.

After the death of Strauss Senior in 1849, **Johann Strauss Junior** rapidly became the first pop star of the modern age. He gained a following of hysterical women, who wrote him fan letters with requests for locks of his hair (not having enough hair to satisfy the demand, he sent them clippings from his poodle instead). But his music was also admired for its technical brilliance by composers of the stature of Brahms and Mahler. His waltz *An der schönen blauen Donau* has become a musical emblem of Vienna and his operetta *Die Fledermaus* is played all over the world at New Year. A workaholic, he ran several orchestras simultaneously in different establishments, pressing his brothers Josef and Eduard into conductor roles, since the public would accept no Strauss substitutes. Yet the family tensions led to Josef's premature death and an act of dreadful barbarism on the part of Eduard, who survived Johann. As revenge for the way this weakest of characters imagined he had been used, he personally supervised in 1907 the burning of a vast body of still unknown Strauss compositions and arrangements. 'Such an *auto-da-fé*', writes Henry-Louis de La Grange in his account of music in Vienna, 'is unique in the history of music'.

An absurd footnote to the history of the Strauss dynasty was written by the Nazis. Not daring to denigrate the fame of such quintessentially Austrian music with their campaign against 'Jewish' art, they had the entry for Strauss's great-grandfather in the marriage register of St Stephen's for 1762 quietly altered. The old register had referred to this Johann Michael Strauss, an immigrant from Hungary in the mid-18C, as a 'baptised Jew.'

After crossing the mouth of Schwarzenbergplatz you soon pass on your right the delightful **Stadtpark** (laid out 1862–63) with its *Kursalon* (originally a tea-dance venue), one of the few examples of the Munich Rundbogen style in Vienna. The highlight of the park is Edmund Hellmer's gilded **statue of Johann Strauß Junior**, the waltz king. The composer is depicted playing one of his immortal melodies; behind him is an icing sugar aureola of marble, studded with relief figures evidently enraptured by the maestro's playing (some identify these with Danube water-nymphs). It certainly captures in plastic form the Viennese sweet tooth for music.

Other (more restrained) busts in the park honour Bruckner, Schubert and the painter Hans Makart.

Österreichisches Museum für Angewandte Kunst

Just beyond the park is the Austrian Museum of Applied Art, now known as **MAK** (Stubenring 5, open Tues 10.00–midnight, Wed–Sun 10.00–18.00). Founded in 1863 (and inspired by what was then the South Kensington Museum in London), the museum has remarkable collections of furniture, textiles, glass, ceramics and jewellery. It also has a fashionable café-restaurant (recommended) and a specialist book shop.

The collection

Items are rather sparsely displayed in a series of interiors, each of the latter having been conceptualised by a different contemporary artist. The idea is to explore the creative tension between historical role and contemporary perceptions of art, both in the presentation of the objects (highlights of the museum's collections grouped according to materials) and in the ongoing temporary shows which reflect current artistic preoccupations. The new arrangement strikes a cunning balance between impressionistic, relatively small-scale displays for the casual visitor and densely packed study areas for students and specialists of textiles, furniture, ceramics and glass in the basement area.

From the **Romanesque, Gothic and Renaissance** periods there is a fine 16C cabinet, perhaps from Augsburg, with secret compartments and beautiful marquetry showing landscapes. The oldest surviving piece of Austrian furniture is a folding stool (13C) used by the abbots of Admont. From the 13C also are the important Göss vestments from Styria.

The 16C majolica includes hand-painted dishes, plates, ewers and vases, many from Urbino. From the **Baroque, Rococo and Classicism** periods there is a complete 'porcelain room' from the Dubsky Palais in Brno, a superb German cabinet (1776) incorporating a flute-playing music box and two lovely marquetry panels by the same craftsman (David Roentgen). Also some unusual hand-painted Chinese wallpaper.

The **Oriental Display** includes an exquisite silk carpet (early 16C) from Egypt, a prayer carpet from Istanbul or Bursa and a silk hunting carpet from Persia, the last-named so finely knotted that 19C experts declared it to be of velvet. In the space between the oriental items and the study area are items of the **East Asian Collection**, including porcelain, an extraordinarily modern looking wooden sculpture of a unicorn's head dating to the Han Dynasty, an ornate Japanese saddle from the 19C and statuettes from China and Japan.

The **Empire Style and Biedermeier** exhibits on the first floor include some of the Duke of Reichstadt's travelling service commissioned personally by his father (Napoleon) in 1811. Also, some furniture from the famous Danhauser factory in Vienna—most notably a lovely cherrywood sofa with dazzling (reconstructed) crimson upholstery—and a substantial collection of glass and jewellery.

The **Historicism, Art Nouveau (Jugendstil)** and **Art Deco** sections contain some interesting furniture, particularly that of 'bentwood' manufacture made by the Thonet firm in the mid-19C. This astonishingly successful undertaking, which still has a shop in Vienna (now, unfortunately, in foreign ownership) selling luxury items to individual order, was founded in 1849 in a small Viennese workshop. By the 1860s, Thonet was making and delivering affordable furniture (mostly for cafés and hotels) all over the Dual Monarchy. Its style of simplicity, with elegant bowed ribs, eventually came to epitomise the serviceable chair for public use. You can also see a variation on the Thonet chair designed by Adolf Loos for *Café Museum*, and developments of the bentwood idea by the leading light of the Wiener Werkstätte, Josef Hoffmann. Perhaps the most celebrated art nouveau item is the huge, **curved desk** by Van de Velde, a complete office in a single piece of elegant furniture.

The section specifically devoted to **Wiener Werkstätte** is not to be missed, and includes many small functional objects (visiting card cases, wallets, cigarette boxes, etc.), together with a controversially 'primitive' set of cutlery by Hoffmann, a secretaire by Kolo Moser, book covers by Hoffmann and Moser and several original designs for objects.

Lastly, the current director, Peter Noever, has chosen a thought-provoking display of items for the showrooms of **20C Design and Architecture** and **Contemporary Art**. It includes Frank Gehry's (1988) chair made from corrugated board (*Hole in One*).

The **Universität für Angewandte Kunst** (formerly High School) for Applied Art adjoins the museum to the north. It was founded in 1868 but its premises were not built until 1875–77. The architect was Heinrich Ferstel (who also designed the museum), and both buildings are in neo-Renaissance style. Now that the museum has been restored, you can see the detail better, in particular the frieze between the socle and upper storey, which features sgraffiti with majolica medallions depicting celebrated applied artists. A hideous extension to the University was added after World War II, but fortunately this can only be seen from the side and rear.

North of the High School is the **Regierungsgebäude**, an overblown neo-Baroque edifice (1913) by Ludwig Baumann, whose façade is crowned with a bombastic eagle and trophies. It was formerly the Ministry of War for the

Habsburg Empire. In front of it is the equestrian statue of Field Marshal Radetzky, hero of the Italian wars before and during the revolutions of 1848, and generally regarded as Austria's greatest general after Prince Eugene of Savoy. The quotation from Grillparzer ('In your camp is all Austria!') on the front of Caspar von Zumbusch's monument reflects the affection in which the Marshal was held, an affection given mythopoeic expression in Johann Strauss Senior's glorious *Radetzky March*. (Radetzky is also credited with introducing Austrians to the joys of *Wiener Schnitzel*, which is, in origin, a *piccata alla Milanese*.)

The Regierungsgebäude looks across the Ring to the Georg-Coch-Platz and Otto Wagner's famous **Österreichisches Postsparkassenamt** or Austrian Post Office Savings Bank (1904–12). The idea for such a bank came from Coch, an anti-semitic official who wanted to provide an alternative to the large, Jewish-dominated merchant banks of the Liberal era (his model system was partly derived from English practice). Coch's statue in front of the bank has been memorably described by Carl Schorske as 'the first monument to an anti-semitic culture hero on the Ringstraße'.

Wagner's bank is an outstanding example of his much proclaimed concept of 'faith to materials', whereby the functional aspects of an architectural construction are an integral part of its aesthetic. The façade is clad in panels of marble secured by 17,000 highly visible metal pins, while the rusticated walls of the base are faced with granite slabs fixed with countersunk aluminium-headed bolts. The light and airy triple-naved interior is glassed over to supply maximum light and the same approach of functional elegance has been applied to pay counters, desks and even to the revolutionary hot-air vents. Wagner's ingenuity extended to ideas such as under-roof heating to prevent snow accumulating and graffiti-resistant glass panels in the public rooms.

Just to the north, the Ringstraße meets the Danube canal close to where the River Wien flows into it. To the right may be seen some extravagantly Post-Modern architecture on Vordere Zollamtsstraße housing the **Ministry of Transport**. Overlooking the canal is Max Fabiani's **Urania** (1910), shaped like the bridge of a ship and having an observatory at the east end. The Urania is modelled on a Berlin predecessor and is the venue for adult education courses, jazz concerts, art films and the like. It is also used for the annual 'Viennale' film festival. It is a short walk from here along Franz-Josefs-Kai to Schwedenplatz.

9 • Dr.-Karl-Renner-Ring to Börse

The junction at Dr.-Karl-Renner-Ring (U3, Trams 1, 2, 46, 49) to the north of the Natural History Museum (p 137) provides a convenient starting point for a clockwise tour of the western half of the Ringstraße. Hard by the tram terminal you will see the **Monument to the Republic**, consisting of three busts of leading Socialist politicians of the First Republic and 'Red Vienna' (1919–34). Of the three (Ferdinand Hanusch, Viktor Adler and Jakob Reumann), Reumann was especially significant for the capital. In his period as mayor (1919–25), the ambitious programme for social housing began in Vienna, paid for by swingeing taxes on the better off. He also presided over the separation of the capital from Conservative-ruled Lower Austria in 1922. Hanusch was one of the founders of the Austrian welfare state, a remarkable achievement in unpropitious economic circumstances, while Adler was the founder of the Social Democratic Party. The monument was removed by the Dollfuß regime and reinstated only in 1948.

Some way behind it, beyond a small park, is the **Palace of Justice**, a pompous work of late Historicism (1881) on a site originally earmarked for the parliamentary Upper House. The building was set on fire by rioting workers in 1927 after a blatant miscarriage of justice by a conservative judiciary and jury. The Social Democratic leaders lost control of their rank and file, and the police shot indiscriminately into the crowd; the incident thus became a dress rehearsal for the civil war seven years later.

Northwest of the Monument to the Republic, you will see Theophil Hansen's neo-Classical **Parlament** (Parliament) (1883), formerly the Chamber of Deputies for the Austrian half of the Austro-Hungarian Empire. (Tours when the Houses are not in session, Mon–Fri 11.00, 15.00, Dr.-Karl-Renner-Ring 3.) At the foot of the approach ramp are four elevated bronze sculptures of horse-breaking, an optimistically chosen symbol to suggest the calming of the passions, although calmness was latterly conspicuous by its absence. The sitting figures flanking the ramp are the great historians of antiquity. On the roof, triumphal chariots mark the corners of the eight chambers of the interior. The relief on the central tympanum shows the granting of a constitution to the Crown Lands by Franz Joseph in 1861.

The modern Parliament is composed of two houses, the Nationalrat (National Council—183 seats) and the Bundesrat (Federal Council). The former is elected quadrennially by proportional representation; the latter is filled with elected representatives of the nine Federal States.

A massive **Pallas Athene Fountain** (Carl Kundmann, 1902) stands in front of the Parlament, a substitute for the originally planned allegory of Austria, which was abandoned to avoid offending the non-Austrian nationalities of the Empire. However the figures representing the main rivers of the Dual Monarchy are carried over from the earlier plan, as are the flanking allegories of *Legislative* and *Executive Power*. Cynics pointed out that the Goddess, in her wisdom, has turned her back on the debating chamber.

Opposite the Parliament is the **Volksgarten**, laid out by Peter Nobile in 1823. Although it was supposed to be a garden for the '*Volk*', the authorities rejected any idea of an intimate English-style garden then in vogue, since they regarded the cover it would provide as an invitation to 'immorality'. Hence the formal French style. Nobile also erected the **Theseus Temple** (1823) in the middle, which originally housed Antonio Canova's statue of *Theseus Fighting a Centaur* (now on the landing of the Kunsthistorischen Museum's stairway). Ironically, the sculpture had been commissioned by Napoleon, but Franz I decided to adopt it as a symbol of Austria's victory over the French.

There are monuments in the garden to two figures held in great affection by Austrians: that to the **Empress Elisabeth** (1907) is at the Burgtheater end and was erected on popular initiative to commemorate the ill-starred Empress after she was assassinated by an anarchist in 1898. At the other end of the garden is a **monument to Franz Grillparzer** (1791–1872), Austria's greatest dramatist. The reliefs round the base of the sitting figure (by Carl Kundmann) are by Rudolf Weyr and show key scenes from Grillparzer's main works.

North of the Parliament is Friedrich Schmidt's grandiloquent **Rathaus** (City Hall; for information about tours ☎ 52 550-0), a potent symbol of Vienna's new-found civic pride and increasing autonomy in the Liberal era of the 19C.

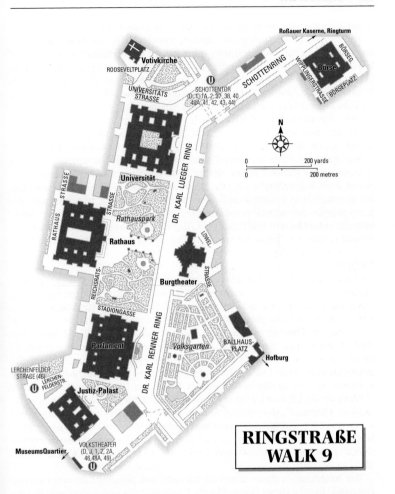

**RINGSTRAßE
WALK 9**

Liberal hegemony in municipal politics lasted from the 1860s to the election of the populist Christian Social mayor, Karl Lueger, in 1897; Lueger's 13-year tenure raised Viennese political consciousness still further. Universal franchise brought the Social Democrats to power, which they have retained in every democratic election up to the present (they were forcibly removed by the clerico-Fascist state and its successor, the Nazi regime).

The models for Schmidt's edifice (completed in 1883) were the town halls of medieval Flemish cities, considered to be emblematic of the self-esteem of a wealthy and successful burgher class. However this model has been inflated to almost megalomaniacal proportions in Schmidt's design. The tower at the front is some 98m high, measured from the tip of the figure placed at the top. This *Rathausmann* (actually a knight) is modelled on the armoured figure of Maximilian I in the weapons collection of the Neue Burg, although the original inspiration for it may have been the medieval 'Roland figures' of many German towns.

The Rathaus is extremely ornate inside, particularly the huge **Festsaal**—a ceremonial hall rising through three storeys, which is embellished with statues of important figures from the Viennese past. In the Magistrature are two paintings by the Baroque artist J.M. Rottmayr, transferred from the Old City Hall (Altes Rathaus) in the Altstadt. There is an impressive Council Chamber with a fresco cycle by Ludwig Mayer depicting scenes of Viennese history.

The main **allée** of the **Rathauspark** is lined with statues of Babenberg and Habsburg rulers, the defenders of the city during the two Turkish sieges and other major figures of the Viennese past, such as Bishop Kollonitsch, Joseph von Sonnenfels and Johann Bernhard Fischer von Erlach. These statues were rescued from the former Elisabeth Bridge over the River Wien, which stood at the southern end of the Kärntner Straße until the Wien was enclosed in 1897. Elsewhere there are monuments to Johann Strauß Senior and Joseph Lanner, who first made the waltz popular (see above). A noteworthy modern addition to all these is Alfred Hrdlicka's **steel bust** of Karl Renner (1870–1950), the Grand Old Man of Austrian Socialism, who was Chancellor in the First Republic and President in the Second.

Burgtheater

Across the Ring from the Rathaus is the richly decorated Burgtheater, another collaboration of Gottfried Semper and Karl von Hasenauer, built to replace the Court Theatre that stood until 1888 on the Michaelerplatz. The crowded façade includes busts of great playwrights and (over the central attic) *Apollo* between the Muses of *Comedy* (Thalia) and *Tragedy* (Melpomene). The frieze below shows the triumphal procession of Dionysius and Ariadne, a reference to the origins of theatre in antiquity. The theatre in history is also the leitmotif of the marvellous decoration of the two lateral stairways inside, carried out by the Company of Artists (the young Gustav Klimt, his brother Ernst, and Franz Matsch). In the left-hand wing are Klimt's *Apollo Altar* and *Thespis Chariot*, an *Antique Theatre* (F. Matsch) and Shakespeare's *Globe Theatre* (G. Klimt). Over the doors of the auditorium, Ernst Klimt painted a *Hanswurst* (the stock figure of Viennese comedy) and Molière's *Le malade imaginaire*. (Tours of the interior of the Burgtheater Mon–Fri, 09.00 and 15.00, Sat 15.00, Sun 11.00 and 15.00, ☎ 51444-4140).

The Burgtheater's cluttered architecture and lush ornament attracted adverse comment, like the Opera House, like the Parliament (bad acoustics), and like the Rathaus (the funereal gloom of many offices); unfortunately Semper did not pay enough attention to the sight-lines from some of the boxes (it was claimed that several actually faced away from the stage!) provoking the famous witticism of the Viennese grumblers: 'In Parliament you can't hear anything, in the Rathaus you can't see anything and in the Burgtheater you can neither see nor hear anything.'

Continuing towards Shottentor on the Ring you pass the fashionable *Café Landtmann*, Sigmund Freud's favourite, and not far beyond it the monument to Andreas von Liebenberg, the Mayor of Vienna who died of the plague during the Turkish siege of 1683. This monument stands opposite the neo-Renaissance **University** by Heinrich Ferstel, which was completed in 1884. It is built around an arcaded courtyard, which serves as an academic hall of fame with busts of distinguished scholars placed along the walls of the loggia; in the central green is a Castalian Spring (by Edmund Hellmer), recalling its namesake on Mount Parnassus, sacred to Apollo and the Muses.

Gustav Klimt and Franz Matsch received commissions for decorating the university aula in 1894. However, Klimt's pessimistic conception of *Philosophy*—and even more his *Medicine* and *Jurisprudence*—so enraged some of the positivist professors when exhibited, that he eventually withdrew them and repaid his fee to the Education Ministry. (Matsch's blandly conformist picture for *Theology, The Triumph of Light over Darkness*, proved more acceptable.)

Votivkirche

Set back from the busy junction of Schottentor is the neo-Gothic Votivkirche.

History

The church was erected as thanksgiving for Franz Joseph's narrow escape from assassination at the hands of a Hungarian tailor in 1853. After the tailor was hanged at Simmering, a cynical rhyme circulated among the populace, who were evidently not so concerned about their emperor's survival as the memorial committee assumed:

> *On Simmering Heath*
> *A tailor's just copped it;*
> *But it serves him right*
> *For stitching so badly ...*

The competition to build the church was won, against 74 competing entries, by the 27-year-old Heinrich Ferstel, who thus embarked in 1856 on the construction of the first Ringstraßen monument; however the enormously high standards of craftsmanship and materials he demanded meant that the church was not completed until 1879. By then its prime mover, Franz Joseph's ill-fated brother, Maximilian who had unwisely accepted an invitation to become Emperor of Mexico, had already been executed (1867). Although Maximilian had headed the committee that raised money for the church, this had not prevented Franz Joseph from forcing him to renounce all his rights in the Austrian succession and even his rights as an Archduke, when he took over a largely hostile Mexico. In the end, Maximilian was deserted by his family, by his Belgian wife who lost her wits, and by the French troops of Napoleon III, who had placed him on the throne in the first place. A celebrated picture by Manet records his fate at the hands of a firing squad, after he had refused an invitation to go into exile.

The Votivkirche's soaring filigree steeples, recalling those of 13C French cathedrals, make it an impressive Viennese landmark, while the generous free space in front of it (Rooseveltplatz) gives it plenty of room in which to exert its grandeur. Yet the rigid adherence to Historicist principles and the grey-white stone of its monumental façade create a rather chilling effect. Moreover, as with the Stephansdom, pollution is making it crumble. About 29 million Euros have been needed for the restoration, now well under way.

The **interior** achieves a more welcoming ambience, being heavily overpainted in subdued but warm colours. Several chapels are dedicated to Austrian regiments, and there is a general orientation to the concept of an Austrian Hall of Fame on the lines of Westminster Abbey; however the choice of figures (for example in the modern stained glass windows) is limited by Catholic orthodoxy. The symbolic role of the Votivkirche was to emphasize the 'unbreakable unity of throne and altar' against revolution, socialism and secularism.

Notable in the interior is the **Renaissance tomb of Count Salm**, defender of Vienna in the first Turkish siege of 1529, which is to be found in the baptismal chapel. A relief of the ambitious young architect by Viktor Tilgner may be seen under the pulpit. Recently efforts have been made to display the church's treasures more effectively and a **museum** has been opened in the U-shaped Kaiser-Oratorium beyond the high altar (open Tues, Thur, Sat, 10.00–12.00). The most important work here is the **Antwerp Altar**, a masterpiece of Flemish Gothic carving, recently transferred from the Diocesan Museum on Stephansplatz. There are also exhibits relating to the founding and building of the Votivkirche.

The last section of the Ring leads down towards the Franz-Josefs-Kai, passing the Hotel de France and the rather appealing post-modern *Hilton-Plaza Hotel* at Schottenring 11, which shows influence of the Vienna Secession. Between the hotels is the site of the Ringtheater, which burned down on the night of 8 December 1881, with the loss of 386 lives. Anton Bruckner lived nearby and observed the catastrophe from his window (indeed he had tickets for that evening's performance, but had not used them). It is said he was so nervous of fire thereafter, he preferred to sit in darkness rather than risk candles or gaslight (the latter having been responsible for the theatre fire). Another person with tickets for the same performance, who also failed to go, was Sigmund Freud. When the Emperor subsequently ordered a 'House of Atonement' to be built on the theatre site, the recently married Freud took an apartment in the block. On the birth of Freud's first child in 1887, an imperial aide arrived on the doorstep with flowers and congratulations from Franz Joseph, to mark the birth of new life where so many had perished.

On the other side of Schottenring is the **Börse** (Stock Exchange, completed 1877), one of Theophil Hansen's most appealingly restrained and elegant buildings. The mellow red brick from the Wienerberg combined with the soft whiteness of stone used for the window cornices, the attic area and arcades, create an effect of grace and dignity. The repeated representation of Poseidon on the two main façades is a reference to world-wide trade on the seven seas. The interior is largely new, following a devastating fire in 1956.

Shortly before the bottom of Schottenring you will see to your left the newly restored **Roßauer Kaserne**, one of three major barracks erected in the wake of the 1848 revolution (although in this case work began only in 1865, when the need for the building had already passed). The pseudo-Renaissance architecture looks more like a creation of Hollywood than an Italian fortress (and has also been described, not with intent to flatter, as 'Windsor Castle style'). The military architects are alleged to have overlooked the necessity for sanitary arrangements, although their defenders say they did provide primitive, wooden 'drop loos' at the corner towers, which unfortunately rotted very quickly.

From here it is a short walk to Franz-Josefs-Kai, passing the modern 23-storeyed **Ringturm** (1955) at Schottenring 30, on top of which is the radio mast of the Austrian weather service. You are now within five minutes' walk of the U-Bahn and tram connections at Schwedenplatz.

Walks beyond the Ringstraße

There are many areas of architectural, historical and cultural interest beyond the Ringstraße and these are covered in the following five walks. Walk 14 is devoted to the palace of **Schönbrunn** to the west—an integrated complex of palace and park. Individual sights near the city borders, which are well worth a visit if time permits are listed (p 196) as are excursions (p 200).

10 • Schwarzenbergplatz to the Belvedere via Karlsplatz, the Secession and Karlskirche

Schwarzenbergplatz

Schwarzenbergplatz (trams 1 and 2 on the Ringstraße and a short walk from the Karlsplatz exit of U1, U2 and U4) is dominated by the equestrian statue (Ernst Hähnel, 1867) of Karl Philipp, Fürst zu Schwarzenberg, described on the plinth as 'the victorious leader of the allied armies against Napoleon in 1813 and 1814'. The unveiling was delayed because of the Austrian defeat at Sadowa (1866).

At no. 1 is the neo-Renaissance **palace** (1866) built by Heinrich Ferstel for Franz Joseph's youngest brother, the Archduke Ludwig Viktor. The latter (known as 'Bubi' and 'Luzivuzi') was notoriously dissolute; the Emperor eventually banned him to Salzburg after a fracas following his attempted seduction of a young man in the public baths. The palace passed to the military and is still partly an officers' club, another part being a rehearsal stage for the Burgtheater, where performances are also given. The industrialist Franz Wertheim (described by Mayor Cajetan Felder as a 'pastmaster of self-advertisement and charlatanism') had Ferstel build him a palace (no. 17) opposite that of Ludwig Victor. Another financial and railway baron, Viktor Ofenheim von Ponteuxin, commissioned the subsequently much altered palace at no. 15, these two being typical examples of the grandiose historicising taste of the *nouveaux riches* of the Ringstrassen era.

Other interesting Historicist buildings on the square include the **Viennese Chamber of Commerce** (no. 7), which combines neo-Baroque and Jugendstil elements, and the **House of Industry** at no. 4 opposite. At the end of the war, the Allied Control Commission for Austria occupied this building and it was here that details of the 1955 State Treaty were later thrashed out.

Turn left at the southern end of Schwarzenbergplatz for the **Akademie Theater** (Lisztstraße 1), completed 1914, which shares a building with the High School for Music and the Performing Arts; just beyond it is the **Konzerthaus** (Lothringerstraße 20), built (1912) by Helmer and Fellner in eclectic style. The inscriptions on the façade are a quotation from *Die Meistersinger von Nürnberg* (but borrowed from Goethe): 'Honour your German masters, for thus will you conjure the benevolent spirits.'

Returning west across the mouth of Schwarzenbergplatz, you soon come to Theophil Hansen's opulent **Musikvereinsgebäude** (Bösendorferstraße 2) (1869), whose main concert hall represents the high point of Historicist decoration. Its side galleries are supported by gilded caryatids and the coffered ceil-

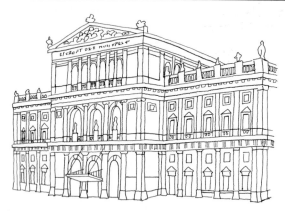

Das Musikvereinsgebäude (1869) designed by Theophil Hansen

ing is richly ornamented with painted panels of *Apollo and the Nine Muses* (by August Eisenmenger) in elaborate gilt frames. The suspended ceiling, structurally divided walls and hollow spaces beneath the floor are responsible for the hall's near-perfect acoustics. The New Year's Concerts of the celebrated Wiener Philharmoniker (founded by Otto Nicolai in 1842), whose base it is, are broadcast live all over the world from here. The orchestra's Sunday morning concerts of Viennese classics are traditionally packed out (mostly by season ticket holders). In the same building are the musical archives and library of the Society of the Friends of Music, founded in 1812 to promote musical performance in the city—an early example of independent middle class (as opposed to aristocratic or state) initiative.

Just beyond the Musikverein at Karlsplatz 5 is the **Künstlerhaus** (1868) by August Weber, similarly built in a lush neo-Renaissance style but without Hansen's flair. On the outside walls are life-size statues of Raphael, Michelangelo, Leonardo da Vinci, Titian, Dürer, Rubens, Bramante and Velázquez, by various hands. It was against the academic painters who commissioned the building (the Viennese Society of Fine Artists, founded 1861), and who held their establishment-oriented triennial 'State Exhibitions' here, that the Secession (see below) rebelled some 30 years later.

Further west is Ferdinand Fellner's Romantic **Academy of Trade and Commerce** (1862) with Josef Cesar's statues of Christopher Columbus and Adam Smith flanking the main entrance. A passage leads from the Künstlerhaus under a busy thoroughfare to Otto Wagner's **Stadtbahn Pavilions** on the edge of Karlsplatz. The 1890–92 plan for the city's expansion envisaged the building of a rapid transit railway from the suburbs to the centre and Otto Wagner was commissioned to design the stations and bridges. He produced a series of delightful, decorative structures which have become Viennese landmarks. In some cases other Secessionist architects assisted in the design process: Joseph Maria Olbrich worked on the imperial station or 'Kaiser Pavilion' at Schönbrunn, which was reserved exclusively for the imperial family (although Franz Joseph himself used it on precisely two occasions); Max Fabiani worked on the Karlsplatz pavilions with Wagner. They now function as a gallery and café.

BEYOND RINGSTRAßE WALK 10

Secession Building

If you walk west, crossing the Rechte Wienzeile and leaving the monument to the great 19C actor, Alexander Girardi, on your right, you will see ahead of you the newly restored **Secession** (Friedrichstraße 12). Joseph Maria Olbrich designed this pioneering exhibition hall (incorporating novelties such as movable partitions for more flexible hanging), which was substantially financed by Karl Wittgenstein (father of the philosopher, Ludwig). It was here that the artists who 'seceded' from the Society of Viennese Fine Artists (see above) in 1897, put on shows of their own work and exhibited avant-garde works from abroad. Prominent among the Secessionists were Gustav Klimt (their leader), Carl Moll and Kolo Moser. They received enthusiastic support, also, from the Academy's Professor of Architecture, Otto Wagner.

The building consists of three stereometric masses balanced round a receding tomb-like entrance, the whole being crowned with a globe of gilded laurel leaves (irreverently called the 'Golden Cabbage' by the Viennese, who also denigrated the ensemble as the Mahdi's Tomb). The controlling architectural metaphor is that of the Grove of Art, hence also the laurel leaf motifs on the walls. The similarly gilded inscription on the façade (meaning: 'To the age its art, to art its freedom') was devised by the critic Ludwig Hevesi, propagandist for, and chroni-

Secession Building (1897–98), designed by Joseph Maria Olbrich

cler of, the Secession. On the left-hand panel of the façade are the words *Ver Sacrum* (Sacred Spring), which was also the name of the important journal published by the artists and exemplifying their aesthetic approach.

On permanent display inside is Klimt's celebrated **Beethoven Frieze**, a complex allegorical work made for the Secession's homage to Beethoven (1902), of which the centrepiece was a monumental statue of the composer by the Leipzig artist, Max Klinger. The three parts of the frieze form a developmental sequence: first comes the *Longing for Happiness*; then the *Hostile Powers*; finally the *Kingdom of the Ideal* achieved through art. The work is regarded as a visual realisation of the choral movement of Beethoven's Ninth Symphony, and indeed Klimt selected two quotations from Schiller's *Ode to Joy* as mottoes for the final panel ('Joy, thou spark from Heav'n immortal...' and '...With one kiss for all the world').

Just to the north of the building is Arthur Strasser's **bronze** representing Mark Antony standing in a chariot drawn by panthers. Aesthetically speaking it is unrelated to the Secession and was placed 'provisionally' in this rather unsuitable location after being exhibited at the Paris World Exhibition of 1900.

Retracing your steps to the east across the Resselpark, you will see to your right the hideous modern building of the Technical University, across the road from Theophil Hansen's **Lutheran School** (1862) at Karlsplatz 14. Next to this is the old Technische Universität (Karlsplatz 13), founded (1816) under Franz I. Two Austrian inventors are honoured with statues in the Resselpark: Joseph Madersperger (1768–1850), a Tyrolean who invented the sewing machine, and Josef Ressel (1793–1857), the first person to develop a workable version of the ship's screw (1827). Ressel's life-story makes depressing reading: he was intrigued against by an Englishman named Morgan, who saw his monopoly of the steamer route between Trieste and Venice threatened. Ressel then unwisely showed his designs to a Parisian firm, which stole them and later seems to have sold them to the British. Insult was added to injury when, in 1850, the Admiralty in London announced a prize for anyone who could show that his design had originated the screw. Ressel's submission was ignored and he later learned that the prize had been distributed amongst the very people in England who had appropriated his invention.

Gustav Klimt (1862–1918)

There has been a steady rise of Gustav Klimt's work to European, and then world, prominence since World War II. The rise dovetails with the discovery of 'Vienna in 1900' as an apocalypse of artistic and intellectual brilliance; according to your point of view, the last effervescence of a dying empire or the glittering avatar of nascent Modernism (perhaps it was both). Klimt's decorative, flat and Symbolist painting departed from the Academicism in which he had been trained, and Klimt himself headed the '**Secession**', a group of nineteen artists that broke away from the Künstlerhaus in 1897. The Secession revolutionised the Vienna art scene.

Klimt excelled even in the artistic tradition he had abandoned—for example, his famous painting of the audience at the Burgtheater is a masterpiece of academic realism. His new style, however, with its overt pessimism and taboo-breaking approach to the secrets of mankind's most intimate lusts and anxieties, outraged many who could not understand any work divorced from their notions of what constituted beauty in art. His bleak faculty studies for the university aula, which depicted *Philosophy* and *Medicine* in a powerfully alienated and non-positivist manner, so outraged the conservatives in the university establishment that he withdrew the paintings and returned the commission payment he had received from the government. These remarkable paintings were lost in the war.

Klimt is better known to the public today for his brilliant portraits of Viennese society women that hang in the Austrian Gallery in the Belvedere (p 177); these richly allusive paintings complement the exercises in pure Symbolism, such as *The Kiss*, and the glowing exotic sensualism of his gold backgrounds influenced by the Byzantine art he had seen in Ravenna. Finally his landscapes, particularly the scenes painted around the Upper Austrian Attersee, are among the most decoratively lyrical evocations of the Austrian countryside ever painted. Only his frieze in the Secession building, created as part of the Secession's homage to Beethoven and celebrating the composer's Ninth Symphony, is generally accounted an ambitious, if tantalising failure.

Klimt is rightly regarded as the mediating link between the fine craftsmanship of academic Historicism and the bleakly erotic, psychologically uninhibited and spiritually oriented Expressionism of Schiele (p 178) and his Austrian peers. Yet his decorative, Secessionist style of flatness and ornament is also a uniquely individual interpretation of the Viennese *Zeitgeist* at the turn of the 19th century.

Karlskirche

As you continue east, a vista opens up of the lovely Karlskirche fronted by Henry Moore's sculpture, *Hill Arches* (1978), the latter set in a shallow pool whose water reflects the noble contours of Fischer von Erlach's great building.

History

The Karlskirche was the most magnificent church built under Karl VI and is one of Europe's finest and most idiosyncratic examples of Baroque architecture. The impetus for building it came from the Emperor himself and its name happily combines the memory of the founder with that of St Carlo Borromeo, to whom it was dedicated. St Carlo was particularly associated with plague relief after his activities in the Milan epidemic of 1576, and it was during the last onslaught of the disease in Vienna in 1713, which claimed some 8000 lives, that the Emperor vowed to dedicate a new church when the scourge receded. Money was raised from all over the Habsburg lands to build it, the intention being to create a symbolic focus for Vienna as the 'new Rome', the seat of the Holy Roman Emperor. Johann Bernhard Fischer von Erlach worked on the project from 1716 to his death in 1723; thereafter construction was in the hands of his son, Joseph Emanuel, until completion in 1739.

The **façade** exhibits a perfect balance of antique elements with swirling Baroque forms, a synthesis of classical regularity with sensuous decoration. Its two Trajanesque columns emphasise the vertical axes of an elongated façade closed at each end with bulky clock-towers. The classical portico is surmounted by an oval cupola with a lantern. The drum of the cupola is girdled by a richly ornamented attic consisting of oval windows interspersed with gesticulating figures of angels. The church is most striking at night, when light gleaming from the windows makes the green copper dome seem almost transparent, floating like a bubble in the velvet darkness.

The extraordinary **columns** are the boldest strokes of Fischer von Erlach's great plan. They recall triumphal monuments in Rome dedicated to Marcus Aurelius and (specifically) Trajan, both of whom played a role in the earliest history of Vienna. They bear in addition a heavy weight of symbolism which had been elaborately worked out for the whole building by the philosopher Leibniz and the court historian, Carl Gustav Heraeus. Thus they were not only plague columns, in the tradition of similar such memorials, but also enduring mementoes of Karl VI's thwarted claim to Spain, the Pillars of Hercules at the western end of the Mediterranean. Even more abstractly, they recall that the Emperor's motto—*constantia et fortitudine* (steadfastness and fortitude, the one a spiritual, the other a military virtue)—indicated that imperial grace rested on two fundamental pillars of human worth.

Lastly, in combination with the façade, the columns were supposed to recall for learned visitors the two huge bronze pillars that stood before the Temple of Solomon in Jerusalem. These were called Jachin (representing Permanence) and Boaz (representing Strength), and thus dovetailed with the allusion to the imperial motto. The reliefs of the columns were originally planned as a glorious pictorial parade of the deeds of Charlemagne and Count Charles the Good of Flanders (ruled 1119–28), seen as forerunners of Karl VI in the Empire as a whole, and in the Netherlands in particular. However, at some point *sacerdotium* seems to have prevailed over *imperium* and it was decided to represent the life and works of St Carlo Borromeo. On the plinths atop the columns crouch suitably grim-looking eagles and on the lanterns above them a crown, the two symbols of Habsburg rule.

The sculptured tympanum over the noble hexastyle portico depicts an angel withdrawing his sword from the city, an image of Vienna's deliverance from the plague. Above it are sculptures of the apotheosis of St Carlo Borromeo and allegorical figures by Lorenzo Mattielli: a snake standing for Penitence, a pelican for Mercy, a cock for Prayerfulness and a unicorn for Religion. On either side of the ceremonial stairway are colossal statues of angels representing respectively the Old and New Testaments.

The massive oval **interior** of the church gives an impression of sublimity and unified space, enhanced by Gaetano Fanti's illusionist architectural effects and the prevailing colour scheme of reddish brown, gold and white. Seemingly very distant in the high cupola is Johann Michael Rottmayr's fresco, which shows *Our Lady lending her support to Carlo Borromeo's Intercession with the Almighty*. Rottmayr also painted the cycle of frescoes round the side walls, *St Cecilia* over the organ, in the left-hand chapel *Trust*, in the right-hand

Karlskirche (1716–39), designed by the Fischer von Erlach, father and son

one *Submission to the Will of God* and on the arch of the choir the *Invocation of God*. There are other fine works by Daniel Gran: *Christ and the Centurion, Saint Elisabeth ministering to the Poor* and Sebastiano Ricci's *Ascension of the Virgin*.

Historisches Museum der Stadt Wien

To the north of the Karlskirche is the **Historical Museum of Vienna** (open Tues–Sun 09.00–18.00. Guided Tours, Sat 15.00, Sun and Hols 10.00 and 15.00), an ugly 1950s building which is fortunately so placed that it does not interfere with the sightlines of the church. It was designed by Oswald Haerdtl, a pupil of Josef Hoffmann. The collection is of great interest, documenting the urban growth and the cultural and historical aspects of the city since pre-Roman times. There is also a rolling programme of temporary exhibitions.

Ground floor This covers the period from the Hallstatt culture (9C–5C BC) up to the Renaissance. There are archaeological remains, inscriptions, sandstone statues and a section devoted to armour.

First floor The highlights of the first floor include Augustin Hirschvogel's circular **plan of Vienna** in 1548 and Eduard Fischer's fascinating maquette of the city in the 1850s. A number of artefacts and pictures relate to the Turkish siege of 1683 (including a portrait of the ill-fated Turkish commander, *Kara Mustafa*). There are important pictures from the period of enlightened absolutism, including Meytens' portrait of *Maria Theresia* and Josef Hickel's portrait of *Joseph II*. The **Viennese Baroque** tradition is further represented by works of Franz Anton Maulbertsch, Paul Troger and J.M. Rottmayr, all of whom left their mark on the city's churches and palaces. Note also the anonymous painting of a freemasons' lodge in Vienna, showing both Mozart and Schikaneder among the initiates.

Second floor The second floor contains works from the **Biedermeier period** to the present. Paintings and other materials relate to the Napoleonic War and the Congress of Vienna. There are several pictures by leading Biedermeier artists, such as Peter Fendi, Friedrich Amerling and Georg Ferdinand Waldmüller. Particularly interesting are the reconstructions of the playwright Franz Grillparzer's apartment in the Spiegelgasse and the reception room in neo-Classical style (1800) of the **Palais-Caprera** in the Wallnerstraße. The finest topographical views of Vienna ever painted (surpassing even Bellotto) were produced by the Alt dynasty, several of whose works are on show.

There are also paintings and artefacts of the **Secession** and **pre-Secession** academicism, as well as pictures by the Austrian **Expressionists** (Gerstl, Schönberg, Schiele). Gustav Klimt's famous academic portrait of high society in the Burgtheater is an interesting example of his pre-Secession brilliance; but he is also represented by major Secessionist works (*Portrait of Emilie Flöge, Pallas Athene, Love*—these are frequently out on loan however). Emanuel Pendl's 1898 model of the Inner City provides an intriguing comparison to Fischer's maquette on the floor below. Finally, the reconstruction of Adolf Loos's open-plan sitting room, with a strong English arts and crafts accent, gives a unique insight into the concept of modern living promoted by this moderniser and functionalist.

A walk down Technikerstraße beyond the museum brings you to the **French Embassy** at the southern end of Schwarzenbergplatz (Technikerstraße 2). The elegant art nouveau building (1909) is by Georges Paul Chédanne. The large gold reliefs at each end of the façade symbolise Austria and France. If you now cross the busy traffic junction southwards, you will reach the mighty **Hochstrahlbrunnen** (High Fountain) built in 1873 to mark the inauguration of Vienna's first mains water supply. Its builder (Anton Gabrielli, a London entrepreneur) was an horometry buff, hence the 365 mini-jets set around the fountain's basin to represent the days of the year. The six jets between the edge and the inner island, together with the island itself, are the six weekdays and Sunday, the twelve high jets are the twelve months, and the 30 island jets the days in the month. At night the fountain is brilliantly illuminated with background colour.

Behind the Hochstrahlbrunnen is the **Russian Freedom Monument** erected in 1945 to mark the 'liberation' of Vienna by Russian troops and in honour of the Red Army's fallen soldiers. On a plinth in front of a balustrade ornamented with groups of fighting comrades, a Russian soldier strides forward, flag in hand. The Viennese saw a rather less heroic side of the Red Army than that celebrated here and christened the striding figure 'The Unknown Rapist' (or 'The Unknown Plunderer'). More affectionately, they also referred to him as the '*Erbsenpepi*', *Pepi* being Viennese dialect for Joseph (as in Joseph Stalin), and *Erbsen* (pea) being an allusion to the rations of dried peas dispensed by the Russians to civilians. Since 1989 there has been some discussion about dismantling the monument, Austria having been obliged to maintain it under a bilateral treaty with the Soviet Union, an entity that no longer exists. However most people feel it is a part of Viennese history and it looks as if it will stay.

Behind the Russian monument is the **Schwarzenberg-Palais**, built in the 1720s for the Chief Equerry to Emperor Karl VI, Fürst Adam Franz Schwarzenberg. It was designed by Johann Bernhard Fischer von Erlach; with his son, Joseph Emanuel, he revised and completed a plan for the previous owner that had been drawn up by Lukas von Hildebrandt. Sadly, Fürst Schwarzenberg was already dead when his palace was completed, accidentally killed by a shot from the Emperor's gun while out hunting.

The ancillary buildings of the palace, which is still owned by a Schwarzenberg, are now a luxury hotel, the gourmet restaurant of which overlooks the terraced park. The younger Fischer von Erlach was proud to have erected in the garden the city's first steam-driven pump, which was used for circulating water to the fountains. A great deal of the Baroque fittings of the palace and garden were damaged or destroyed by allied bombing during the war. (The current owner once thanked the Queen of England at a reception for 'bombing my palace into a profitable hotel'.)

If you take the **Rennweg**, the road to the east of the Russian monument, you will shortly pass the **Gardekirche**, which has been the Polish National Church in Vienna since 1898, and before that belonged to the Imperial Polish Bodyguard. It began as the Imperial Hospital Church, built to a design by the architect of Schönbrunn, Nikolaus Pacassi, but altered in 1769 by Peter Mollner. The oval interior with gilded stucco is pleasing. The Polish pope, John Paul II, dedicated a new organ on his visit to Vienna in 1983.

You continue up the Rennweg, which is so-called from the races (dubbed *Scharlachrennen* after the prize of scarlet cloth for the winners) instituted by Duke Albrecht III in 1382. The nobles and knights had their horse races, but the entertainment most keenly awaited by the populace was the closing gallop of the 'public prostitutes'. In the streets to the east of the Rennweg, you will see numerous embassies and diplomatic missions, eloquent embodiments of tax-payers' generosity to their foreign representatives. At no. 27 is the palace occupied by Prince Metternich after his exile in England. From its windows he claimed he could see the Balkans, which he memorably described as beginning at the Landstraße, just to the east.

If you walk down Jaurésgasse, you will see in the grounds of the Russian Embassy, at no. 2, the **Russian Orthodox Church** (1899), designed to evoke the great orthodox cathedrals of the 16C and 17C.

Continuing to Rennweg 6A, you arrive at the gates of the Unteren Belvedere (Lower Belvedere; see below), and just beyond them, the **Salesianerinnen-Kirche** (Rennweg 10), built for the convent of the Salesian Order that was called to Vienna by the widow of Josef I (1678–1711), Empress Amalia. A school for daughters of the aristocracy was attached to the convent, and its graduates had the right to reside there as widows in the evening of their days, as did the Empress herself. The buildings were designed by Donato Felice d'Allio (who had made the plans for Klosterneuburg for Karl VI; p 202), and Joseph Emanuel Fischer von Erlach, who worked on the façade.

It is often difficult to gain access to the church, but its interior is impressive. The fresco in the cupola represents the *Ascension of Mary* (Giovanni Pellegrini, 1727) and the high altar is by Antonio Beduzzi (1726). Antonio Bellucci painted the altarpiece (*The Visitation*), while the side walls of the choir were painted by Jacob van Schuppen (the *Annunciation* and the *Adoration of the Shepherds*).

The Belvedere

Return to Rennweg no. 6A, and enter the gardens belonging to the greatest example of profane Baroque architecture in Vienna, indeed in Central Europe. The complex is divided into the Lower Belvedere (Unteres Belvedere), which now contains the **Austrian Baroque Museum**, the Orangery which houses the **Museum of Austrian Medieval Art**, and the Upper Belvedere (Oberes Belvedere), Prince Eugene of Savoy's palace, now containing the **Österreichische Galerie** and Austria's most important collection of 19C and 20C Austrian paintings.

History

Prince Eugene of Savoy was the most successful campaigner and general the imperial armies ever had, distinguishing himself in a subordinate rank when the Turkish siege of Vienna was lifted in 1683, and going on to liberate Hungary and the Balkans as far as Belgrade. In the War of the Spanish Succession (provoked by the extinction of the Spanish Habsburg line in 1700), he joined forces with the Duke of Marlborough and won several great victories over the French in the Low Countries, where he was subsequently Governor from 1716. Because of budget constraints imposed by war, it was not until the end of the 17C that he received his full rewards from a grateful emperor. He acquired the site for his great summer palace in 1697, but was only able to begin construction in 1714 (employing in the process 1300 Viennese desperate for work, many of them army veterans). His now enormous wealth enabled him to have the Lower Belvedere (Unteres Belvedere) built in only two years (1714–16), and the huge Upper Belvedere (Oberes Belvedere) with astonishing speed in a single year (1721–22). The architect for both was Lukas von Hildebrandt, whose association with the Prince went back to his role as military engineer in Eugene's early campaigns.

• **Opening times** The three Belvedere museums are open Nov–Mar Tues–Sun 09.00–17.00, Apr–Oct, Tue–Sun 10.00–18.00.
Austrian Baroque Museum (Lower Belvedere)
Museum of Austrian Medieval Art (Orangery)
Österreichische Galerie (Upper Belvedere)

Lower Belvedere and Baroque Museum

The Lower Belvedere (Rennweg 6A) was both living quarters and an administrative centre for Prince Eugene's burgeoning estates, although its representational and aesthetic features somewhat overwhelm its ostensible domestic functions. Its most spectacular room is the central **marble hall**, with a fresco by Martino Altomonte showing the *Apotheosis of Prince Eugene after the Battle of Peterwardein*; the prince is here identified with the sun-god Apollo, banishing the shades of night and protecting the muses.

The building, home to the Austrian Baroque Museum, includes a number of fine bronze and marble **reliefs** (Room 10) by the leading sculptor of the age, Georg Raphael Donner (1693–1741), as well as (in the Marble Hall) the latter's original lead figures for the Providentia Fountain on the Neuen Markt (p 122).

To the west of the hall was **Prince Eugene's state bedroom**, appropriately decorated with Altomonte's lunettes of *Apollo and Clytie* and *Luna and Endymion*. The choice of themes develops the hall's imagery of day and night, at the same time drawing attention to the adoration of earth-bound beings by celes-

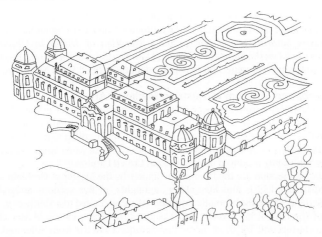

Schloß Belvedere

tial godheads: the moon embraces the sleeping shepherd (*Endymion*) nightly, while the ocean nymph (*Clytie*), metamorphosed into a sunflower, turns through the sun's course, following her erstwhile lover's progression from dawn to dusk. As in the hall, the *trompe l'oeil* architecture of the bedroom is by the Bolognese artists, Marcantonio Chiarini and Gaetano Fanti.

The Hall of Grotesques at the southwest corner is devoted to extraordinary busts with extravagantly grimacing faces by Franz Xaver Messerschmidt. These surreal physiognomies are a far cry from idealised Baroque representation. The impulse for Messerschmidt's work, produced around 1770, came from the then fashionable 'science' of physiognomy, vigorously promoted by its founder, a Swiss clergyman named Johann Caspar Lavater. He claimed that a study of the facial traits of humans offered reliable insights into their characters, a doctrine so seductive that, according to a contemporary English journal, 'a servant would ... scarcely be hired till the descriptions and engravings of Lavater had been consulted'. (In reality, Lavater's descriptions were often *post hoc* applications of physiognomic theory to what was already known about historical figures from other sources.)

Next comes the mirrored **Marble Gallery** in the west wing, in which the Prince's collection of antiquities (the so-called *Herkulanerinnen*—the statues were all female) was housed. The mythological figures in the wall niches are by Domenico Parodi. The over-life-size statues of Franz Stephan of Lorraine and his wife, Maria Theresia (represented as Queen of Hungary—legally, she was never Empress) are earlier and more conventional works by Messerschmidt.

The last room is the **cabinet doré**, along the walls of which are huge mirrors with gilded Baroque frames. It contains Balthasar Permoser's ***Apotheosis of Prince Eugene*** (1721), an ambitious sculpture that greatly displeased its commissioner. This may have been because Permoser (who pocketed 2400 Taler for the work) did not trouble himself to travel to Vienna from his home in Dresden and created his (albeit idealised) representation from existing portraits.

The Lower Belvedere's individual rooms are also devoted to displays of the leading painters of the Austrian Baroque, including Johann Michael Rottmayr

(Room 4), Paul Troger and Daniel Gran (Rooms 5, 19, 20), 'Kremser' Schmidt (Room 5), and Franz Anton Maulbertsch (Rooms 5 and 18). Highlights include Rottmayr's *Lamentation of Abel*, Gran's *Reception of Diana in Olympus*, Troger's *Christ on the Mount of Olives* and Maulbertsch's *Self-Portrait*, together with his striking representation of a figure doubtfully titled *Saint Narcissus*.

Orangery and Museum of Austrian Medieval Art

The display (access from Rennweg 6A) of Austrian medieval art in the adjacent Orangery does not give a comprehensive overview of the period's ecclesiastical art, not least because so many major works are happily still in situ. The emphasis of the collection is instead, on the late Gothic period, when works of superb quality were being produced in the Austrian Crown Lands.

In the first section are the lovely stone figures by the Master of Großlobming, created in the 1370s and 80s. Other highlights, in five sections altogether, include the vividly polychromatic **Znaimer Altar** attributed to a Viennese workshop of the early 15C, a votive panel of the *Crucifixion* by the Master of St Lambrecht (around 1420), a carved Romanesque **Crucifix** from Stämmerberg (mid-12C and the oldest treasure of the museum), a mid-15C *Pietà* by the Master of the Schottenaltar (p 97), Conrad Laib's *Crucifixion* (1449) and five superb works by the great Tyrolean painter and sculptor of the 15C, Michael Pacher. Two important Renaissance works are Rueland Frueauf's painted panels of *The Passion*, the events of which are placed in an Austrian setting, and Urban Görtschacher (or Görtschader)'s *Ecce Homo* (1508).

An important part of the Baroque prince's self-glorification was the **great garden**, laid out by Dominique Girard, a Bavarian of French origin and pupil of Le Nôtre. It was designed in such a way as to celebrate the Prince's qualities by means of a complex programme of statuary. Work could only begin on this when Prince Eugene had successfully negotiated the purchase of a parcel of land from his neighbour, Prince Schwarzenberg, thus creating the potential for a glorious and uninterrupted vista from the windows of the Upper Belvedere across the city to the Kahlenberg beyond—the departure point for the young soldier's first triumphs of leadership.

The **statuary** of the western part of the park had an Apollonian theme, an allusion to the Prince's cultural interests and statesmanship; the eastern part explicated the deeds of Hercules, thus celebrating the successful military general. At the lower end of the garden, the elemental forces of nature were represented, while the middle area was devoted to sculptural evocations of the prince's virtues. The upper part was dominated by the Olympian gods, the Upper Belvedere standing for Olympus itself. To the east (where the **Botanical and Alpine Gardens** now are) was the menagerie containing the first giraffe to survive in captivity in Central Europe; also a lion that performed the appropriately Baroque ritual of expiring on the same night as the prince himself. Little of the garden's original ornament survives, but the plantings of the northern and southern regions have been partially recreated. Still extant is the magnificent cascade (symbolising the Parnassian source of rivers) in the north garden and, in the southern one, the huge stone water basin (showing the influence of Versailles). In its water the reflection of the Schloss shimmers and glimmers, dazzling or sombre according to the weather.

Upper Belvedere and Österreichische Galerie

The Upper Belvedere (Oberes Belvedere, access from the park, as on this walk, or direct from Prinz-Eugen-Straße 27, Tram D) is now resplendent after recent total renovation. This was once the representational palace, where the Prince staged great festivities, receptions and political negotiations. With its harmonious division into seven architectural components, its ceremonial portal at the centre and four domed, corner pavilions on the Renaissance model, it exhibits a unique yet restrained grandeur. Montesquieu, on his visit to Vienna, disliked its façade but was impressed enough to observe: 'how pleasant it is to travel in a land where a subject evidently lives better than his Emperor.'

The now enclosed **sala terrena** (originally carriages could drive up to the foot of the staircase and on through) is notable for the muscle-bound Atlas figures supporting the vaulting and Santino Bussi's stucco of trophies. The neighbouring 'Painted Room' retains its original wall **frescoes** and Carlo Carlone's *Triumph of Aurora* on the ceiling. From the *sala terrena* itself, a noble, double-flighted Baroque stairway climbs to the first storey with fine views of the south garden. The stairwell is shaped like a general's tent, its surfaces decorated with stucco reliefs of the life and exploits of Alexander the Great, drawing a historical parallel to Prince Eugene.

From the landing you enter the great **Festsaal**, which is clad in red marble (said to recall the blood spilled in battle) and richly stuccoed. The ceiling shows an allegory of *Fame and Glory* by Carlo Carlone, again with flattering allusion to the Prince. It was in this room that the *Staatsvertrag* (State Treaty), which freed the country after ten years of post-war occupation, was signed by Dulles, Macmillan, Molotov and Pinay (for the allies) and Leopold Figl (for Austria) in 1955. A famous news-clip of the time shows Figl on the Belvedere balcony holding up the treaty to the cheering masses in the garden below. To the east of the Festsaal is the secret conference room where the Prince himself had held negotiations beneath Giacomo del Pò's apotheosising ceiling fresco. At the southeast corner of this first floor, a glass door leads onto the gallery overlooking the chapel. The latter was frescoed by Carlone and has an altarpiece of the *Resurrection* by Francesco Solimena.

After Prince Eugene's death, his unsatisfactory and spendthrift niece (known to the Viennese as 'the frightful Viktoria') inherited the Belvedere, but was forced to sell out to the imperial family. Thus the Prince's pictures and his superb library of 15,000 volumes also passed to the Habsburgs. In 1776 Joseph II installed the imperial picture collection in the Belvedere; from 1783 it was the first collection in the world to have a scientific catalogue, and also the first to allow the general public free entry. By 1891 the collection had been moved to the new Kunsthistorische Museum; four years later the heir to the throne, Franz Ferdinand, set up his rival court to the aging Franz Joseph in the Belvedere.

The Österreichische Galerie

The Upper Belvedere is home to the country's most important collection of 19C and 20C Austrian painting. The gallery now also includes the contents of the **Neuen Galerie** (formerly in the Stallburg), consisting of 19C and early 20C European paintings, many of them bought on the initiative of the Secession. In addition, acquisitions of foreign works, made between 1914 and 1938 under Director Franz Martin Haberditzl, served to put the work of Austrian masters in an international perspective.

The periodisation and stylistic groupings of the collection are as follows: Classicism, Romanticism and Biedermeier; Realism and Impressionism; Historicism; Vienna 1900, Classical Modernism; Early Expressionism; Art of the Twenties and Thirties; Art since 1945.

Classical and Romantic Highlights of the Classical and Romantic collection include David's florid depiction of *Napoleon on the St Bernhard* (1801), Caspar David Friedrich's atmospheric *Sea-Shore in Mist* (1807), and Leopold Kupelwieser's *The Three Holy Kings* (1825). An interesting product of **early romantic Historicism** is Ludwig Schnorr von Carolsfeld's *Rudolf of Habsburg and the Priest* (1828). It depicts an oft-cited legend that the pious Rudolf offered his horse to a priest, enabling him to cross a swollen stream and minister to a dying man.

Biedermeier, Realist and Impressionist There are a number of fine Biedermeier landscapes and several works by the Alt painter dynasty, who specialised in atmospheric topographical pictures: some of the loveliest views ever made of Vienna were painted by Rudolf, son of Jakob, in particular, his *Stephansdom* (1832). There follow idealised family portraits or evocations of domestic bliss by leading Biedermeier artists such as Georg Ferdinand Waldmüller, Friedrich von Amerling and Josef Danhauser. Their contemporary, Peter Fendi (1796–1842), painted sharply observed social vignettes, often of serving girls, street vendors, soldiers and others from the underprivileged classes. Fendi overcomes the Biedermeier tendency to sentimental quietism with his empathy for his subjects and his undertow of social criticism.

One of the best known of the Austrian Realist painters is **Emil Jakob Schindler**, the father of Alma Mahler (*Steamer at Kaisermühlen in Dazzling Sunshine*; c 1872). Schindler shares a passion for rural scenes with the gifted Tina Blau (*Spring in the Prater*; 1882), but perhaps the masterpiece of *plein air* naturalism in the collection is **Carl Moll**'s beautiful *Naschmarkt in Wien* (1894). Moll, who was later a leading member of the Secession, has here painted a quintessentially atmospheric evocation of a Viennese landmark, in the background of which can be seen the dome of the Karlskirche bathed in sunlight. Contemporary French genre painting and Realism is represented with pictures by Delacroix, Corot, Courbet (*The Wounded*; 1854) and Daumier (*Sancho Panza Resting under A Tree*; 1860–70).

The collection of Impressionists is not as impressive as elsewhere, but there is a pleasant Renoir (*After the Bath*; 1876), a Monet (*A Path in Monet's Garden in Giverny*; 1902) and a van Gogh (*The Plain at Auvers*; 1890). More interesting are the few representatives of German Impressionism, in particular the *Woman by the Goldfish Bowl* (1911) by Lovis Corinth and Max Liebermann's *Man out Shooting on the Dunes* (1913).

Historicism is represented by leading painters and sculptors of the Ringstraßen era, many of whom (like Anton Fernkorn, Hans Canon and Hans Makart) had received major commissions both from the state and from newly enriched, often newly ennobled, private patrons. Canon painted *The Circle of Life*, a cycle of frescoes for the Natural History Museum's stairway, the sketch for which is in the Austrian Gallery; here also is his neo-Baroque *The Lodge of St John* (1873), a remarkable composition in which all the branches of the Christian faith from Orthodoxy to Protestantism are symbolically united in common obeisance to the dual *fons et origo* of Christianity, Moses and Christ. A Munich painter, who decorated the ceremonial hall of the Academy of Fine Arts (p 151), is Anselm Feuerbach, here represented with several major works, among them *Orpheus and Eurydice* (1869).

The most successful painter of the age was Makart, who painted huge and sensual historical or mythological canvases; some of these would be acted out as tableaux by the art-oriented liberal bourgeoisie, a form of entertainment that now seems bizarre. Besides his large-scale works showing the twin influences of the Venetian cinquecento and Rubens (*Venice Welcomes Catherina Cornaro* and *Bacchus and Ariadne*), he also excelled at genre pictures and flattering portraits of Ringstraßen beauties.

A very different sort of painter was Anton Romako (1832–89), whose uncompromising realism met with incomprehension in Vienna, particularly in the now iconic, but non-heroic, depiction of Admiral Tegetthoff on the bridge of his ship at the victory of the Austrian fleet over the Italians at Lissa (1866) *Tegetthoff at the Battle of Lissa*; 1878/80).

Turn of the 20C painting—Classical Modernism and Secession

There is no doubt that the chief attraction for today's visitors to the Belvedere is the marvellous collection of turn of the century paintings, especially the works of **Gustav Klimt**. He is equally well represented here by his superb, flatly painted landscapes, perhaps the most beloved of which is the van Gogh influenced *Allee in the Park at Schloß Kammer* (1912), as by his decorative and sensual portraits of well to do middle-class ladies, or the richly symbolic works of his gold period. Of the latter, the most celebrated is *The Kiss* (1907/8), regarded as an emblem of *fin de siècle* Vienna's *hortus conclusus*, an aestheticised world where art permeates all aspects of life. The picture is at once symbol and sensuality, a perfected harmony of human desires and love from which threatening elements (such as the precipitous edge on which the lovers are perched) are by no means absent. The differing gold symbols (inspired by the Ravenna mosaics that Klimt had recently seen) of the lovers' all-enveloping robes symbolise the opposing qualities of yin and yang that are melted together and reconciled in the kiss. Klimt's famous *Beethoven Frieze* is also owned by the Austrian Gallery but displayed in the Secession building (p 166).

The collection possesses other important Symbolist works from the turn of the century, notably Carl Moll's menacing *Dusk* (1899), where an empty boat (Charon's?) drifts in the gloaming amongst the trees of a flooded wood. The treatment owes a lot to the Belgian symbolist Fernand Khnopff, who is also represented in the gallery, together with the Italian symbolist master, Giovanni Segantini (*The Evil Mothers*; 1894), the Swiss Ferdinand Hodler (*Emotion*; 1901) and Edvard Munch (*Summer Night on the Shore*; 1902).

The two stars of Austrian early **Expressionism** are **Egon Schiele** and **Oskar Kokoschka**. The Schiele collection boasts many of the classic works, vividly documenting the artist's tortured sexuality and his preoccupation with transience and death. Examples are *Death and the Maiden* (1915), and *The Family* (1918). The latter was painted just before he died in the devastating epidemic of influenza of that year, which is said to have killed more people over the whole of Europe than the First World War itself.

Egon Schiele (1890–1918)

The young Egon Schiele got to know Gustav Klimt in 1907 and his early work was influenced by the great Viennese master. As with Klimt, Schiele's work was unrestrained in its searingly honest depiction of sexuality—both men were superb draughtsmen and their erotic drawings (some of Schiele's made for private collectors of erotica) are astonishing both in their sensuality and in their avoidance of cliché. But while Klimt's drawings are infused with sensual warmth and tenderness, Schiele's treatment of sexuality (and especially of his own) can be alienating and bleak. This bleakness is particularly evident in *The Family* (Austrian Gallery, Belvedere) painted just before his death in 1918, where the viewer is reminded of the cruel paradox of Eros and Thanatos, of the procreative act leading ultimately and inexorably only to death.

Feelings of alienation and isolation are also evoked by Schiele's Expressionist studies of landscape or towns, perhaps the most remarkable of which is his *Small Tree in Late Autumn* (Leopold Museum, p 182). Works of this type have an unmistakable anthropomorphic element. As Patrick Werkner has written, the tree 'gives the impression of being marooned ....[and] seems to be in lonely communion with itself.' Likewise his marvellous imagined townscapes, bearing titles like *Dead City*, refer directly to mankind, while his depiction of villages in the Wachau region or the little town of Krumau 'only succeed when they function as metaphors for emotional (and usually melancholy) states' (Frank Whitford).

Although labelled an Expressionist, Schiele's art is a highly individual contribution to Modernism, and one that is still anchored in the tradition of figurative naturalism. The most personal element is the feeling of claustrophobia his work evokes, at its noblest of human love striving to carve out a niche in all-pervading death and decay, at its most nihilistic, of alienated mankind as the prey of the blind forces of fate.

Kokoschka is represented by some powerful portraits, as well as his enigmatic masterpiece, *Still-Life with Dead Wether* (1910), a *memento mori* whose odd assemblage of detail (a tortoise, an axolotl in an aquarium, a white mouse and a hyacinth) achieve what Werner Hofmann has called an 'emancipation of dissonance'. Two other important Expressionists are featured, Kokoschka's great rival, **Max Oppenheimer**, and Richard Gerstl, whose lacerating *Laughing Self-Portrait* (1908) brilliantly and disturbingly indicates the mental instability that ended in suicide.

Art of the 1920s and 1930s Another superb Kokoschka is hung amongst the art of the Twenties and Thirties, namely *The Tiger-Lion* (1926), inspired by a unique experimental cross that the artist saw at the London zoo (Kokoschka describes how he arrived with paints and easel early in the morning and sleepily leant against the bars of the cage, only to be terrified into wakefulness as the suddenly released beast roared towards him 'as if he would tear me to rags').

Besides works by Boeckl, Albert Paris Gütersloh and sculpture by Viennese masters such as Fritz Wotruba, this section is distinguished by Oskar Laske's spell-binding *Ship of Fools* (1923). The famous 15C satire by Sebastian Brant is here reinterpreted in contemporary terms. The ship of the world with its patched and torn sails drifts on an oily green swell; on board, all the follies and horrors of mankind are brutally enacted in a continuum of violence, lust, fear, hatred and stupidity.

Art since 1945 Of the art since 1945, the highlights include Fritz Wotruba's *Large Sitting Figure (Cathedral)* (1949), Anton Lehmden's delicately evocative *Summer and Winter* (1951) and *The Great Way* (1955) by Friedensreich Hundertwasser. The late Hundertwasser was the best-known artist and architectural designer in post-war Austria, whose Viennese monument is the multi-coloured **Hundertwasser Haus** (at Löwengasse/Kegelgasse; 3rd District), completed in 1985.

If you leave the Upper Belvedere on Prinz-Eugen-Straße, it is a short walk southwards towards the busy Gürtel (ring road) to Goldeggasse (first street on the right) and the unique, characteristically Viennese **Bestattungsmuseum** or **Burial Museum**, (Goldeggasse 19; ☎ 50 195 Ext: 4227 for appointment, Mon–Fri 12.00–15.00). Those of a morbid disposition will enjoy such items as the re-usable boxes with drop-flaps ordained by Joseph II for economic burials, but resisted by the populace. Also an early 19C coffin equipped with a bell-pull to alert people on the surface, should you unfortunately discover you had been buried alive (to avoid such a fate you could write into your will that you should be stilet-toed through the heart before inhumation—there is a nice stiletto on display).

Schweizer Garten

Continuing south on Prinz-Eugen-Straße, you arrive shortly at the busy **Gürtel**, the Outer Ring Road that follows an ancient line of peripheral fortification formerly known as the Linienwall. Crossing the Gürtel, with the Südbahnhof on your right, you enter the Schweizer Garten, a pleasant park which has been so-called since 1918 in recognition of financial contributions by the Swiss to Austria for reconstruction after the First World War. In the park with its picturesque rosarium is the never previously beautiful, but now absolutely hulk-like **Haus des 20. Jahrhunderts** or **20C House**, (Arsenalstrasse 1), formerly a venue for contemporary art exhibitions. The modern building (1962) is the work of Karl Schwanzer and is a slightly altered version of the Austrian pavilion he designed for the Brussels World Exhibition (1958). The modern art hitherto displayed here has been transferred to the Museum of Modern Art and Stiftung Ludwig, Wien in the MuseumsQuartier (p 182 and below), which opened in September 2001.

Arsenal and Museum of Military History

Following the signs eastwards through the park, you come to the Arsenal (1854), and the **Heeresgeschichtliches Museum** or Museum of Military History (Arsenalstraße, Objekt 1,8; open Mon–Thur, Sat, Sun 09.00–17.00) and one of the noblest examples of Romantic Historicism, in this case the militaristic style of the Italian Renaissance.

History

After the revolution of 1848, four large barracks and arms depots were planned at strategic points of the city, in order to avoid a repeat of the plundering of the civil armoury Am Hof, as happened in 1848. Of these four forts, only the Arsenal and the Roßauer Kaserne (p 162) remain. In any case, the need for them no longer existed by the time they were ready. The huge

Arsenal (eight barrack-blocks linked by lower lateral wings, in all 72 sections, making an enormous built-in square), was the combined work of leading architects of Historicism—August von Siccardsburg, Eduard van der Nüll, Karl Roesner, Ludwig Förster and Theophil Hansen. Besides the barracks, the complex included a cadet school for gunners, an arms depot and munitions factory, a hospital, a chapel and a patriotism-inspiring military museum: the **Heeresgeschichtliches Museum** (1856), designed by Hansen with Ludwig Förster. This last is well worth a visit, if only to admire the superb and exotic architecture, the first Historicist building in Vienna.

From outside, the Byzantine dome and Moorish windows give the museum block an oriental look. The sculptures in the tower niches are allegories of military virtues—*Strength, Alertness, Piety* and *Wisdom* (on the higher, central elevation), together with (below) *Courage, Loyalty to the Flag, Personal Sacrifice* and *Military Skill*.

Inside, in the vestibule area, is a **Hall of Honour** with 56 statues of Austrian military heroes, leading to an impressive stairway with frescoes by Carl Rahl, and at the top Johann Benk's marble allegory of *Austria*. A further **Ceremonial Hall** on the upper floor has frescoes by Carl Blaas, apotheosising Austrian military achievements in the Turkish and Napoleonic Wars.

To view the collection chronologically, begin on the **first floor** with the exhibits relating to the Turkish siege of Vienna in 1683, which include a captured Turkish banner emblazoned with a text from the Koran, and the Grand Vizier's tent. On this floor also, there is material relating to the Thirty Years War (1616–48), the War of the Spanish Succession (1701–14), Maria Theresia's wars against Frederick II of Prussia and the Napoleonic Wars (note the captured Montgolfier balloon and Johann Peter Krafft's dramatic rendering of the *Battle of Aspern*).

On the **ground floor** is the display of 19th and 20C military history. A high-light (in the west wing) is the car in which the Archduke Franz-Ferdinand, heir to the Austrian throne, was assassinated on 28 June 1914 (his bloodstained uniform is also displayed). Noteworthy is the painting of a Tyrolean artist, Albin Egger-Lienz, dedicated to *The Unknown Soldier* (1916), a grim stylised evocation of mass warfare, surprisingly pacifist for such a setting. The East Wing covers the history of the Austrian navy. An interesting exhibit documents the expedition to the North Pole (1872–74) which discovered and named Franz-Josefs-Land (claimed by the USSR in 1926).

A short walk north from the Arsenal brings you back to the Gürtel and trams running to the traffic connections at Südbahnhof or Südtiroler Platz (U1).

11 • Mariahilf, the MuseumsQuartier, Josefstadt

The 6th District of Vienna is best known for its shopping area, the **Mariahilfer Straße**, roughly equivalent to London's Oxford Street. The U-Bahn (U3) now runs along its length. The liveliest part stretches from Babenberger Straße at the northeastern end as far as the Gürtel, which crosses near the Westbahnhof.

The MuseumsQuartier

To the southwest, as you leave the U4 at Babenbergerstraße, you will see the vast complex of the former **Messepalast**: a long, raking, Baroque building designed

N

| 0 | | 750 yards |
| 0 | | 750 metres |

General Hospital (AKH)

ALSERSTRAßE

Schönborn Palais (Museum of Folklore)

LAUDONGASSE

GÜRTEL

JODOK FINK-PLATZ

Maria Treu Church

JOSEFSTÄDTER STRAßE

Theater in der Josefstadt

JOSEFSTADT

LERCHENFELDER STRASSE

BURGGASSE

SPITTEL BERG

MuseumsQuartier

MUSEUMSPLATZ

BABENBERGER STRASSE

MUSEUMSQUARTIER (2A, 57A)

Stiftskirche

NEUBAUGASSE (2A, 13A, 14A)

GÜRTEL

West Bahnhof

MARIAHILFER STRASSE

Mariahilfer Parish Church

MARIAHILFER STRASSE

SECHSHAUSER STRASSE

HADIKGASSE

Wien

by the Fischer von Erlachs (1723) for Karl VI, and originally the court stables. It could accommodate 600 horses and also housed a carriage remise, an armoury for hunting-weapons, and apartments for officials, not to mention a substantial palace for the *Oberststallmeister*. It has been a site for commercial fairs since 1921 and latterly for performances of the Wiener Festwochen.

This whole area has now been turned into the **MuseumsQuartier** (**'MuQua'**) (Museumsplatz 1, ☎ 523 58 81, 🖹 523 53 86), a multifarious cultural centre sensitively designed (1990) by the Ortner brothers. The new complex, adapted to house nine museums in former commercial exhibition halls and the Court Stables, became fully operational in the autumn of 2001. The fine Baroque buildings have been kept as a backcloth, while the **Leopold Museum** (a cream cube), the **Museum of Modern Art** (a loweringly graphite-coloured bunker) and the **Kunsthalle**, an exhibition hall transferred from Karlsplatz (post-modernist brick and tiles) have been placed in the courtyard area. Some institutions, like the **Architektur Zentrum**, have been established here for some time.

- **Transport** U2 (MuseumsQuartier), U3 (Volkstheater); Bus 48A (Volkstheater), City Bus (Hopper); 2A (MuseumsQuartier). Tram 49 (Volkstheater), underground parking Parkgarage am Museumsplatz.

Museums within the MuQua complex

Opening times, entry prices and current events can be checked on the website ▩ **www.mqw.at**. or in *Wien Programm*. There is a visitor reception and information post at the main entrance. The first three institutions mentioned are intended to be participatory or interactive, as forums, archives, displays etc.

- **Architekturzentrum Wien** Staatsratshof, ☎ 522 31 15.
  ▩ **www.azw.at**. A *mediathek*, archive and databank, with an interactive programme of events for architecture buffs.
- **Art Cult Center 'Tabakmuseum'**, Klosterhof, ☎ 526 17 16.
  ▩ **www.austriatabak.com**. The centre is more interesting than it sounds (open Tues–Fri 10.00–17.00; Sat, Sun 10.00–14.00), and includes among the exhibits several amazingly ornate pipes. It has now turned itself into an 'Art Cult Center' offering a lively and extremely varied programme of events.
- **basis wien–Kunst, Information und Archiv** Staatsratshof, ☎ 522 67 94. ▩ **www.basis-wien.at**. The institutions include a **cyber forum** for art (▩ **basisarchiv:kunst** is an online databank for contemporary Austrian art, ▩ **medien.kunst.archiv wien** is concerned with video art), and new research facilities concerned with the history of ideas and Austrian Modernism.
- **Depot–Kunst und Diskussion** Staatsratshof, ☎ 522 76 13.
  ▩ **www.depot.or.at**
- **Karst- und Höhlenkundliche Abteilung des Naturhistorischen Museums** (Spelaeology Department of the Natural History Museum) Stiege 10, ☎ 523 04 18-0.
- **Kunsthalle Wien** Haupteingang links, Büro, Stiege 6, ☎ 521 89-0.
  ▩ **www.kunsthallewien.at**. The Kunsthalle is an exhibition hall for contemporary art.
- **Leopold Museum** Stiege 5, ☎ 52570-0. ▩ **www.leopoldmuseum.org**. Rudolf Leopold's unique collection of turn of the century and early 20C Viennese art including many works by Schiele, Klimt, Gerstl, Kokoschka and Albin Egger-Lienz. The whole project was made possible by a 'Lex Leopold', whereby the disputed tax bill of the celebrated collector, Rudolf Leopold, was amortised into a Foundation (1994), in the care of which his unique collection was placed, Leopold himself becoming its curator for life.
- **Museum of modern Art** (Museum moderner Kunst, Stiftung Ludwig Wien). Major collection of post-Kandinsky art: Pop Art, Photo Realism, Fluxus, Nouveau Réalisme, Viennese Actionism, etc., recently transferred from the Liechtenstein Garten-Palais (soon to house the major Liechtenstein collection of pictures, p 186) and the 20C House (Haus des 20. Jarhunderts) ▩ **www.mumok.at**.

- **Public Netbase to Media~Space!** A non-profit Internet provider, supporting individual artists and cultural initiatives, ✉ **www.tO.or.at.**
- **Quartier 21**. In a wing of the former Baroque Imperial stable building, Quartier 21 is envisaged as a 'seismograph of future developments in design, architecture, fashion, music, video, visual arts, cultural studies and new media'. It will offer a unique working environment for artists in residence, academics and art managers and there will be a multifunctional event area. Due to open summer 2002.
- **Tanzquartier Wien**. A new centre for contemporary dance and performance, ✉ **www.tqw.at.**
- **Theaterhaus für Kinder**. Exciting co-productions for children aged 4–12. Theatre, dance, puppet theatre, musicals and even opera. ✉ **theaterfuerkinder-mq@gmz.at.**
- **Wiener Festwochen (Vienna Festival).** ✉ **www.festwochen.at**. An annual arts festival of international renown (p 43).
- **wienXtra-children's information** A service which provides information on children's cultural events, games, sports, animation (also answers questions on childcare, education and other child-related issues). ✉ **www.kinderinfowien.at**
- **Zoom Kindermuseum** (Children's Museum). Fürstenhof, ☎ 522 67 48. ✉ **www.kindermuseum.at**. A unique attraction and Austria's first museum for children providing opportunities for play and discovery.

Further along Mariahilfer Straße, on the right, is the **Stiftskaserne** (1749), previously a cadet school and war archive. One of the hideous bunkers with roof-platforms for anti-aircraft batteries designed by Friedrich Tamm stands in the grounds at the Stiftgasse end; unfortunately these disfiguring monstrosities (in the Augarten, Esterházypark, and Arenbergpark) cannot be safely demolished without damaging the surrounding buildings. They contained their own power and water supplies and could accommodate up to 30,000 people inside their 5m-thick walls of reinforced concrete. The only one to be used is that in the Esterházypark, which has been turned into an aquarium.

The **Stiftskirche** (Mariahilfer Straße 24), a church doubtfully attributed (1739) to Joseph Emanuel Fischer von Erlach, was turned into a military store by Joseph II but reconsecrated in 1799 under Franz I. Now the garrison church, its most notable feature is the elaborate stucco depicting the *Passion of Christ* in the elevated niches of the interior.

A little further, on the left, is the **Mariahilfer Parish Church**, which gives the area its name, the church possessing a copy of the famous Passau Madonna, said to have assisted those who prayed to it. The frescoes (1760) of the interior ceiling are by the school of Paul Troger and show scenes from the *Life of Mary*. The altarpiece of the Chapel of St Anne is by J.M. Rottmayr (*Saint Anne and Saint Joachim*) and another Baroque master, Johann Dorfmeister, worked on the tabernacle and angels of the high altar (1776).

Some of the great stores that once graced Mariahilfer Straße are casualties of changing consumer tastes, although *Gerngross* and *Leiner* go on. Near the former is the *Virgin Megastore*, and towards the western end is the excellent international book and CD store, *Amadeus*.

Viennese café interior

Josefstadt

Some way to the north of Mariahilf is the attractive Josefstadt (8th District, named after Emperor Josef I), the most fashionable place to live outside the Inner City (conveniently approached with Tram J from the Ring). Much of its Baroque fabric remains and there are pleasant restaurants and cafés, notably the *Alte Backstube* (Lange Gasse 34), a bakery continuously in service from 1701 until 1963, and now a charming café-restaurant with a small museum of the bakery trade. The sandstone relief (1701) above the entrance symbolises the Holy Trinity.

If you get off the tram at the first stop on the Josefstädter Straße, you are not far from the **Theater in der Josefstadt** at no. 26, one of Vienna's best-loved theatres. The present building was designed by the neo-Classical architect, Josef Kornhäusel, in 1822, and boasts an elegant, compact auditorium with the first chandelier to be mechanically raised and lowered. Beethoven composed an overture for the reopening (there had been a theatre here since 1788); he conducted it himself, according to onlookers, 'looking wild and unkempt'. Max Reinhardt, the celebrated founder (with Hugo von Hofmannsthal) of the Salzburg Festival, took over the theatre in 1923 and made it famous for productions of quality modern drama. Nowadays it plays mainstream material, leaving experimentation to the Burgtheater and the fringe.

Maria Treu (or Piarist) Church

From the corner to the west of the theatre, the Piaristengasse runs towards Jodok-Fink-Platz, on which stands the beautiful Maria Treu (or Piarist) Church (c 1751). The pleasing sweep of the convex façade of this lovely late Baroque and Rococo church is elegantly balanced by its two lateral towers, and the cobbled square in front of it has a distinctly Roman ambience.

History

Although Lukas von Hildebrandt submitted the original plans, which were partially realised, the building clearly bears the imprint of the great Prague master, Kilian Ignaz Dientzenhofer (designer of St Nicholas' Church in Prague Old Town and co-builder, with his father, of the famous Basilica in Mala Strana). Dientzenhofer seems to have submitted his plans for the façade and cupola in 1721; after his death in 1751, Matthias Gerl continued with the work in the 1750s, finishing touches being added by Franz Sitte in the 19C. The coat of arms over the entrance is that of Sigismund, Count Kollonitsch, patron of the church and of the Piarist Order for which it was founded. The order's school is adjacent (it is still one of the most esteemed in Vienna). Kollonitsch was the first Archbishop of Vienna, following the fulfilment (1722) of Karl VI's request to Innocent XIII that the city be raised to an archbishopric.

The interior is notable for superb **ceiling frescoes** (1753) by Franz Anton Maulbertsch, which narrate the sacred story from *Adam and Eve* through the *Coronation of Mary* (as Queen of Heaven), the *Fall of the Angels* (to be seen above the organ loft), the *Ascension of Mary* and the *Four Evangelists* (in the choir); in the side-chapels, the *Parable of the Good Shepherd* (to the right) and *Jacob at the Well* (to the left). Carl Rahl's *Marriage of Mary* (1841) over the high altar replaces a work with the same theme by Maulbertsch that is now lost. The church takes its name from its copy of the *Madonna* in San Pantaleo in Rome. To the left of the entrance in the Chapel of the Crucifix is a wooden *Pietà* dating from the early 15C.

The **organ** has the distinction of being the one on which **Anton Bruckner** took his composition test when applying for entry to the Music Academy in 1861. In the stunned silence that followed his performance, one of the professorial adjudicators was heard to whisper: 'He should be examining us!' (Bruckner, on receiving an honorary DPhil. from the University of Vienna in 1891, simply said: 'I cannot find the words to thank you as I would wish, but if there were an organ here, I could tell you.')

Also of interest in the Josefstadt is the **Schönborn-Palais** (Laudongasse 15–19), reached if you continue north from Maria Treu along Kochgasse and turn right. The palace was designed (1714) by Lukas von Hildebrandt (who was later appointed Inspector General of the Schönborn estates), and altered in early neo-Classical style by Isidore Canevale in the 1760s (the architect died here 20 years later). Inside the palace, only the vestibule and Baroque staircase have been preserved of the original. The palace now houses the **Österreichische Museum für Volkskunde** or Museum of Austrian Folklore (open Tues–Sun 10.00–17.00). The display documents everyday life in the Austrian territories down the ages, and includes some rustic furniture and two typical '*Stuben*' (parlours) from Montafon and Tirol.

12 • Alsergrund, Strudlhofstiege, Berggasse

Alsergrund, Vienna's 9th District adjoins Josefstadt and includes the city's medical quarter. The starting point of our walk can be reached on foot from Schottentor, or by Trams 43 and 44 (one stop), bringing you close to the **Trinity Church** (Dreifaltigkeitskirche or Alser Parish Church ; Alser Straße 17). This church was founded by the Trinitarians (a Spanish order known as the *Weißspanier* on account of their white habit) under Leopold I, but became a parish church with responsibilities for attending the inmates of the new general hospital established across the street by Joseph II. There is a fine relief (1730) representing the *Trinity* over the main entrance and a plaque on the wall recalls the funeral of Beethoven here in 1827. (A solid line of mourners ran from Beethoven's last residence in the Schwarzspanierstraße to the church, and 15,000 accompanied the coffin to Währing cemetery.) Another plaque refers to the hymn (*Faith, Hope and Charity*) composed by Schubert for the consecration of the church bells shortly before he died.

Opposite the church is the main entrance to the huge former **Allgemeines Krankenhaus** (General Hospital) founded by Joseph II in the 1780s and constructed to plans by Isidore Canevale and Matthias Gerl. It was extended in 1834 and 1859 and encompasses a dozen internal courtyards. It now plays second fiddle, however, to the ultra-modern AKH further west, the construction of which produced the greatest of the many corruption scandals in Austria since the beginning of the Kreisky era. The university has partly moved into vacated buildings.

For the tourist, the bizarre **Narrenturm** or Fools' Tower in the sixth courtyard (nearest Sensengasse) is the star attraction. A revolutionary cylindrical building (1784) by Isidore Canevale, it was commissioned by the Emperor as a 'lunatic asylum' (not all the inmates appear to have been mental cases—Count Seilern had his son committed for refusing to marry the girl of his parents' choice). The Viennese call it the *Gugelhupf* after a pound cake much prized locally, which it is said to resemble. It is now the **Museum for Pathological Anatomy** (nearest street entrance, Spitalgasse 2; open Wed 15.00–18.00; Thur 08.00–11.00), and contains an unrivalled collection of medical horrors (deformed skeletons, lungs eaten away by nicotine and the world's largest collection of gall and kidney stones).

Währinger Straße skirts the AKH on the northeast side; if you walk towards the city you come to the **Josephinum** (at No. 25), commissioned by Joseph II from Canevale (1785) as an academy for military surgeons. It has a fine neo-Classical library with Corinthian columns and a coffered ceiling. The main attraction, however, is the collection of wax anatomical models made (1775–1785) by a Florentine craftsman according to plans by Felice Fontana and Paolo Mascagni, for instructing the apprentice surgeons, now in the **Museum of the History of Medicine** (open Mon–Fri 09.00–15.00).

Retrace your steps northwestwards along Währinger Straße as far as Strudlhofgasse, which is to your right. Towards the end of it, again on your right (no. 10), you will see what is now the Embassy of Qatar, but was formerly the **Villa of Count Berchtold**, the Austrian Foreign Minister in 1914, who pushed Franz

Joseph into his disastrous ultimatum against Serbia. The Hellenistic building was built in 1873 on the site of the Strudlhof, so-named after its owner, the court painter, Peter von Strudel (1660–1714). The painter's name is also preserved in the adjacent **Strudlhofstiege**, a beautiful *art nouveau* flight of steps (1910) by Theodor Jäger, that drops from the Strudlhofgasse to the Liechtensteinstraße below. The steps have become an even more famous landmark since featuring as backcloth to Heimito von Doderer's period novel of the same name.

Strudlhofstiege (1910) designed by Theodor Jäger

Turn right at the bottom of the steps, then left off the Liechtensteinstraße along Fürstengasse to reach the magnificent wrought-iron gates of the **Liechtenstein-Gartenpalais** (Fürstengasse 1). The Baroque palace was built between 1691 and 1711 to plans by Domenico Martinelli. The *sala terrena* is decorated with frescoed medallions (1708) by Johann Michael Rottmayr and a double-flighted stairway leads to the **Ceremonial Hall** with a ceiling fresco (the

BEYOND RINGSTRAßE WALK 12

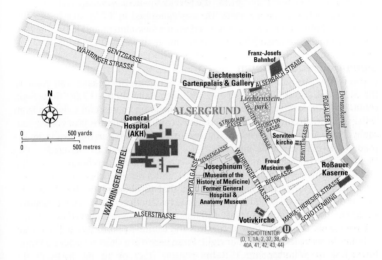

SCHOTTENTOR
(D, 1, 1A, 2, 37, 38, 40
40A, 41, 42, 43, 44)

Apotheosis of Hercules; 1708) by Andrea Pozzo. A further room is painted with allegories on the walls, the work of Marcantonio Franceschini. The Museum of Modern Art, formerly here, has been transferred to the new MuseumsQuartier (p 182) and the palais will, after refurbishment, house the major Liechtenstein collection of pictures (Flemish, Italian and German works of 15C–19C) and applied arts, currently in Vaduz. At present, opening is planned for 2003, by which time the Rottmayr and Pozzo frescoes will have been restored; and a library and archive, originally transferred from a Liechtenstein palace on the Herrengasse (now demolished) will have been installed. Prolonged negotiations with the Austrian state regarding the superb picture collection, which was already under Nazi-inspired 'national protection' when removed to Vaduz in 1938 (and therefore in theory removed illegally), appear to have been resolved and these marvellous works of art will now doubtless reach a wider public.

Servitenkirche

Leave the Liechtenstein Palace by continuing along Fürstengasse, then turning right into Porzellangasse, and left down to Grünentorgasse, which will bring you on the right to the **Servite Church**. Built for the Servite Order in the late 17C to designs by Carlo Canevale, the church has a notable **interior**, of which the most striking part is the *stucco lustro* by Giovanni Battista Bussi, Giovanni Barbarino and their assistants. Their works (in the chapels to the right and left under the towers) show respectively the *Death of St Juliana Falconieri* (founder of the Servite nuns) and the *Martyrdom of Saint John Nepomuk*, the courageous Vicar-General of Prague drowned in the Vltava on the orders of Wenceslas IV in 1393. There is also a fine **pulpit** (1739) with representations of the four evangelists and personifications of the Virtues by Balthasar Moll and Franz Joseph Hilber. Off the main church to the right is the **chapel** dedicated to the Servite saint, Peregrine Laziosi, a fanatical Ghibelline who once struck the leader of the Servite order, Philip Benizzi, when the latter was mediating between Guelfs and Ghibellines at Forlì. So impressed was Peregrine by the Servite's patient acceptance of the blow, that he himself became a Servite. He was canonised in 1726, just before this chapel was built. Saint Peregrine suffered from a foot ailment and his shrine here has traditionally attracted fellow sufferers, among them Joseph Haydn.

Sigmund Freud Museum

If you follow Servitengasse south and turn right into **Berggasse**, you come to the Sigmund Freud Museum at no. 19 (open daily 09.00–17.00, July–Sept, 09.00–18.00), located where he had his consulting rooms and lodgings from 1891 to 1938. Freud (1856–1939) is now a contentious figure, years of hagiography having been undermined by recent critical scholarship exposing his pseudo-scientific methods and failure to deal honestly with his critics. The Viennese satirist, Karl Kraus, memorably remarked that 'psychoanalysis is the disease of which it purports to be the cure' and a distinguished contemporary scientist (Sir Peter Medawar) has observed that psychoanalytic theory may be 'the most stupendous confidence trick of the twentieth century'. The museum is strictly for devotees and has about 420 items (letters, books, objets d'art, etc.).

If you walk to the northeast, towards the Danube Canal, you will pass the Roßauer Kaserne (p 162) on your right. From here it is a short walk along Franz-Josefs-Kai to Schottenring U-Bahn station (U2) or (a bit further) the Schwedenplatz transport connections (U1, U4, Trams 1 and 2).

13 • Leopoldstadt, Augarten, Prater

The 2nd District of Vienna (conveniently reached on foot or by Tram N from Schwedenplatz) became the Jewish quarter by order of Ferdinand II in 1625, when it was still an area of marshy islands between arms of the Danube known as the Untere Werd. In 1670 the Jews were expelled by Leopold I, their synagogue demolished, and the **Leopoldkirche** built on the site. Subsequently members of the aristocracy built their summer palaces here, among them Cardinal Kollonitsch, a prime mover in persecuting the Jews, although he also had a record of outstanding leadership through the plague years and the siege of Vienna. In the 18C and 19C, the Leopoldstadt was again home to immigrant Jews, the poorer Orthodox Jews remaining in the area and having nothing in common with the wealthy, assimilated ones engaged in business, the professions and the arts, who lived in the city's fashionable quarters. All the Viennese Jews were expelled by the Nazis, although there were isolated exceptions, such as a branch of the Wittgensteins, who bought themselves immunity by turning over assets held in a Swiss bank.

The area holds sparse interest today for the sightseer. Anton Ospel's Leopoldkirche (Große Pfarrgasse 15) having been badly damaged in the war and reconstructed without the rich Baroque ornament of the interior. A new, if somewhat macabre, attraction is the **Kriminalmuseum** (Crime Museum; Große Sperlgasse 24, open Tues–Sun 10.00–17.00), whose 20 rooms chronicle wrong-

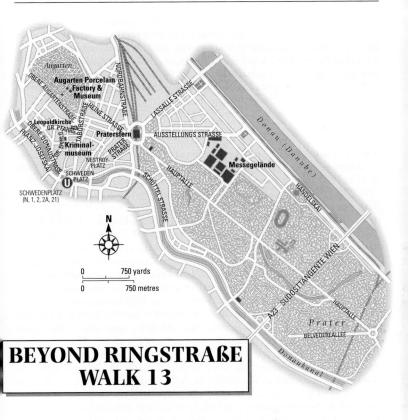

NORDBAHNSTRASSE

OBERE AUGARTENSTRASSE

Augarten

Augarten Porcelain Factory & Museum

TABORSTRASSE

KLEINE STRASSE

LASSALLE STRASSE

Leopoldkirche

GR. PFARR..

OBERE DONAUSTRASSE

FRANZ-JOSEFS-KAI

Pratersfern

AUSSTELLUNGS STRASSE

PRATER STRASSE

Kriminal-museum

NESTROY-PLATZ

SCHWEDEN-PLATZ

SCHWEDENPLATZ
(N, 1, 2, 2A, 21)

SCHÜTTEL STRASSE

HAUPTALLE

Donau (Danube)

HANDELSKAI

Messegelände

A23 - SÜDOSTTANGENTE WIEN

HAUPTALLE

Prater

BELVEDEREALLEE

Donaukanal

N

0   750 yards

0   750 metres

BEYOND RINGSTRAßE WALK 13

doing in Vienna through the ages, with a distinct emphasis on murder and violence. There is also material relating to the development of the criminal justice system in Austria. If you have a penchant for mummified heads of executed villains, death masks and murder weapons, this is the place to visit. Nearby at Karmelitergasse 9 is the **Circus and Clown Museum** (open Wed 17.30–19.00; Sat 14.30–17.00; Sun 10.00–12.00).

The Augarten

A pleasant excursion may be made to the Augarten (Obere Augartenstraße 1; Bus 5A from Nestroyplatz or U1), a park laid out in 1712 by Jean Trehet on earlier Baroque gardens destroyed in the Turkish siege. Joseph II opened the park to the public in 1775 and later had the lodge known as the **Joseph-Stöckl** (1781) built by Isidore Canevale. Canevale also built the triumphal arch over the park entrance, with Joseph's ingratiating slogan on it: 'A place of leisure dedicated to all men by one who esteems them.'

The old, much-altered Baroque Palais of the Augarten is now home to the **Vienna Boys' Choir**, while the nearby Saalgebäude (attributed to J.B. Fischer von Erlach) houses the **Augarten Porcelain Factory and Museum**. The firm's products may be admired and also purchased here (museum/shop open Mon–Fri 09.00–18.00; Sat 09.00–12.00. Guided Tours: Mon–Fri 09.30, or on application ☎ 21 124 Ext. 11). Founded in the early 18C, the business is the second oldest of its kind in Europe after Meißen; notwithstanding the acknowledged excellence of its ware, it had to be rescued several times by the state from bankruptcy.

Behind the factory is the **Gustinus Ambrosi Museum**, part of the Austrian Gallery. In the former atelier of the sculptor (1893–1975) is a display of his works, many of them portrait busts of the leading figures of his day (open Tues–Sun, 10.00–18.00).

If you leave the Augarten at the Klanggasse exit, near the Joseph-Stöckl, and walk the length of Heine Straße, you arrive at the large traffic hub of Praterstern, on which is a column commemorating Admiral Tegetthoff's victory at Lissa (p 177).

The Prater

To the east is the vast area of the Prater, with its fun-fair, planetarium, Prater Museum, Ferris Wheel and other attractions (in the **Wurstelprater**). There are also acres of parkland and allées, a commercial exhibition centre (**Messegelände**—the site of the 1873 World Exhibition), sports centres of various kinds, race-courses and trotting stadia at **Freudenau** and at **Krieau**, and a rather shabby golf course. The luna park is as lugubrious as such places usually are, but the **Ferris Wheel** (built in 1896/7 by an Englishman, Walter Bassett) affords marvellous views of the city. The ride will be familiar to fans of Graham Greene's *The Third Man* (Holly shares a ride with Harry Lime, who seems to contemplate throwing him to his death from the top of the wheel). There are plans to modernise the attractions in the Prater. Since the 15C the Prater had been imperial hunting grounds and was first opened to the public by Joseph II in 1766. In the 19C, part of it became a workers' playground, while the carriages of the well-to-do would parade (the *Praterfahrt*) along the chestnut-lined allée, especially in the spring when a special event was the *Blumencorso*. This promenade of the prominent, watched by the curious masses (and a field day for pickpockets) was instituted by Princess Pauline Metternich in 1886. An entrance fee was charged, the proceeds going to the Viennese polyclinic. Everyone tried to outdo each other in the floral decoration of their carriages, for which no expense was spared. A distributor of Hungarian paprika even wanted ornamentation consisting only of paprika bouquets, but had to abandon the idea when the horses became tetchy from the irritation of the paprika, while both animals and passing public were wracked with sneezing fits. Quite another sort of event in the Prater was the May Day parade of the workers, an annual fixture from 1890. The first to be held frightened the wits out of the authorities and the middle classes, but nevertheless passed off peacefully. Ilsa Barea's poignant description of that day's events ends as follows: 'Everyone, the adversaries of a new social order, as much as its champions, agreed that something new had entered history...'

14 • Schönbrunn

The monument most associated with Maria Theresia in Vienna is the imperial **Lustschloß** at **Schönbrunn** (Schönbrunner Schloßstraße, 13th District. U4 to Schönbrunnm, or Hietzing for the park and zoo).

History

In the late 17C, Johann Bernhard Fischer von Erlach (then tutor in civil architecture to the Habsburg heir) drew up plans for a splendid palace and park to rival that of Versailles. These plans are featured in his *Entwurf einer historischen Architektur* published in 1721, and envisaged a sky-line building on top of the hill to the south, where the Gloriette now stands.

A new and less expensive design, ordered by Leopold I for his heir (later Josef I), moved the palace to its present location, and down-graded it to a *Jagdschloß* (hunting lodge). Although Josef I occupied the unfinished building for a while, little use was found for it by his successor Karl VI. Maria Theresia, however, not wishing to live in the Favorita residence, where her adored father had died, commissioned her court architect, Nikolaus Pacassi, to remodel Fischer von Erlach's building as a Rococo palace, chiefly for summer use.

The construction continued from 1744 to 1749, the end result being a palace imposing in size, relatively undistinguished architecturally, but much enhanced by its magnificent Baroque park. Here the Empress enjoyed informal, almost bourgeois, family life as mater patriae, the unstuffy atmosphere of which is recorded in anecdotes: the child Mozart jumping into his ruler's lap after she had praised his playing, or the chorister Joseph Haydn being given a furious scolding by a concerned Empress, after he climbed on the scaffolding against her express instructions. Schönbrunn soon set the tone elsewhere—the familiar yellow ochre (*Schönbrunnergelb*) of the walls was copied from Trieste to Czernowitz, while *Schönbrunnerdeutsch* (the Viennese dialect sprinkled with French idioms favoured by the imperial family) left its mark on café society.

Opening times

- The palace is open Apr–Oct 08.30–17.00; Nov–Mar 08.30–16.30. Audioguides are included with the tickets, which have timed admission. The rooms can be visited with a **Grand Tour** (40 rooms out of 1441, c 50 minutes), or the **Imperial Tour** (22 rooms, c 35 minutes).

- From April to October a discounted VIP pass is available which is valid for all the attractions of the Schloss and the Park, including exclusive access for passholders only to the frescoed Bergl rooms. This may be the best solution for a family (family ticket: 2 adults plus up to 3 children) wanting to spend a whole day at Schönbrunn.

- Semi-privatised Schönbrunn is extremely (excessively?) tourist-friendly, with everything from a café in the 'Emperor's Breakfast Pavilion' to a 'Sissy' (Emperor Elisabeth) souvenir shop.

Approaching via the **main entrance** (the Haupttor, flanked by two eagle-topped obelisks), you will pass on your right the Pacassi-designed **Schloßtheater**, now used for productions of the Wiener Kammeroper in July and August and by the Max Reinhardt School of Dramatic Art. Its interior decoration was designed by

Schloß Schönbrunn in the snow

Ferdinand von Hohenberg and executed in 1766/67. Further to the southwest is the Wagenburg or **Carriage Museum** (formerly the Riding School) with a display of coaches, including the hearse used at Franz Joseph's funeral in 1916, and Maria Theresia's carousel carriages. In summer, booths offering culinary specialities from all parts of Austria are set up before the palace.

The Palace

In the east wing is Fischer von Erlach's **chapel** (open on Sundays) with a ceiling fresco by Daniel Gran (*The Apotheosis of Mary Magdalene*, 1744), an altarpiece by Paul Troger of the *Betrothal of Mary* and a relief by the school of Georg Raphael Donner; also the **Bergl-Zimmer** (1777; recently restored) which is entirely overpainted with exotic landscapes by the Bohemian artist, Johann Wenzl Bergl.

Both the **Grand Tour** and the **Imperial Tour** start from an entrance east of the external ceremonial stairway. Passing through the billiard room (where petitioners kicked their heels), and an audience chamber (known as the Walnut Chamber from the elegant wainscoting), we reach Franz Joseph's study and bedroom, the latter containing the iron bedstead in which he died. At the exit is the Emperor's lavatory. Some way beyond (Room 9) is the gloomy, shared bedroom of Franz Joseph and Elisabeth, with religious pictures on the walls by Carlo Dolci and Guido Reni.

At the southwest corner of the palace, after the **Marie Antoinette Room** and the **Nursery**, is Maria Theresia's **Breakfast Room** (from which fine views of the park), where the appliqué floral designs were made by the Empress and her daughters. The **Mirror Gallery**, where the child Mozart performed in 1762, is part of the following **Ceremonial Apartments**. The large **Rosa Room** takes its name from the artist Joseph Rosa (born 'Roos'), whose North Italian and Swiss landscapes are painted on the wall panels. Flanking the Small Gallery (see below) are the **Round Chinese Room** and the **Oval Chinese Room**, containing striking ensembles of oriental porcelain, mirrors and gilt panelling inset with Chinese landscapes. A hidden staircase from the Round Chinese Room climbs to Chancellor Kaunitz's apartment above; a ready-laid table could be hoisted through the floor to obviate the need for servants at secret conferences.

We come now to the **Great Gallery**, decorated with Guglielmo Guglielmi's ceiling frescoes (1761), representing the *Territories of the Empire Paying Homage to Maria Theresia and Franz Stephan* at the centre, flanked by *The Glories of War* and *The Blessings of Peace* (the fresco to the east is a reconstruction after a bomb fell through it in 1945). This impressive and lushly decorated space (42.67m long) was used as a ballroom during the Congress of Vienna; governmental receptions are still held here from time to time, a significant one being the 1961 meeting between President Kennedy and Khrushchev. The **Small Gallery** is effectively an extension of the Great Gallery on the park side, and also has a fresco by Guglielmi (*The Union of the House of Habsburg-Lorraine with the Holy Roman Empire*). It was used primarily for smaller banquets, concerts and children's parties.

There follows a **Carousel Room** that recalls the mounted quadrille led by Maria Theresia to celebrate the reconquest of Prague (1743). Next to it is the **Ceremonial Hall** (Zeremoniensaal) with a sumptuous painting of the entry into Vienna of Joseph II's bride in 1760 (94 six-horse carriages are depicted), and Meytens' finest portrait of Maria Theresia. The Imperial Tour ends here. The Grand Tour continues with the **Blue Chinese Salon** where Karl I abdicated on 11 November 1918.

The subsequent **Vieux Laque Zimmer**, designed by Isidore Canevale around 1770 is so-called from the black lacquered wall-panels featuring Japanese landscapes picked out in gold. It was here that Maria Theresia spent much of her time in widowhood, no doubt often in contemplation of Pompeo Batoni's portrait of her husband. The same artist painted the double portrait of her two sons and imperial successors, Joseph II and Leopold II.

Passing through the room where Napoleon's unfortunate son, the 21-year-old Duc de Reichstadt, expired in 1832 after a period of virtual captivity in Schönbrunn, and Maria Theresia's study (the **Porcelain Room** with ink drawings in the panels which were executed by her husband with two of his daughters), we enter the **Millionenzimmer**, whose rosewood panelling inset with Indian and Persian miniatures which in the 18C reputedly cost a million florins to build.

In spite of its name, the **Gobelinsalon** actually contains Brussels tapestries of the 18C, featuring scenes of Antwerp fishermen. Beyond it is a room dedicated to the abandoned **Aiglon** ('eaglet' as the Duc de Reichstadt was known), with a child portrait, death mask and the stuffed corpse of his pet lark. In the **Red Salon** (covered in scarlet damask) are several Habsburg portraits and beyond that the apartments of Franz Joseph's parents, including the chamber in which the Emperor was born. In the adjoining room are portraits of Maria Theresia's family (most of her 16 children can be seen).

The Park

The area of Schönbrunn had been in possession of the Habsburgs since Maximilian II acquired the Katterburg (a small *Schloß* next to a corn mill owned by the Augustinians of Klosterneuburg). He converted this to a hunting lodge in 1569. Under Emperor Matthias (1612–19) the 'beautiful spring' (from which Schönbrunn takes its name) was discovered—its properties still being prized three centuries later by Franz Joseph, who served his guests with the pure and healing water. The stone with Kaiser Matthias's monogram can be seen at the spring, which is in the woods to the southeast of the Schloß. In a **grotto** here (by Isidore Canevale, 1771) is a **statue** of the fleshly nymph *Egeria* (by Wilhelm Beyer, 1779) holding a pitcher from which the water flows.

Under Leopold I (1705) the 500-acre Baroque park was laid out by Jean Trehet, most of the earlier gardens having been destroyed by Turkish action in 1683. After Nicholas Jadot de Ville Issey (or possibly Louis Gervais) had completed the formal **Kronprinzengarten** (so-called from 1880 after Crown Prince Rudolf) and the **Kammergarten** at the east and west ends of the *Schloß* (1745–50), a team of Lorraine and Dutch gardeners, the best known being Adriaen van Steckhoven, radically altered the park in Rococo style in the 1750s. Bernardo Bellotto's view of Schönbrunn in the Kunsthistorischen Museum gives a vivid impression of the great central parterre flanked by woodland divided into star shapes by allées as it looked in the 1760s.

Ferdinand von Hohenberg supplied numerous ideas for decorative ornament and it is to him we owe the elaborately faked **Roman ruins** (1778), partly built from Maximilian II's Renaissance Neugebäude (the latter had been destroyed by Hungarian rebels under Rákóczi in 1704). The ruins were originally called *Carthago* and symbolised the destruction of the enemies of the Empire. Hohenberg also created the **Obelisk Fountain** (1777) at the end of the eastern diagonal allée.

The 32 garden statues of the great parterre were commissioned in 1773 from a team led by Wilhelm Beyer, who had discovered a source of high quality marble in Tyrol. All are figures from antiquity, their iconographical function being to draw a parallel and show continuity between the Empire of Rome and its Habsburg-dominated successor in the west, the Holy Roman Empire.

The broad gravel way of the great parterre to the south of the palace sweeps down to Wilhelm Beyer's remarkable **Neptune Fountain** (1781). On the hill above is Hohenberg's neo-Classical **Gloriette** (1775), a colonnaded triumphal arch built on the urging of Chancellor Kaunitz as a symbol of peace achieved through victory. More specifically, it was a tribute to Maria Theresia's survival skills, especially in the face of aggression from her arch-enemy, Frederick of Prussia. The sculptural trophies are by J.B. Hagenauer, and the stucco by Benedikt Henrici. From the colonnade there is a magnificent view over the western outskirts of Vienna.

Some way to the west is F. Segenschmid's **Palm House** (1882), a replica of the one at Kew and (together with the glass-house in the Burggarten) the most important surviving glass and iron construction from the 19C still standing in Austria. Sir Joseph Banks, visiting in 1814, had described Schönbrunn Park as the world's only rival to Kew; he was impressed by the adjacent **Botanical (or Dutch) Garden** (1754), which owes its origin to Franz Stephan's passionate interest in the natural world and the expeditions he financed to collect rare species (see also Natural History Museum, p 137). A little later, in 1755, the great Orangery was laid out to the northeast.

In 1752 Franz also revived the **Tiergarten** (**Menagerie**). Maximilian II having had one at the Neugebäude. (The origin of animal pelts sported on the uniforms of some Hungarian regiments lies in the bleeding skins of the slaughtered menagerie animals that the warlike Magyars slung over their shoulders when they laid waste the area in 1704.) The main architectural feature of the zoo, which houses some 750 animals, is the **octagonal pavilion** (1759), designed by Jadot de Ville Issey, which is surrounded by twelve radially arranged animal enclosures. Now a restaurant, the pavilion was originally used by the imperial family for viewing the animals. Menagerie, botanical gardens and park were regarded as having a pedagogic, as well as an ornamental, function and from 1779 the public were admitted for free.

Schönbrunn was symbolically at the heart of the Empire under Maria Theresia and Franz Joseph: references to it abound in domestic and foreign literature. Fanny Trollope wondered that the 'black and vilely smelling' River Wien nearby was allowed by Maria Theresia 'to flow between the wind and her regality'. Joseph Roth immortalizes it in his novel of the late Empire, *The Radetzky March* (1932) where Herr von Trotta has a secret audience at Schönbrunn with Franz Joseph, whose life his father had saved at Solferino. Joseph Lanner wrote a '*Schönbrunner Waltz*'.

Technisches Museum für Industrie und Gewerbe

A short walk to the north of Schönbrunn is the **Technical Museum** (Mariahilfer Straße 212, open Mon–Sat, 09.00–18.00, Sun, 10.00–18.00, Thur, 09.00–20.00) reopened in 2000 after massive restoration. It is now one of the most impressive among Vienna's museums utilising video, electronic data transfer and listening stations in the interactive displays (of which more are still being developed). Founded in 1908, it documents, inter alia, the development of transport, industrial processes and mining, as well as illustrating inventions by Austrians, the latter being more numerous than is generally thought. There is also a substantial archive, a library and pleasant café. Many of the guided tours and programmes are aimed (but not patronisingly) at children.

Sights further afield

Kirche am Steinhof

- Baumgartner Höhe 1, Psychiatrisches Krankenhaus. Bus 48A from Dr.-Karl-Renner-Ring. About half an hour from the city centre.

This spectacular late work (1907) by Otto Wagner may be visited only with a guided group on Saturday afternoons, starting at 15.00 (☎ 91 060, ext. 20031). It was commissioned by the Lower Austrian government to serve the inmates of the adjacent psychiatric clinic. Wagner has taken account of the patients' needs in his design, which thus incorporates hygienic features (a stoop with running water, easily cleaned surfaces, excellent acoustics), as well as some to increase security (the short and easily accessible benches of dark oak).

The church is now resplendent after major restoration of the exterior. Two kilos of gold leaf were used to regild the cupola; as a result, the church is once again being called by its Viennese nickname the '*Limoniberg*' (Lemon Mountain), the cupola flashing in the sunlight having reminded its first viewers of a citrus fruit cut in half. Complete refurbishment, costing 155 million Schillings is expected to continue until 2005.

Kirche am Steinhof

The monumental domed **exterior** is dominated by Richard Luksch's bronzes, seated figures of Sts Leopold and Severin, the patrons of Lower Austria. Three vast angels of gilded copper by Othmar Schimkowitz are situated above the portals in front of an arched mosaic window. Under a suspended ceiling with gilt decoration reminiscent of a star-studded sky, the light-flooded **interior** slopes down towards a raised altar under a gold baldachino (the latter framed by gilt reliefs of angels, again by Schimkowitz). Vivid mosaics by Remigius Geyling (above the altar) and Rudolf Jettmar (above the side altars) testify to Wagner's determination to use only the most durable vitrified materials, and to avoid what he called the 'unreliable fresco technique'.

The most exciting realisations of the Secession's interest in alternative materials are Kolo Moser's lovely blue mosaic **windows** (above the side altars, in the organ loft and the crossing of the vault), which serve to complement the dazzle of the interior's gold and white friezes. These effects provoked J.A. Lux (Wagner's monographer) to comment: 'Whoever believes that the mystical-religious impulse is nurtured in the semi-darkness of a poorly ventilated, cold and damp interior is brilliantly contradicted by Wagner's building.'

Hermesvilla

- Tram 60 from Hietzing (Kennedybrücke) to Speising, then Bus 60B to Lainzer Tiergarten. Allow a good hour from the city centre.

A present from Franz Joseph to Elisabeth, who did not much care for it, the Hermesvilla (open Wed–Sun and holidays 09.00–16.30) was designed by Karl von Hasenauer (1884) in the tradition of Baroque garden pavilions. It is set in an extensive park, now a nature reserve abounding with wild boar and deer. Notable are the sgraffitoed exterior walls and delicate arcaded balconies of the façade.

The villa takes its name from a statue by Ernst Herter that stands on the side of the formal garden, and is otherwise distinguished by the sumptuous, if gloomy, murals of *A Midsummer Night's Dream*, which Hans Makart had planned for Empress Elisabeth's first floor bedroom. They were carried out after Makart's death in his distinctive style, the latter being rudely described by the painter Anselm Feuerbach as 'diarrhoea-type productions' of the type that were on show in great profusion in Makart's 'asiatic junkshop' of an atelier. But the subject matter was appropriate, as Elisabeth had begun characterising herself as 'Titania' in her melancholy poems, one of which describes the villa as 'Titanias Schloss'. Gustav Klimt and Franz Matsch also decorated parts of the house. It is now used for nostalgic exhibitions of the Monarchy era, staged by the Historical Museum of the City of Vienna.

Wotrubakirche

- The nearest bus to the church, which stands at the junction of Georgsgasse and Rysergasse in Mauer, is the 60A to Kaserngasse from Atzgersdorf-Mauer station, which in turn is reached by S-Bahn 1 or 2. About 1 hour from the city centre.

It is a long—but worthwhile—trek to the **Church of the Holy Trinity**, designed by the sculptor Fritz Wotruba (1907–75), and completed in 1976 (open between 14.00 and 16.00, Thur, Fri; 14.00–20.00 Sat, 09.00–17.00 Sun and holidays. Guided tours by appointment; ☎ 888 5003). It is constructed from irregular rectangular concrete slabs, light being filtered by the narrow glass panels between them. It is very much a sculptor's work, a daring (and, many think, successful) experiment in creating the atmosphere of a religious sanctuary by means of uncompromisingly brutalist forms and materials.

The Josef-Hoffmann Villa Colony

- Tram 37 from Schottentor to end stop (Hohe Warte). About 40 minutes from the city centre.

A colony of turn-of-the-twentieth-century villas, mostly built for well-to-do artists, is situated in the area flanked by Steinfeldgasse and Wollergasse in the 19th District. The idea of creating something similar to an English garden suburb with custom-built villa-ateliers came from the painter Carl Moll. Joseph Maria Olbrich (designer of the Secession building) began the work, and Josef Hoffmann took over when Olbrich was called to Darmstadt in Germany. The houses were built between 1900 and 1907, all having a similar internal plan: service quarters were in the basement, reception and dining room on the main floor and an independent studio on the top floor, from the terrace of which there were fine views of the Wienerwald. Among the owners were the artists Carl Moll and Kolo Moser, as well as Hugo Henneberg (a Secession photographer) and various patrons of the Secession.

Geymüller-Schlößchen (or Schlößl)

- Tram 41 to end stop. Bus 41a. About 40 minutes from the city centre.

The Geymüller-Schlößl (Khevenhüllerstraße 2) is an attractive late Empire villa and was built c 1808 for the banker, Baron Geymüller. Open 1 Mar–Oct only, Mon–Wed 10.30–15.00. Thur–Sun by appointment. Guided tours available, ☎ 71 136 Ext: 232 (opening times change, so it is best to confirm by telephone). Its chief source of interest is the fine collection of Biedermeier furniture and about 200 clocks made between 1780 and 1850. The house is in the care of the Museum of Applied Arts.

Karl-Marx-Hof

- Tram D from Schottentor or U4, U6 to Heiligenstadt station. About 40 minutes from the city centre.

The apartment block is the most spectacular of the *Gemeindebauten* (social housing apartment blocks) built by the socialist council between 1919 and the civil war of 1934. The ambitious building programme of '*Rotes Wien*' (63,000 apartments were created) was financed by a steeply progressive tax on the wealthier citizens, together with an import tax on luxury services and goods. The Karl-Marx-Hof (built 1926–30) was designed by Karl Ehn, a pupil of Otto Wagner. It originally contained 1325 flats, the smallest of them only 26 sq. m, and extends for more than a kilometre along Heiligenstädter Straße (nos 82–92). In the complex were included a laundry, bathing facilities (individual apartments had none), a kindergarten, a library, a chemist, a post office, a surgery and shops. In the Civil War of 1934 it was occupied by rebels and bombarded by the troops of the Dollfuß clerico-Fascist regime. Traces of this conflict could be seen on the walls up to the restoration of 1989. The ceramic figures on the façade (J.F. Riedl, 1930) represent Socialist slogans: *Child Welfare*, *Liberation*, *Physical Culture* and *Enlightenment*.

UNO-City

- Reached by U1 (alight at Vienna International Centre). Visitors must bring their passports with them. About 15 minutes by U-bahn from the city centre.

The UNO-City (tours Mon–Fri at 11.00 and 14.00, but check first by telephone on ☎ 26060 3328 or ▤ 26060 5899 in case of security alerts) on the north bank of the Danube was built in the 1970s, after Chancellor Bruno Kreisky had successfully lobbied to make Vienna the third UNO centre after New York and Geneva. The vast futuristic and impersonal blocks housing the UNIDO, the IAEO, the UNHCR and the Commission for Infectious Diseases, which rent their offices from the Austrian government, were designed by Johann Staber.

Adjacent is the **Austria Centre**, offering 14 auditoria with varying capacities up to 4000 people.

The **Danube Park** nearby is dominated by the 249 metre (820 ft) high **Danube**

Tower (open daily Apr–Oct 09.30–midnight, Nov–Mar 10.00–22.00) with revolving restaurants at 158.49m (520 ft) and 170.68m (560 ft) above ground. It offers panoramic views over the Danube Valley, the Marchfeld to the north and the Wienerwald to the west.

Zentralfriedhof (Central Cemetery)

- Tram 71 from Schwarzenbergplatz to Simmeringer Hauptstraße 234, S-Bahn to Zentralfriedhof.

Vienna is famous for its death cult, its obsession with obsequies (what the locals call *a schöne Leich*—literally translated as 'the lovely corpse'), and generally for its Baroque interest in the minutiae of death and interment (p 179). Those with a similar penchant might visit the Central Cemetery (open May–August, 07.00–1900, Mar, Apr, Sept, Oct, 07.00–1800, Nov–Feb, 08.00–1700) on All Saints Day (1 November), when much of Vienna sets out on what is often the first frosty day of the year to lay wreaths on family graves or the tombs of the famous.

The 238.77 hectare (590 acre) cemetery was opened in 1874 to the south of the city (Simmeringer Hauptstraße 234). Among the circa three million graves are those of great Viennese actors, writers, musicians and composers (including a striking modern cube by Fritz Wotruba that marks the remains of Arnold Schönberg). The focal point is the **Dr-Karl-Lueger-Church** (1910), named after the populist Viennese mayor (1897–1910), who numbered among his good works the founding of a municipal undertakers to undercut the rapacious private firms. (The latter were notorious for staking out the houses of the dying and for hustling those who could ill afford it to invest in costly funerals, complete with carriages drawn by plumed black horses.) The church, inside which Lueger is buried, was designed by an Otto Wagner pupil, Max Hegele; its architecture clearly quotes from its great Viennese antecedents, such as Wagner's Kirche am Steinhof (p 196) and Fischer von Erlach's Karlskirche (p 167).

There are separate areas of the cemetery for those of Jewish, Islamic, Orthodox or Protestant faith. On the far side of Simmeringer Hauptstraße at no. 337 is Clemens Holzmeister's formidable **Crematorium** (1923), incorporated in the ruins of Maximilian II's celebrated Neugebäude (p 194). The official and somewhat bleak nomenclature for the crematorium is *Feuerhalle der Stadt Wien*, and it was built in the teeth of opposition from the Catholic Church during the period of Socialist hegemony on the city council. Social Democrats could pay monthly dues to an organisation called *Flame*, which then arranged for free cremation on death. Holzmeister was himself a Catholic and built several churches in Austria, but is best known for the Salzburg Festival Theatre and the government buildings in Ankara, a project undertaken in exile from the Nazis.

Excursions

Heurigen villages

A favourite entertainment for the Viennese is to spend an evening in one of the traditional taverns known as *Heurigen*. The young, petillant wine of the current vintage (dated from 11 November) is known as a *Heuriger*, a tipple of little sophistication for which the locals have an unaccountable passion. Genuine Heurigen obey the rules originally laid down by Joseph II, remaining open until their own production of wine (usually from a vineyard backing onto the Heurige) is exhausted. In the Heurigen villages a signpost in the main street indicates which Heurigen have '*ausgsteckt*', a reference to the pine twigs hung over the door as long as the tavern is in operation. However, in popular areas such as Grinzing, Heiligenstadt and Neustift am Walde, a number of the Heurigen now resemble folksy restaurants, open all the year round, serving wines in addition to the '*gemischter Satz*' (a blend of local grape varieties) and offering traditional *Schrammelmusik*. (The latter gets its name from the 19C brothers Schrammel, who performed folk music and songs in Viennese dialect, some of which, for example *Wien bleibt Wien*—'Vienna will always be Vienna', have become classics of Viennese folk culture.)

Grinzing

* Tram 38 from Schottentor.

The best known of the Heurigen villages is Grinzing to the northwest of the city, a favourite haunt of Franz Schubert. The village was twice destroyed by the Turks and only recovered slowly—the pretty, yellow ochre houses are thus mostly neo-Classical. Despite excessive tourism, it retains a countrified charm, but is under threat from land speculation. To combat this, a club has been formed, each of whose members buys a single vine in the targetted vineyards, which he or she undertakes to protect (glamorous owners of vines include the Pope, the Dalai-Lama, Sophia Loren and the somewhat less glamorous Kurt Waldheim). Two good Heurigen in Grinzing are **Martin Sepp** (Cobenzlgasse 34) and **Reinprecht** (Cobenzlgasse 22). Those with a musical sweet tooth can book into the touristy evening show (April–Jan) of Wiener Walzer, operetta, and Wiener Lieder at the Kronprinz Rudolfshof (☎ 524 74 78).

Gustav Mahler is buried in Grinzing cemetery (Gruppe 7, Reihe 2) under a monumental headstone designed by Josef Hoffmann. So also is Mahler's wife, the indefatigable turn-of-the-century groupie, Alma Mahler-(Gropius)-Werfel (1879–1964), daughter of the painter, Emil Jakob Schindler (p 176).

Heiligenstadt

* U4, U6 to Heiligenstadt, then two stops with Bus 38A. Check night bus services before departure, otherwise taxis are available at all hours.

Not far from Grinzing is Heiligenstadt which has associations with Beethoven. At Probusgasse 6 is the house where he wrote the *Heiligenstadt Testament* on

6 October 1802—a desperate and tragic letter to his brothers describing his incipient deafness. The memorial rooms are worth a visit. In the pleasant Heiligenstädter Park, south of Grinzinger Straße, is an idealised **Beethoven Monument** by Robert Weigl (1910). On Grinzinger Straße itself, at no. 64, Beethoven shared a house briefly in 1808 with the playwright Franz Grillparzer, but quarrelled with him when he caught Grillparzer's mother listening at the door as he played the piano. Beethoven also lived on Pfarrplatz at no. 2 (he moved constantly during his 36 years of Viennese residence), which is next to the Parish Church of St James.

The origins of this church lie in Roman times and it retains Romanesque and Gothic elements. The empty grave found in the interior is said to have been that of St Severin (d. 482), a Roman who proclaimed the gospel along the Danube from Passau to *Favianae* (Mautern) in the Dark Ages. According to tradition, his hermitage was in the neighbouring vineyard. After his death, retreating Roman troops carried his body back to Italy (p 45). A congenial Heiligenstadt Heurige (Mayer am Pfarrplatz) is now located in the Beethoven house next to the church.

Other wine villages

Other pleasant Heurigen villages include **Neustift am Walde** (reached by Bus 35A from the junction Krottenbach/Silbergasse or Tram 38 from Schottentor) and just above it the peaceful **Salmannsdorf**. Aficionados may like to venture further afield to the villages across the Danube to the northwest, specifically **Jedlersdorf** and **Stammersdorf**, both reached with Tram 31 from Schottenring, or **Strebersdorf** (Tram 32). These villages are all in the 21st District and tend to be frequented by Viennese of modest means; traditions are thereby preserved and prices are kept moderate. **Gumpoldskirchen** (S-Bahn from Südbahnhof) is close to Baden (p 204) in the south. An attractive village with wine festivals in late June and late August, it is famous for its indigenous white wines (*Zierfandler, Rotgipfler, Neuburger*) and has a number of surviving Renaissance houses. In the south-western 23rd District of Liesing there are also charmingly unpretentious Heurigen in the villages of Mauer, Rodaun and Atzgersdorf (Bus 58B from Kennedy-Brüche (Hietzing) for Atzgersdorf and Mauer. Tram 60 from the same station for Rodaun.

Kahlenberg and Leopoldsberg

• Both hills are reached by Bus 38A from the U4/U6 terminus at Heiligenstadt.

The last northeastern spur of the Alps peters out to the west of Vienna with these two hilltops overlooking the city. **Leopoldsberg** is thought to have been the earliest inhabited part of the area, once occupied by prehistoric peoples, then by the Celtic Boier tribe, who the Romans compelled to re-settle in the Danube basin below.

The bus takes you up the scenic and winding **Höhenstraße**, built between 1934 and 1938 as a job creation scheme under the clerico-Fascist Dollfuß/Schuschnigg regimes. From the **Leopoldkirche** on the outermost hill there are wonderful views over the city, the historic Marchfeld and the Napoleonic battlefields of Aspern and Wagram.

Built on the site of a Babenberg fortress destroyed by the Turks in 1529, the 17C Baroque church was again badly damaged in 1683, but renovated and extended by Antonio Beduzzi between 1718 and 1730. It contains documentation relating to the last Turkish siege and the liberation by the imperial armies. The church and hilltop are named after St Leopold (III) of Babenberg, the founder of nearby Klosterneuburg (see below).

A little to the east is the **Kahlenberg**, literally the 'bald mountain', a reference to the fact that both hilltops were deforested by Viennese collecting firewood over the years, but earlier called the Sauberg in the days when wild boar roamed its slopes. The **Church of St Joseph** has a memorial recalling the dawn Mass on 12 September 1683, at which King Jan Sobieski, Polish Commander-in-Chief of the relieving army, was a ministrant. After the Papal Legate and confessor to Leopold I, Marco d'Aviano, had concluded the Mass, the armies swept down upon the Turks, the city falling to them by nightfall. In 1906, the Polish Redemptorist Order took over the church and instituted the Sobieski chapel with frescoes by J.H. Rosen. Nearby is the 1930's *Kahlenberg Restaurant*, which dates from the construction of the Höhenstraße, offering marvellous views of Vienna.

Klosterneuburg

- S-Bahn from Wien Franz-Josefs-Bahnhof.

Klosterneuburg (open May–Nov, Tue–Sun, 10.00–17.00) was the last seat of the Babenberg rulers before they transferred to Am Hof in Vienna under Duke Heinrich II in 1156. Founded by Margrave (later Saint) Leopold III in the early 12C, the Augustinian monastery and church should have been expanded in the 18C according to the ambitious plans of Karl VI's Milanese architect, Donato Felice d'Allio. The idea was to create a combined palace, dynastic shrine and mausoleum similar in scale and symbolic majesty to that of the Spanish Habsburgs, Philip II's Escorial. However, only two of the planned nine domes were completed before Karl's death in 1740 and the project languished. What survives is the original Romanesque and Gothic church with alterations to the towers carried out in the Baroque period and again in 1879 by the Ringstraßen architect, Friedrich Schmidt.

The **interior** has Baroque frescoes in the vault by H.G. Greiner (completed in 1689 and including a contemporary depiction of the Turkish siege of 1683 featured next to J.G.Freundt's organ of 1642). In the cupola are frescoes by J.M. Rottmayr, while the elegant decorative scheme of the altar and its surround is the work (1723–30) of Matthias Steinl. Steps descend to the Gothic cloister and the St Leopold Chapel. This contains the monastery's greatest treasure, the marvellous **wing-altar** (1181) by Nicolas of Verdun (c1130–c1205), made of gilded copper with 51 plaques of champlevé enamel. It consists of rows of biblical scenes narrating the unfolding of the divine plan of world history from the Creation through the Old and New Testaments. Read vertically, the scenes, as divided between the old teaching and the new, also correlate in a closely worked out typology, whereby the featured events of the Old Testament symbolically prefigure specific aspects of the Life of Christ. This two-way vertical reading is organised so that the upper row shows the Old Testament epoch, before Moses and the reception of the Holy Law from God; the middle row shows the fulfilment of the prophecies and redemption through Christ; the bottom row reverts to the Old Testament and the period following the adoption of the Holy Law. On the rear, the oldest datable painted panels in Austria have been attached—the work of an unknown Central European artist, which shows early attempts at perspective. The relics of St Leopold are kept in an enamelled shrine above the altar.

In the southern wing of the monastery, on the upper floor, is a genealogical tree of the Babenbergs in the form of a triptych made by Hans Part. It was commissioned to celebrate Leopold's canonisation in 1485, but only completed in 1492. In the ovals are scenes from Babenberg lives, while the backgrounds show Viennese landmarks, as well as the dynasty's religious foundations at Melk, Heiligenkreuz and elsewhere. The Sebastianikapelle on the Stiftsplatz contains the huge (but largely rebuilt) **Albrechtsaltar** (1439), described by historian Felix Czeike as 'the most important work of Gothic realism in Austria'. However Joseph II had much of it dismantled and the reconstruction dates to 1965.

The Kafka Memorial Room

• It is a long walk from the monastery but you can take bus 241 to the corner of Kierlinger Hauptstraße.

The memorial room (Kierlinger Hauptstraße 187, Kierling by Klosterneuburg) is located in the former sanatorium where the author Franz Kafka spent his dying days. It is open Mon–Sat, 08.00–12.00 and 14.00–17.00 (key obtainable in the house). Various Kafka memorabilia are on display in the form of photographic documentation, letters and the case notes of the progress of his illness.

Sammlung Essl

• S-bahn (S40) from Heiligenstadt; U4, U6 to Klosterneuburg-Weidling. Bus 239 from the Heiligenstadt Terminus to Leopoldsbrücke–Sammlung Essl. For a minimum of 6 persons there is a shuttle service from the Oper (Tue–Sun) at 15.00, price inclusive of museum entrance fee.

The impressive purpose-built gallery (An der Donau, Au 1, Klosterneuburg, open Tue–Sun 10.00–19.00, Wed to 21.00) for the collection, completed in 2000, and slightly reminiscent of the Getty Centre in California gives a broad overview of Austrian painting since 1945, complemented and contextualised by international works of the same period. There are over 4000 works in the collection and the gallery also hosts concerts of modern music. In addition there is a bookshop and café.

Heiligenkreuz and Mayerling

• Bus 265 travels to both Heiligenkreuz and from Südtiroler Platz.

The **Cistercian abbey** (1133) at **Heiligenkreuz** was one of Saint Leopold's many foundations. Open Apr–Oct daily 09.00–11.30, 13.30–17.00; Nov–Mar 13.30–16.00. Guided tours in German (obligatory if you wish to see everything) five times daily from 10 a.m. Its name refers to its most famous relic, a fragment of the True Cross collected by Leopold V on a crusade. The chapter-house is also a Babenberg tomb and Babenberg portraits are to be seen in the glass panels of the enneagonal well-house. The fountain (1739) and plague column (1737) in the courtyard are by Giovanni Giuliani, who also worked on the Heiligenkreuzer Hof in the Inner City (p 128). The originally Romanesque church has a beautiful, soaring Gothic choir. About 60 Cistercian monks occupy the monastery, one of whom will act as guide.

It was in the **cemetery** at Heiligenkreuz that Crown Prince Rudolf's lover, an adventuress named Marie Vetsera, was buried after the couple's joint suicide at the nearby hunting lodge of **Mayerling** on 29 January 1889. Her grave bears the legend: 'Like a flower blooms mankind, only to be crushed.' (Her coffin was stolen by an eccentric Linz businessman in the 1980s, but was later recovered.) After the suicide, Franz Joseph ordered the lodge to be turned into a Carmelite convent. The **chapel** may be visited (closed during lunch, 12.30–13.30. Ring the bell for admission).

There is a vivid account of the suicide and its aftermath in Frederic Morton's *A Nervous Splendour* (1979), a welcome corrective to the sugar-coating so often given to this unsavoury episode and its unhappy protagonists.

Hinterbrühl

Between Vienna and Heiligenkreuz is the Brühl valley, through which flows the River Mödling. The village of Hinterbrühl's main attraction is the **grotto**, the largest underground lake in Europe (6200 sq metres), which was used by the Nazis as a bunker-cum-factory. Motor boat trips are possible all year round, but there is a break for lunch between 12.00 and 13.00. Warm clothes are essential.

On the edge of the village is the **Höldrichsmühle** (Gaadner Straße 34) a hotel and restaurant. According to legend, Franz Schubert was inspired by the miller's daughter-in-law to write *Die schöne Müllerin* song cycle in 1823. The lime trees and the well featured in *Am Brunnen vor dem Tore* are supposed to be those near the house. There has been a mill here since the 12C and a restaurant for 200 years.

Baden

- A *Lokalbahn* (suburban tram) runs from the Oper to Baden at regular intervals.

The sulphurous **spa** at Baden has been uninterruptedly exploited since Roman times. We read in Mozart's letters that Constanze was continually taking the waters here. Mozart himself wrote the lovely *Ave Verum* chorus for his friend, Anton Stoll, the local schoolmaster and director of the church choir. The heyday of Baden was the Biedermeier age, when Emperor Franz I made it popular with the emergent bourgeoisie by spending the summer months in the town. The leading neo-Classical architect of the day, Josef Kornhäusel, rebuilt many of the baths after a destructive fire in 1812.

It was in Baden that Leopold von Sacher-Masoch underwent his six months of pleasurable pain at the hands of Baroness Pistor, as described in the scandalous novella, *Venus in Furs* (1870). Although Sacher-Masoch was a gifted story-teller, Krafft-Ebing's identification of him in *Psychopathia Sexualis* as the discoverer of masochism has, in the words of William Johnston, 'foisted upon the unhappy writer a notoriety that has eclipsed his literary merits'.

Laxenburg

- Bus from Südtiroler Platz to Maria Enzersdorf, thence on the Gießhübl bus to the end stop. About 17km from the city centre.

The imperial complex of Laxenburg (open Easter–end Oct, daily 10.00–12.00 and 14.00–17.00) lies to the southeast of Vienna. It consists of Nikolaus

Pacassi's **Neues Schloß** (also known as the Blauer Hof, 1752) and the **Alte Schloß**, a 14C building rebuilt in the late 17C by the court architect, Ludovico Burnacini, and now containing the Austrian Film Archives (films shown here at weekends May–Sept).

In the English-style **park**, liberally supplied with temples, artificial ponds, grottoes and bridges, is the moated **Franzensburg**, an imitation of the original Swiss medieval castle of the Habsburgs built on the lake for Franz I between 1796 and 1836. This was his Biedermeier retreat from the cares of office and the the threatening advance of industrialisation, French armies and new-fangled political ideas. Architecturally and aesthetically it is an exercise in Habsburg nostalgia, a junk room of objects and exploded aspirations, which, as the Emperor rather pathetically expressed it, 'if nothing else, the French should leave for me.' Recently restored, Michael Riedl and Franz Jäger's Romantic folly (actually a panopticon of architectural styles from Gothic to Neo-Classicism) is well worth a visit. Highlights of the Franzensburg include the **Habsburg Hall**, with 17 marble statues of archdukes and emperors (1700, mostly the work of Peter and Paul Strudel) up to the time of Maria Theresia, the Throne Room, the Chapel, the Lorraine Hall and a recreated medieval dungeon. (In the dungeon there is an imprisoned knight whose realistic groans can be heard on a background tape.) The unfortunate last Emperor, Karl I, lived here periodically between 1916 and 1918.

Glossary

Architecture

Romanesque typically characterised by round arches, powerful vaults and massive articulated wall structures, the Romanesque style in Vienna has mostly been subsumed in later Gothic (q.v.) building. However, remnants survive in the Ruprechtskirche, the earliest church still standing in the city, and in the Stephansdom (the two so-called 'Heathen Towers' of the west façade). Romanesque edifices were being built in the Babenberg period (976–1246), and until the late 13C.

Gothic pointed arches, flying buttresses and beautiful rib vaulting are the hall-marks of Gothic architecture, the first examples of which were to be seen in the churches of the mendicant orders that came to Vienna in the early 13C. For some 300 years Gothic churches were built in the city; two of the loveliest exam-ples are the Stephansdom, particularly its Albertine choir (1304–40) and the marvellous south tower (1359–1433); and the choir of Maria am Gestade, built by Michael Knab (1394–1414).

Renaissance relatively little Renaissance architecture was built in Vienna in the 16C. This was due partly to a prolonged period of absence of the imperial court, which might otherwise have patronised it, but another factor was the use of funds for the construction of city fortifications after the alarming Turkish attack of 1529. A few Renaissance gateways and burgher houses survive, while the most striking imperial contribution was the Stallburg, an extension of the Hofburg built after 1558 for the Archduke Maximilian, later Emperor Maximilian II. Its beautifully rhythmic, open loggias, rising over two levels around an open courtyard, recall a characteristic feature of the Italian Renaissance.

Baroque the dramatic, sometimes theatrical, style of Baroque, with its prefer-ence for strong plasticity, intricate interpenetration of spaces, great domes and sweeping vistas, is associated with the Counter-Reformation. The early Baroque architects in Vienna, who built both churches and great palaces for the aristocracy, were almost all Italian (Burnacini, Martinelli, Tencala and others). Later Viennese Baroque, which also produced its greatest master-pieces, was the work of Austrian masters after the defeat of the Turks in 1683. The two finest examples are the Karlskirche (1716–39) by Fischer von Erlach, father and son, and the Belvedere Palace (1714–22), built by Lukas von Hildebrandt.

Rococo the mid-18C saw the creation of Vienna's most impressive example of Rococo, namely the imperial palace of Schönbrunn, built between 1744 and 1749 for Maria Theresia by Nikolaus Pacassi, who adapted earlier Baroque plans. The palace was designed to rival Versailles and the playfulness of imported French taste is most evident in Schönbrunn's glittering interiors, a dazzle of gilded decoration and mirrors.

Classicism Rococo was followed by a revival of the stateliness and sobriety of classical Greek and Roman architecture, which enjoyed a vogue from the late 18C to the mid-19C. The leading architect of Classicism was Josef Kornhäusel, whose work includes the synagogue (1825–26) in Vienna and several buildings in Baden bei Wien. A fine neo-Classical work is Alois Pichl's Erste Österreichische Spar-Casse on the Graben, while a notable interior in the same style is that of the Albertina.

Historicism the Ringstraßen era of the second half of the 19C saw an explosion of construction both in the public and private spheres. The great architects of the day—Theophil Hansen, Heinrich Ferstel, Karl Hasenauer and others—designed monumental public buildings in neo-Hellenistic style (the Parliament), neo-Renaissance style (the University), neo-Byzantine style (the Greek Church), in short whatever seemed symbolically appropriate to the building's function. Many other houses were built in an eclectic style that mixed elements of different periods. The most exotic Historicist interior consists of the arcade, marble stairway and upper chambers of the so-called Ferstel-Palais between Herrengasse and Freyung. The era of Historicism, more than any other, characterises the face of average Viennese architecture today, especially in the inner suburbs.

Secession and Jugendstil reaction to the increasing repetitiveness and sterility of Historicism set in with the adoption of Jugendstil (also identified with Secession) in the 1890s. Jugendstil was the Germanic and Central European version of *art nouveau*, characterised by organic and dynamic forms, curving design and whiplash or floral ornaments. Some of its most interesting products are the villas designed by Josef Hoffmann, the Secession building itself (1897–98) by Joseph Maria Olbrich, and the Kirche am Steinhof (1905–7) by Otto Wagner.

Socialist Architecture during the period of Socialist hegemony in the City Council after the First World War ('Rotes Wien', 1919–34) a massive programme of social housing was undertaken. The most famous of the resulting housing estates is the Karl-Marx-Hof (1926–30) by Karl Ehn. Such estates may be seen all over the city, except in the historic core, and all bear a plaque stating when they were built and indicating that they were financed out of the city housing tax.

Functionalism and Modernism an early, if idiosyncratic, exponent of Functionalism was Adolf Loos, whose Loos-Haus (1910–12) is justly famous. Contemporary, or near-contemporary Viennese architects of distinction tend to be individualists who have left their mark on the city with a few highly original buildings. A remarkable example is Fritz Wotruba's angular play of concrete blocks, the Wotrubakirche (1965–76), and a recent controversial one is Hans Hollein's Haas-Haus (1985–90), the vast bow-fronted glass façade of which reflects the Stephansdom opposite.

Post-Modernism Vienna's most vivid example of Post-Modernism is Friedensreich Hundertwasser's multi-coloured Hundertwasser-Haus (1983–85). The same architect also designed a coloured and gilded tower for the city rubbish burner, which has become something of a landmark.

Art, Music and Literature

Gothic Art Gothic painting and sculpture was produced in a period roughly coinciding with that of Gothic architecture, from the 12C to the 16C. Its strongly transcendental religious works (sculptured crucifixions, madonnas, altarpieces and the like) exploit the gentle plasticity of flowing drapery and bodily movement, especially in the works of Italian-influenced International Gothic. The earliest artefacts that have survived in Vienna may be seen in churches, the Diocesan Museum on Stephansplatz, the Historical Museum of the City of Vienna and the collection of Austrian Medieval Art in the Orangery of the Lower Belvedere. This last collection is notable for paintings by the local Danube School (Albrecht Altdorfer, Lucas Cranach and Wolf Huber). This dramatically intense version of late Gothic painting cultivated by artists working in Vienna at the turn of the 16C looks forward to the Renaissance fondness for realistic landscapes. The most celebrated of locally produced Gothic works are the Wiener Neustadt altar in the northern choir of the Stephansdom, the late Gothic tomb of Friedrich III in the south choir; also the late Gothic views of Vienna incorporated into the so-called Schottenaltar, now in the Schottenstift Museum.

Renaissance Renaissance art, broadly interpreted as incorporating qualities of serenity and harmony founded on classical ideals and realistic depiction of nature, had an impact on 15C and 16C Vienna through collecting and scholarship. The great masters of the Italian Renaissance were collected by the Habsburg ruling house and may be seen in the Kunsthistorischen Museum. A star item is Benvenuto Cellini's celebrated salt-cellar, a High Renaissance work with elongated Mannerist features made for Francis I of France in 1543. Locally produced Renaissance work, as with architecture, does not amount to a great deal. There are some examples in the Dom-und Diözesanmuseum, including a beautiful relief of the *Carrying of the Cross* (1523). In Stephansdom are the marble memorial plaques to leading humanist scholars of the Renaissance, such as Conrad Celtis and Johannes Cuspinian. Fine Renaissance carving may be seen on the portals of the Salvatorkapelle, part of the Altes Rathaus.

Mannerism Mannerism, which deliberately broke Classical and Renaissance 'rules', especially by distortion or elongation of human figures, also heightened the desired emotional effect by devices such as strained poses and discrepancies of scale between figures. The Emperor Rudolf II (1576–1608), who surrounded himself with scientists and artists in his Prague castle, had a distinct taste for Mannerism, including its more bizarre or erotic elements. The Kunsthistorische Museum has many of the pictures by Mannerist painters collected or commissioned by Rudolf: they include works by Bartholomäus Spranger (1546–1611), who worked in Prague, and the extraordinary compositions of Giuseppe Arcimboldo (1527–93), which made human figures or heads from vegetables, flowers, fruits and fragments of landscape. He was Court Painter in Prague between 1562 and 1587 and was made a Count Palatine by Rudolf.

Baroque following the Council of Trent (1545–63) and the calling of the Jesuits to Vienna by Ferdinand I in 1551, the Counter-Reformatory campaign to win the hearts and minds of the people was driven forward by means of preaching, didactic theatrical spectacle and, not least, art. Like the architecture,

Baroque art was intensely emotional and dramatic, using illusionism and chiaroscuro effects to manipulate the viewer's feelings. In the 17C and 18C, the services of a host of painters and sculptors were required to decorate the newly built or barockised churches. Among them were men of real genius such as the Italian Lorenzo Mattielli and the native Austrian, Georg Raphael Donner. A notable work of the former is the sculpture of St John Nepomuk in the Peterskirche (c 1714); and of the latter, the Providentia Fountain for the Neuer Markt (1739), the original of which is now in the Lower Belvedere.

Leading **painters** of the Viennese Baroque include Daniel Gran, Johann Michael Rottmayr and Martino Altomonte. Perhaps the greatest late master of the style, whose work already shows the dancing lightness of the Venetian Rococo, is Franz Anton Maulbertsch, who painted the cycle of frescoes in the Maria Treu Church (1752–53).

Baroque music in Vienna was dominated by Italian composers (such as Mozart's rival, Antonio Salieri) until the advent of Christoph Willibald Gluck (1714–87). His great reforming operas (*Orfeo*, *Iphigenie in Aulis* and *Alceste*) successfully placed the music at the service of the text, in contrast to the then dominant rules of the Court Poet, Pietro Metastasio, where recitative moved the plot forward and over-ornamented arias apostrophised abstract feeling.

Wiener Klassik the term often used to describe the musical style established and elaborated in the great flowering of musical composition of late 18C and early 19C Vienna, typically in the work of Joseph Haydn (1732–1809), Wolfgang Amadeus Mozart (1756–91) and Ludwig van Beethoven (1770–1827). Beethoven's work makes the transition to full-blown Romantic music.

Biedermeier the term Biedermeier refers to the cultural products of the period between the Congress of Vienna (1814–15) at the end of the Napoleonic Wars and the Revolution of 1848. The architecture of this period is sturdy neo-Classicism, while the furniture and applied art displays an elegant harmony and simplicity. The works of Franz Schubert are the epitome of the Biedermeier soul in music (the composer's modestly Bohemian lifestyle even more so); in the fine arts, painters such as Friedrich von Amerling and Georg Ferdinand Waldmüller evoked a domestic idyll in their portraits. Their works can be seen in the Austrian Gallery (Österreichische Galerie, Belvedere), while Biedermeier furniture by Josef Danhauser and others can be seen in the Museum of Applied Arts (Österreichisches Museum für Angewandte Kunst—MAK).

Romanticism Biedermeier Romanticism is evident in the popularity of picturesque landscapes, often wild mountain scenes painted with a scrupulous attention to detail. Idealisation of landscape and man's relation to the natural world reaches its apogee in Adalbert Stifter's lengthy philosophical novel, *Indian Summer* (1857). Stifter's near-contemporary was Austria's greatest dramatist, Franz Grillparzer (1791–1872) whose works, especially the historical dramas, show a Romantic preoccupation with the psychological conflict of the individual having to choose between duty to anointed authority and personal conscience. (Grillparzer himself had trouble with the censor, but rejected the violent revolution of 1848.)

However, it was in Austrian **music** that Romanticism had its most dramatic impact, whether in the lyricism of Franz Schubert (1797–1828), or the hymns to liberty and exalted human feeling of Ludwig van Beethoven (1770–1827). In the late 19C a battle raged between the faction favouring the elegance and somewhat restrained perfectionism of Johannes Brahms (1833–97) and that supporting the elemental, massively architectonic compositions of Anton Bruckner (1824–96), the hero of the Wagnerites. A sophisticated late flowering of Romanticism, full of existential agonising and emotional extremes, was evident in the work of Gustav Mahler (1860–1911). As the long-standing director of the opera, he applied the Secession's idea of *Gesamtkunstwerk* (unified work of art) to the staging of operatic works.

Historicism the '*Gründerzeit*' or 'founders' period' of Ringstraßen Liberalism (1861 to the turn of the century) brought many commissions for artists and sculptors who produced works in the spirit of Historicism. The demand for monuments was strong (Franz Joseph was particularly keen on statues of military heroes) and the economic boom provided plenty of opportunities for artists to decorate the palaces of the *nouveaux riches*. Men like Anton Fernkorn made a good living from such commissions as the bombastic neo-Baroque equestrian statues of the Archduke Carl (1860) and Prince Eugene of Savoy (1865) on the Heldenplatz; the Artists' Company of the brothers Klimt and Franz Matsch were employed for interiors, most notably that of the new Burgtheater. The quintessential painter of Historicism was Hans Makart, whose vast historical canvases and luxuriously decadent mythological scenes attracted admirers from all over Europe. His work can be seen in the Austrian Gallery (Österreichische Galerie)of the Upper Belvedere.

Secession as in architecture, a reaction set in amongst artists against the heavy and monumental style of Historicism and the academic realism practised at the Academy. The same Gustav Klimt who had begun his career working in the latter style led the rebellion of the artists who 'seceded' from the Association of Fine Artists and formed their own group with its own patrons in 1897. Otto Wagner underwent a similar artistic transformation, although remaining an influential member of the establishment as Professor of Architecture at the Academy and a planner for the city's public transport. Although a parallel development to *art nouveau*, the Vienna Secession was *sui generis*, encompassing a broad range of talent from Klimt, to Carl Moll, to Kolo Moser. In particular, it was influenced by Symbolist art; perhaps the most famous work of the Secession, Gustav Klimt's *The Kiss* (1907/8), is a symbolist painting incorporating eastern decorative elements. In the applied arts, Josef Hoffmann, and others identified with the *Wiener Werkstätte*, produced furniture and everyday objects showing the influence of the Scottish architect and furniture designer, Charles Rennie Mackintosh, and the English Arts and Crafts designer, C.R. Ashbee. A hallmark of the *Wiener Werkstätte* was the so-called '*Würfelstil*, characterised by plain black and white (or silver) diaper patterns.

Expressionism Austrian Expressionism—a confrontational style which abandons naturalism in favour of exaggerations or distortions of line and colour to achieve a more direct emotional impact—produced three great masters: Egon

Schiele (1890–1918), Oskar Kokoschka (1886–1980) and Richard Gerstl (1883–1908). Gerstl's *Laughing Self-Portrait* (1908) or Schiele's *Death and the Maiden* (1915) are just two of the works in the Austrian Gallery which exemplify the Expressionists' concern with the extremes of the human condition and personality. The latter picture was painted against the background of the economic and social collapse of the First World War.

Modernism the breakthrough to Modernism in **music** occurs with the atonal work of Arnold Schönberg (Schoenberg) (1874–1951) and his followers, Alban Berg (1885–1935) and Anton von Webern (1883–1945), who developed Schönberg's 'twelve-note' technique.

In the fine arts, the move to abstraction in post-war art is exemplified by leading Austrian painters such as Arnulf Rainer (b. 1929), Friedensreich Hundertwasser (1928–2000) and the lyrical Max Weiler (b. 1910–2001). From the 1960s, the school of so-called 'Magical Realism' (Ernst Fuchs and others) achieved widespread recognition. More extreme was the work of the 'Viennese Actionists', whose best-known protagonist is Hermann Nitsch. The movement's early happenings involved music, dance and ritualistic sacrifice of animals (in one case, the self-sacrifice of a participant).

Sun — morning — Vienna   dept.to
    — night   — Vienna

Monday — Vienna

Tuesday — Salzburg
    ↳ morning — dept. @ 10am
    — night in Salzburg
        (or Italy)

Wed. — dept. to Venice
    — aftern. in Vienna
    — stay Vienna

Thursd — morning Vienna
    — aft. dept. to Bard.
    — night at Bardalino

Friday — dept. to Sermione

Sat — shopping Milano

Sun — mount. hiking
    — castle

Monday — Balsano

Index

M

N